Fortress Russia

To my parents, Olga and Aleksandr

Fortress Russia

Conspiracy Theories in Post-Soviet Russia

Ilya Yablokov

polity

Copyright © Ilya Yablokov 2018

The right of Ilya Yablokov to be identified as Author of this Work has been asserted in accordance with the UK Copyright, Designs and Patents Act 1988.

First published in 2018 by Polity Press

Polity Press
65 Bridge Street
Cambridge CB2 1UR, UK

Polity Press
101 Station Landing
Suite 300
Medford, MA 02155, USA

All rights reserved. Except for the quotation of short passages for the purpose of criticism and review, no part of this publication may be reproduced, stored in a retrieval system or transmitted, in any form or by any means, electronic, mechanical, photocopying, recording or otherwise, without the prior permission of the publisher.

Library of Congress Cataloging-in-Publication Data

Names: Yablokov, Ilya, author.
Title: Fortress Russia : conspiracy theories in post-Soviet Russia / Ilya Yablokov.
Description: 1 | Cambridge, UK ; Medford, MA : Polity, 2018. | Includes bibliographical references and index.
Identifiers: LCCN 2017055177 (print) | LCCN 2018009984 (ebook) | ISBN 9781509522699 (Epub) | ISBN 9781509522651 (hardback) | ISBN 9781509522668 (paperback)
Subjects: LCSH: Russia (Federation)--Politics and government--1991- | Conspiracy theories--Russia (Federation) | Political culture--Russia (Federation) | Authoritarianism--Russia (Federation) | Intellectuals--Political activity--Russia (Federation) | Russia (Federation)--Foreign relations--Western countries. | Western countries--Foreign relations--Russia (Federation) | BISAC: SOCIAL SCIENCE / Sociology / General.
Classification: LCC DK510.763 (ebook) | LCC DK510.763 .Y33 2018 (print) | DDC 001.90947--dc23
LC record available at https://lccn.loc.gov/2017055177

ISBN-13: 978-1-5095-2265-1 (hardback)
ISBN-13: 978-1-5095-2266-8 (paperback)

A catalogue record for this book is available from the British Library.

Typeset in 10.5 on 12 pt Sabon by
Servis Filmsetting Ltd, Stockport, Cheshire
Printed and bound in the UK by Clays Ltd, St Ives PLC

The publisher has used its best endeavours to ensure that the URLs for external websites referred to in this book are correct and active at the time of going to press. However, the publisher has no responsibility for the websites and can make no guarantee that a site will remain live or that the content is or will remain appropriate.

Every effort has been made to trace all copyright holders, but if any have been inadvertently overlooked the publisher will be pleased to include any necessary credits in any subsequent reprint or edition.

For further information on Polity, visit our website: politybooks.com

Contents

Acknowledgements	*page* vii
Introduction	1
1 Building 'Fortress Russia'	14
2 The Spectres of Conspiracy Mythmaking	24
3 In Search of the 'Agents of Perestroika'	50
4 Sovereign Democracy and its Enemies	79
5 Battling against 'Foreign Agents'	112
6 Shadows of the Revolution	132
7 The War has Begun	162
Conclusion	185
References	196
Index	230

Acknowledgements

From the moment that the idea of this book was conceived to the day the final version of the manuscript was sent to my editors, eleven years have passed. Throughout this long and eventful period there were many people who helped me design the arguments, change my views, dig deeper and think more critically. Firstly, this project would never have been realized without the advice of Viktor Muchnik, my mentor and academic guru at Tomsk State University. His suggestion of looking more closely at conspiracy theories, made over a cup of coffee, turned out to be decisive and laid the groundwork for past and future achievements. Rashid Kaplanov, Viktoria Mochalova, Semion Goldin and all of the staff at 'Sefer', the Moscow centre for Jewish studies, were the first to support me financially and helped me begin collecting the resources for this project. Daniel Romanovsky and Viktor Shnirel'man gave advice for my first academic steps. Oleg Khazanov at Tomsk State University, Michael Miller at Central European University, Michael Tuval at the Hebrew University of Jerusalem and Rani Jaeger in Stockholm showed me how academic research could actually be fun. Gevorg Avetikyan, Istvan Pal Adam, Sanja Tepavcevic, David Karas, Anastas Vangeli, Vadim Nigmatov and Yulia Likhacheva-Kuzmane were always there (mainly in Budapest) to run by me many ideas that later appeared in the book.

The key person who made the production of this book possible is Vera Tolz, who had faith in this project from the very first day we met. Vera's knowledge and academic achievements, as well as her critical and thorough analysis of texts, have provided me with academic inspiration and a scholarly role model. Her kindness and willingness to help in every possible situation greatly contributed to the successful completion of this book. She taught me how to be a teacher and mentor, which I shall always remember. I am indebted to Peter Knight for his extraordinary help in developing the conceptual framework required to approach such a peculiar topic. As a student in Tomsk, Peter's book on American conspiracy culture was the first that I read on the subject and indeed it was sheer luck and, of course, an absolute privilege to have him as second supervisor of my project. As a young scholar, I am also indebted to Stephen Hutchings for providing invaluable academic opportunities. Stephen's critical comments, a deep understanding of Russian culture and readiness to share knowledge helped me look at my project in a different way and has laid the foundations for future research. Lynne Attwood was extremely helpful during the work on my project in Manchester and, at a later stage, was a key figure in turning my often unbearably academic language into a (hopefully) fascinating read. Luke March's opinion on the PhD dissertation and the further evolution of the text have been crucial in turning what was a postgraduate thesis into a proper book.

A friendly and creative atmosphere at the School of Arts, Languages and Cultures at Manchester also contributed to the outcome of the book. Elizaveta Alentaeva, Elena Simms, Paul Richardson, Svetlana Rapin, Kenzie Burchell, Alistair Dickins, Jan Gryta, Piotrek Andrzejewski, Marina Henrikson and Ana Barazal Barreira were at every moment very supportive of my work on the book, both in the office space and at our house in Victoria Park. Of all people in Manchester I am especially indebted to Alistair, who was very kind in sharpening my skills as an entry-level writer. Manchester was also the place where I met my co-author and close friend Elisabeth Schimpfossl. Since then we have shared the happiness and sadness of our first steps in the field while working in parallel on our first books and numerous fascinating projects about Russian media. I am very lucky to have a colleague and friend from whom I learn every day.

The final part of the book has been written in Leeds where my colleagues/friends, James Harris, Natasha Bogoslavskaya, James Wilson, Pavel Gudoshnikov and Robert Hornsby, have done everything within their powers to ease the teaching workload, inspire me with new ideas and challenge me at every turn.

The young generation of scholars in Russian studies has not only provided me with feedback and useful criticism of my ideas, but also has become a source of inspiration and support in all the possible circumstances that face the young academic in Britain. Arsenii Khitrov, Olga Zeveleva, Tom Rowley, Nathan Brand, Vsevolod Samokhvalov, Jon Roosenbeek – these words are dedicated to you.

ACKNOWLEDGEMENTS

I should like to thank my colleagues and friends around the world – Vasily Gatov, Alexey Kovalev, Alexander Etkind, Peter Pomerantsev, Viktor Vakhshtayn, Marlene Laruelle, Mark Bassin, Samuel Greene, Gulnaz Sharafutdinova, Peter Rutland, Steve Norris, Alexey Miller, Peter Duncan, Andrew McKenzie-McHarg, Sergei Samoilenko, Eliot Borenstein, Joe Uscinski, Mark Fenster, Tigran Amiryan, Samuel Volfson, Anastasiya Stepanyants, Irina Baulina and Andrey Goryanov. Their words of advice have been extremely well received during the work on the book and helped me navigate through the murky waters of Russian politics, which is full of conspiracies – real and imagined.

I am grateful to John Thompson and the team at Polity Press, who were very supportive during the book production process, from the first email to the final editing.

Finally, the two people without whom this book would never have been produced are my parents, Olga and Aleksandr. The unreserved encouragement, patience, love and time they have invested in making me a better man was a key factor in my personal development. No words will ever be able to express my gratitude to them. I am sure my father would have been very proud to hold a copy of this book in his hands.

Leeds, November 2017

Introduction

The attempted coup in August 1991, and the collapse of the Soviet Union in December of that year, produced a sense of bewilderment in Russians, from top-ranking politicians down to ordinary Russians. One explanation crops up again and again: conspiracy. Understood as a malevolent plot underlying historical and current events, the conspiracy theory has become a popular tool for interpreting the social and political realities of post-Soviet Russia. Its essential element – that there is an omnipotent secret group of people plotting to increase their own power at the expense of ordinary people – is espoused by people in all walks of Russian life.

In the post-Soviet period, the West, which is very often seen by Russians as a single entity, has emerged as an essential protagonist in conspiracy discourse. However, in 2016 and 2017 the West began engaging in its own conspiracy theories. The spirit of the Cold War and the witch-hunt for Russian agents both made a comeback. Today, the Kremlin is portrayed as the global puppet master who has successfully managed to appoint a loyal man to deal with the White House. 'Russiagate' and the media hype which surrounds it – that is, the Kremlin's alleged meddling in the US elections, and its attempts to influence elections in the UK and France – revived the old fear of Russian spies. Hysteria about the Russians became a central element of the US domestic political agenda, and an almost mythologized Russia became the source of many of the troubles plaguing the American people (Beauchamp, 2017). Russian hackers were found to be behind the worst cyberattacks (Calabresi, 2017); indeed, who but Russians could cause such havoc? Foreign intelligence officers shared with journalists, albeit anonymously, the claim that Trump's aides had contacts with Kremlin envoys (Schmidt et al., 2017), and that experienced villain Vladimir Putin was sending killers to neutralize all witnesses who could testify about Russian plots against the West (Bearak, 2017; Blake et al., 2017). Russian politicians and journalists loyal to the state have tried to convince the public that Russia's very existence is dependent on Putin. The wave of Western conspiracy theories about Russia's intrusion into US and European politics, in turn, made Russian politicians proud of 'hacking the States' (Cohen, 2017). The fears of Americans thus nurtured the feelings Russians had of being superior to their geopolitical enemy, and encouraged them to believe that they had, indeed, conspired to hack America.

Conspiracy theories have always been a fundamental element of popular culture and political thinking in America, prompting some scholars to define the country as an 'empire of conspiracy' (Melley, 2000). In this respect, despite their socio-economic and political differences, the USA and Russia have much in common. Russian history over the last few centuries has been filled with fears of conspiracy: Jews, Freemasons and Catholics have been considered major enemies (Davis, 1971; Bagdasarian, 1999). Furthermore, as in the USA, the messianic idea of the 'City upon the Hill' (Goldberg, 2001) and Moscow as the Third Rome (Duncan, 2005) provided fertile soil for suspicion and fear of others who wanted to prevent it from fulfilling its global mission. Yet, there is one major difference between these two cases. In the USA, conspiracy theories normally emerge from grassroots movements and are kept at the margins of official political discourse. In post-Soviet Russia the political and intellectual elites are major producers and disseminators of conspiracy theories. The top-down spread of these theories in Russia is reminiscent of countries in the Middle East, where the state is a 'conspiracist narrator' (Gray, 2010). As Gray shows, these theories provide the legitimization of political regimes and social cohesion in the face of mounting social and political challenges and the declining popularity of political leaders. What is special about the Russian case is that these ideas were initially employed to increase the popularity of the country's leaders at a time of economic growth.

Years before the annexation of Crimea, and Russian accusations that the USA was out to destroy the Russian economy by means of economic sanctions, Mikhail Iur'ev, a businessman and member of parliament, published an article entitled 'Fortress Russia: The Concept for the President' (Iur'ev, 2004). He praised Russia's radical economic and cultural isolation from the rest of the world, particularly the West; indeed, he called for complete severance of all ties with the West. He also argued that openness to the world would result in the destruction of the nation. This publication became iconic: from 2004, anti-Western conspiracy theories calling for isolation from the West began to infiltrate Russia's public domain, and by 2017 had become an integral part of public debates, television programmes and state legislation. A careful analysis of the ideas proposed by Iur'ev in the book-length study (Leont'ev et al., 2005), reveals that this isolationist ideology contains elements both of traditional anti-Westernism in Imperial Russia, and Soviet Cold War narratives that criticized the Russias' major rival, the USA. The crux of these ideas is the notion that ordinary Russians must unite with the authorities to deal with conspiracies on the part of the West, and that this unity will eventually turn Russia into a great world power. The Kremlin is not ready to cut all ties with the West at present. On the contrary, many Russian businessmen who keep loyalty to the Kremlin, prefer to keep their savings and invest money in assets in Europe and the USA (Maxwell, 2015; Cowdock, 2017). However, when fear of losing power begins to increase, political elites unhesitatingly attempt to turn Russia into a bastion of anti-Westernism.

Just as in the United States, conspiracy theories have long been a feature of Russian political discourse. This book will demonstrate that by the mid 2010s, the Russian political authorities, with the help of the media and public intellectuals (writers, journalists, media personalities, political scientists, spin doctors and those pseudoacademics who produce and disseminate conspiracy theories), had found a way of transforming these theories into an essential element of official political discourse that strengthened their legitimacy and helped keep society under control. In recent years we have learnt from Vladimir Putin that the Internet is an invention of the CIA and therefore part of the anti-Russian conspiracy (MacAskill, 2014); from Putin's economic adviser, Sergei Glaz'ev, that the Russian government has been infiltrated by foreign agents that undermine its economic stability in the face of sanctions (Adrianova, 2016); and from first deputy prime minister, Arkadii Dvorkovich, that the price of oil is in decline because foreign plotters are trying to destroy oil-rich Russia (Kuvakin, 2015).

In simple terms, this study investigates the reasons why Russian politicians are so keen on conspiracy theories and explores how these ideas help Russian leaders to exercise power through anti-Western conspiratorial rhetoric. As this rhetoric is aimed primarily at the domestic audience, the book will explore how conspiracy theories become the means of achieving popular mobilization, nation-building and community cohesion.¹ What role do public intellectuals play in developing and disseminating anti-Western conspiracy theories? What are the key events in Soviet and post-Soviet history that have generated the notion of anti-Western conspiracy? How do the political and intellectual elites of post-Soviet Russia use concepts which emerged in the Imperial and Soviet periods to produce and disseminate conspiracy theories? How do conspiracy theories enable political elites to reinforce their power? What is the impact of conspiracy theories on electoral campaigns? What role did anti-Western conspiracy theories play in framing the Ukraine crisis of 2014–16, and how were they used to help shape the unfolding crisis? These are some of the questions that this book tries to answer.

Because of the growing impact of conspiracy theories on Russian society today, I will focus on the post-Soviet period. The emergence of democratic and market institutions in Russia after the collapse of the USSR transformed society and opened the way for democratization. However, the rise of authoritarian trends has gradually undermined existing democratic institutions in the country, and this has led to doubts about how successful the Russian state's transition from state socialism to democracy has been. Russia does still demonstrate many elements of a democratic state, but these have acquired a specific form, leading to a 'hybrid regime'. Conspiracy theories play a crucial role in Russia's turn to authoritarianism and have served as a trigger for numerous public campaigns to justify repressive legislation. Yet these ideas are also often marginalized and perceived as eccentric and paranoid and therefore their study lacks academic depth and rigour. This book aims to demarginalize conspiracy theories and approach them as an integral part of the political process. To do so, it will examine the extent to which models for studying conspiracy theories developed in Western democracies can be applied to a non-Western transitional regime.

Conceptual Framework

The topic of conspiracy theories is gradually gaining popularity in the field of Russian, East European and Eurasian studies. Academics have analysed the role of conspiracy theories in fiction and memoirs

---

[1] Although in the 2010s Russian foreign policy strategy also includes the application of anti-US and anti-EU conspiracy theories (Yablokov, 2015), this would require a separate book-length study.

(Livers, 2010; Fedor, 2011; Amirian, 2013; Borenstein, 2017), popular films and documentaries (Razuvalova, 2015), and as a form of modern folklore (Panchenko, 2015; Astapova, 2015). Conspiracy theories as a form of national and social cohesion across post-Soviet states are also getting more attention (Golunov, 2012; Laruelle, 2012; Ortmann and Heathershaw, 2012; Yablokov, 2014; Radnitz, 2016).

Among the works that have studied specifically Russian conspiracy theories is Vardan Bagdasarian's (1999) analysis of conspiratorial literature. The author documents a large set of theories which appeared in the nineteenth and twentieth centuries and concentrates on the concept of conspiracy in the intellectual thought of Imperial and Soviet Russia, only briefly describing its evolution in post-Soviet Russia. According to Bagdasarian, conspiracy theories emerged in Russian society in the mid nineteenth century, because of the Russian defeat in the Crimean War of 1853–6, and of the liberal reforms carried out by Aleksandr II in the 1860s to 1870s. They were then disseminated by various conservative groups in Russian society such as the Slavophiles and radical nationalists, who resisted these reforms. Although he offered a thorough exploration of the conspiracy concepts Bagdasarian failed to develop a clear and systematic methodology of how to approach conspiracy theories in the specifically Russian context.

The lack of a clear methodological framework also characterizes Mikhail Khlebnikov's work on the subject (Khlebnikov, 2012). Khlebnikov traced the emergence of conspiracy theories in Russia from two sources: the movement of Judaizers (*eres' zhidovstvuiushchikh*) in the late medieval period, and secret societies, most notably Freemasonry, in the eighteenth century. Taking these two groups as the progenitors of conspiracy theories in Russia, the author documented the secret societies and various conspiracy theories which existed in Russia in the past. As with Bagdasarian, the lack of a clear methodology significantly reduced Khlebnikov's ability to investigate the roots and development of the phenomenon, as well as its social and political impact on post-Soviet Russia. Russian anthropologist Viktor Shnirel'man (2017) also focuses on conspiracy theories in his study of eschatological fears and anti-Semitic attitudes among Russian nationalists. This work does contribute to our understanding of the phenomenon within the Russian context. However, given the growing presence of conspiracy theories in mainstream political discourse, more has to be done.

A clearer conceptual framework can be designed using the US scholarship on the subject. In the USA conspiracy theories have been an object of scholarly research for almost seventy years, starting with Karl Popper's *Open Society and its Enemies* (1973, vol.2). Almost a decade later, Richard Hofstadter's concept of 'paranoid style', a term he coined in the 1960s, became a significant lens through which to analyse the phenomenon. Hofstadter's approach is sometimes referred to as 'symbolic' due to its emphasis on the symbolic dimension of politics and its stress on the non-rational part of political logic (Rogin, 1987, pp. 272–300). Hofstadter described how conspiracy theorists perceived the world by means of a merging of the clinical term 'paranoid' with historical analysis. He saw the conspiracist as a paranoid person who understood everything as part of an overarching plan to rule the world and perceived himself as involved in a struggle with an infallibly rational and evil enemy; who believed that the history of humankind itself was a grand conspiracy that could be packed into one theory (Hofstadter, 1996, pp. 29–37).

This judgemental conceptualization of conspiracy theories was the dominant approach to the subject for many years. Hofstadter, who developed his ideas in the era of McCarthyism, thought the main threat of conspiracy theories lay in right-wing populism. Daniel Pipes (1997), however, under the influence of the Cold War, extended the 'paranoid style' to left-wing politicians, focusing on conspiracy theories which were popular among Communists. Pipes carefully set out the structural elements of conspiracy mythmaking, depicting the adherent of conspiracy thinking as someone who interprets history as a process directed exclusively towards the realization of a grand plan. Lust for power and a firm belief that nothing happens by accident but is always the result of secretive agreements on the part of powerful people become the crucial pillars of the paranoid mentality, resulting in an oversimplification which is always a part of conspiracy theories (Robins and Post, 1997).

Neither Hofstadter nor his followers offered a robust framework for dealing with conspiracy theories. Pipes, instead, suggested that everyone concerned about the popularity of conspiracy theories should join a 'perpetual struggle' against conspiracy thinking whenever its elements were exposed (p. 49). As some scholars have noted, judgemental suggestions about how to define a conspiracy theory render authors advancing such arguments not entirely dissimilar to the objects of their studies (Dean, 2002, pp. 63–4). The 'symbolic' approach is certainly helpful in detecting conspiracy theories in public narratives. However, it fails to provide the necessary tools for a balanced analysis of the causes and prerequisites for conspiracy fears in the modern world.

INTRODUCTION

Another approach sees conspiracy theories as tools of political manipulation and is often described as 'realist' or 'rationalist'. Scholars who adopt this position argue that 'it is neither accurate nor useful to portray right-wing populists as a "lunatic fringe" of marginal "extremists" since they represent ordinary people, our neighbours and co-workers, whose rhetoric and actions have mundane reasons' (Berlet and Nemiroff Lyons, 2000, pp. 3–4). This approach sees conspiracy theories as the product of small marginal groups (mostly on the Far Right) who exploit populist anti-elitist rhetoric to scapegoat certain groups. Consequently, conspiracy theories become a tool of manipulation for right-wing groups and politicians for the purposes of mobilization and the delegitimization of their opponents. Unlike 'symbolists' such as Hofstadter, scholars of the 'rationalist' approach argue that popular conspiracy fears become part of comprehensible projects that are used by the political leaders to achieve political and economic goals. Although these fears sometimes seem bizarre and exaggerated, their rationalist core points to the clearly identified interests of certain groups.

The 'realist' concept is relatively instrumentalist and is based on the perception of conspiracy theories as a political tool. However, the emphasis on the psychological component of beliefs in conspiracy theories gives it common ground with the 'symbolist' approach. Yet the evocation of psychopathology and references to anxiety among advocates of conspiracy theories (which at times is indeed manifested) are still unable to explain the popularity of conspiracy theories in modern culture. Moreover, it would be incorrect to label as paranoids many people who believe in conspiracy theories, as they often express the ideas that reflect key social issues (Harambam and Aupers, 2016). While the 'symbolist' approach overlooks the 'functional' aspect of conspiracy thinking, the 'realist' approach is unable to clearly locate the conspiratorial mode of thinking in various domains of political and popular culture. A common shortcoming of the concepts we have discussed is their over-stigmatization, even though both Hofstadter and Berlet point out that sometimes conspiracy theorists could be 'on to something', and that their beliefs might have some factual basis in real politics – that is, that there are some real conspiracies.

The extraordinary development of conspiracy theories in the USA in the 1990s in all spheres of public life demonstrated that they were not merely tools enabling deranged people to comprehend the world. Accordingly, in the late 1990s a new approach was introduced which considered the possibility that conspiracy theories could, in fact, constitute a mode of rational thinking, a portal 'through which social phenomena were discussed' (Bratich, 2008, p. 6). Its adherents pointed out that existing interpretations failed to explain the popularity of conspiracy theories among people with different political views, and that while they had previously been associated with particular social or political groups, they had evolved into a more widespread way of interpreting reality. No longer seen as marginal, the idea of conspiracy was now considered to be a regular feature of cultural life, even a mainstream concept, which was used by writers, filmmakers and musicians (Birchall, 2006).

The dilemma of how to analyse conspiracy mythmaking still had no clear-cut solution. To what extent could a certain story be regarded as a conspiracy theory? To what extent did conspiracy theories contain some factual elements? The real conspiracies of the past largely determine the perception of conspiracy ideas in the present, leading to public trust in conspiratorial explanations (Olmsted, 2009).

The new approach to conspiracy discourse, freed from the old dismissive attitudes, could help us to navigate our way through the complexity of modern politics and understand that conspiracy ideas have some social, even positive functions. They might serve as a legitimate tool for the interpretation of power relationships in the modern world. They could challenge the existing social and political state of affairs to transform it in a positive (or, conversely, a negative) way. They could constitute an important 'creative response' to social change. As Fenster (2008, p. 10) argues, conspiracy theories could serve as 'a means to rally support' and at the same time delegitimize opponents 'by branding their beliefs as paranoid'. This new approach, then, is based on the recognition that conspiracy theories can become an important tool for the redistribution of power and an efficient political strategy to expose inequities within the political, economic and social order.

This inevitably leads us to a discussion of the ways in which conspiracy theories are used to persuade the centres of power to redistribute their resources. Populist rhetoric is the principal method of vocalizing conspiracy theories on a political level. Accordingly, Fenster concludes that conspiracy theory is a populist theory of power (p. 89). It possesses an important communicative function by helping to unite 'the people' against the imagined 'Other' represented by the secretive 'power bloc'. The ability of conspiracy discourse to express popular fears and hence foster unity among 'the people' explains its widespread use in the populist rhetoric of authoritarian and fascist regimes. However, since theories are not confined to authoritarian regimes, particularly in the present day, Fenster defines conspiracy mythmaking as an 'ideological misrecognition of power relations' which may occur in any political system (pp. 84–90).

Fenster's argument rests on the broad interpretation of populism introduced by Francisco Panizza and Ernesto Laclau, who see it as 'a mode of identification available to any actor operating in a discursive field in which the notion of the sovereignty of the people and its inevitable corollary, the conflict between the powerful and the powerless, are core elements of its political imaginary' (Panizza, 2005, p. 4). A key feature of this interpretation is the division of society into two antagonistic camps: 'the people', united on the basis of popular demand, oppose the 'Other', the power bloc; this represents the typical juxtaposition of 'Us' versus 'Them'. In Laclau's words, these two camps constitute 'the power' and 'the underdog'. 'The underdog's appeal is based on popular demands and its role is to challenge the social order and gain power, thereby fulfilling popular demands' (Laclau, 2005b, pp. 37–8). Populism also performs the function of gathering different elements of the social into a new identity (Laclau, 2005a, pp. 93–101). This reading of populism accepts that it can exist in a democratic society; it can provide a necessary challenge to the existing democratic order when the latter fails to address certain cutting-edge issues.

Populism, according to this interpretation, has an obvious connection to conspiracy theory. The invention of 'the people' in its various forms (depending on a given 'demand') very often requires a clear and persuasive image of the 'Other', and this can be provided by the conspiracy narrative through generation of fear of foreign or internal deception or subversion. This 'communicative' function of conspiracy theory plays an important role in political discourses and helps to create political identities. Such discourses also address concerns about the inequities of the social system and occasionally pose a positive challenge to the existing social order (Fenster, 2008, pp. 89–90). As we shall see, this understanding of conspiracy theory will prove useful in analysing Russian conspiracy mythmaking and its place in domestic politics.

As Ortmann and Heathershaw (2012, p. 554) noted, conspiracy theories in the post-Soviet context should be studied as a social phenomenon and a specific discursive approach. Fenster's understanding of conspiracy theories provides a useful set of instruments with which to analyse the Russian situation. Firstly, it enables us to abandon the traditional reading of conspiracy theories as easily dismissible paranoia, and study the role of conspiracy fears in the process of nation-building and the formation of collective identities.

INTRODUCTION

The emergence of nation-states established a path to democracy and set conditions for populism. The populist rhetoric, in turn, enabled politicians to search for an 'Other' to correspond to 'the people' (an essential development since it is only possible to identify 'the people' by identifying its 'Other' (Panizza, 2005, p. 6).

In the case of Russian national identity, the ultimate 'Other' has historically been the West, often imagined as 'a single undifferentiated entity ... regarded either as a positive model for Russia to emulate or as a negative example to be rejected', and this has served to define the borders of national identity and its place in world history (Tolz, 2001, p. 70). Fears of anti-Western conspiracy arise as a part of the so-called 'ressentiment' that was born from the recognition of the discrepancy between Russia and its ideal or opponent, the 'West', and which demonstrate Russia's equality or superiority to it (Greenfield, 1992, p. 234). In the mind of a typical Russian nationalist with anti-Western views, the West appears as an ultimate and insidious 'Other' seeking to undermine the progress of the Russian nation.

Secondly, when used to analyse domestic politics in post-Soviet Russian society, this approach enables us to explore the creation of political identities and the struggle for power within the country. The acknowledgement that conspiracy theory is an inherent feature of the popular political discourse of most societies, even democratic ones, allows us to see the post-Soviet Russian political process as a set of specific 'demands' that reflect the vital issues of a transitional society. Used by various Russian political actors to explain the enormous changes in Russia post-1991 and the complexities of its economic and social relations, domestic developments, international relations and cultural processes, the language of conspiracy offers a symbolic resolution to the issue of who is responsible for the problems which have emerged in Russian society, and serves to oversimplify the nature of events (Knight, 2000, p. 32). This approach enables us to see how various actors in Russian political life have employed the rhetoric of conspiracy to strengthen their position in competing for public support in the state.

Fenster uses the theory of populism to study the division of a nation into the 'treacherous elite' and the 'trustworthy people'. His methodology is applied to specific aspects of domestic politics in a democratic state, in which the divisions in society are used to frame discussion of different issues in the domestic agenda. Acknowledging the methodological value of Fenster's study, this book also uses his methodology to study how conspiracy theory, as an element of populist politics, is applied to the fostering of national cohesion in post-Soviet Russia.

INTRODUCTION

It demonstrates that the use of anti-Western conspiracy theories by political elites divides the world into the West on the one hand, presented as a single entity with a powerful elite, and Russian political leaders and intellectuals on the other, who are speaking on behalf of 'the people'.

This book analyses political discourse both in political documents, and the public speeches of politicians. It also explores the writings of public intellectuals, showing how politicians selectively use conspiracy concepts, ideas and theories which have been elaborated by those intellectuals. The sources are analysed through a close reading of the texts, against the background of the historical and political situations at the time of their publication. Attention is paid to the interpretative frames used by authors and some promoters of conspiracy theories. I use a set of tools drawn from discourse analysis to analyse my material and see how a particular type of discourse, that of the anti-Western conspiracy, attempts to construct social reality (Phillips and Hardy, 2002). Following Erving Goffman's (1974) definition of frames, i.e. that one specific interpretation of events prevails over others, I present conspiracy theories as a specific type of social frame which identifies the origins of events as the outcome of secret plots. The application of conspiracy frames allows various social actors and social movements to define and problematize social, political and economic issues to pursue their political goals (Benford and Snow, 2000).

In my analysis of texts, I also apply Critical Discourse Analysis (CDA), which provides a wide set of tools for the study of both language and the social developments reflected through it. CDA understands discourse as a form of social practice 'which both constitutes the social world and is constituted by other social practices' (Jørgensen and Phillips, 2002, p. 61). CDA can reveal how language is employed to exercise power and the extent to which linguistic elements can determine social reality. This approach implies that discourse possesses an ideological effect which contributes to the creation and reproduction of unequal power relations between different social groups, and shows how language contributes to the maintenance of power (Jørgensen and Phillips, 2002, p. 63).

Given that this book is primarily concerned with the use of conspiracy theories by political and intellectual elites in Russia, three groups of people in these categories are identified and analysed in terms of their salience, their impact on domestic politics and the degree to which conspiracy theories are used.

The first group consists of public intellectuals, journalists and various media personalities. In many respects, these people shape the intellectual framework of public conspiracy discourse and develop its conceptual apparatus, making it relevant to the current political agenda. They support the political actions of the authorities, justify political decisions and explain political events through journal articles, interviews and public appearances. The second group consists of politicians who are members of political parties and political movements.[2] It is, though, difficult to accurately determine who is a member of this group because the Russian political arena includes so many political movements and parties, and only a minority are represented in the legislative branch of government. Being a member of parliament would not be an accurate indicator of inclusion in this group because even the so-called 'non-systemic opposition' has sufficiently powerful resources to enable it to disseminate conspiracy theories. All the same, the impact which members of parliament and political movements have on domestic politics cannot be compared with the political power of the executive branch of the government, which constitutes the third group. This includes the President and the Prime Minister of the Russian Federation and members of their staff. This group also includes leaders of the United Russia party whose influence and decisions are pivotal in determining the domestic political agenda.

Structure of the Book

Chapter 1 outlines the history of conspiracy theories in Russia from the end of the eighteenth century, and shows how the tradition of searching for enemies developed among political and intellectual elites of Imperial and Soviet Russia.

Chapter 2 studies the role of public intellectuals in producing and disseminating conspiracy theories in post-Soviet Russia. It investigates the collaboration of Russian intellectuals with the authorities, and how prominent public intellectuals and media personalities introduce conspiracy theories into mainstream political discourse.

Chapter 3 analyses conspiratorial narratives relating to the collapse of the USSR in 1991, and their function in domestic politics. It demonstrates how the application of conspiracy discourse to two major events – the August 1991 coup and the subsequent collapse

---

[2] The analysis does not include the groups of the so-called 'non-systemic' opposition such as right-wing extreme nationalists because it would have required a significant widening of the research focus.

of the Soviet state in December 1991 – became a powerful political instrument.

Chapter 4 examines the impact of conspiracy theories on the nation-building policies of the Kremlin in the 2000s. It studies the Kremlin's attempts in the 2000s to create a Russian national identity based on the concept of sovereign democracy, a term coined by the Kremlin's 'grey cardinal' Vladislav Surkov when he was Deputy Head of the Presidential Administration.

Chapter 5 focuses more specifically on the utilization of anti-Western conspiracy theories in domestic politics. Its primary focus is the Yukos affair and the three campaigns against non-governmental organizations (NGOs) which were based on the notion of a subversive 'fifth column' within the state. The chapter also examines the dynamics of the anti-Western conspiracy narratives and the evolution of political strategies which have been used against the Kremlin's political opponents.

Chapter 6 investigates the domestic application of anti-Western conspiracy theories and the role of conspiratorial narratives in the electoral campaigns of 2007–8 and 2011–12. Following Fenster's definition of conspiracy theories as a tool for redistribution of power between political actors, this chapter looks at the place of conspiracy theories in electoral campaigns.

Chapter 7 looks at the use of anti-Western conspiracy theories during the Ukraine crisis of 2014–16. It demonstrates how the corpus of conspiracy theories, which were developed throughout the post-Soviet era, has been taken up by television, and used for unprecedented public mobilization against the West.

1
Building 'Fortress Russia'

The Imperial Period

Conspiracy theories have a long history in Russia. According to Andrei Zorin (2001), the concept of conspiracy originated in European intellectual thought and arrived in Russia in the eighteenth century. Zorin analysed a poem by a court poet, Vasilii Petrov, that described an alliance of European countries against Russia, which they perceived to be a growing power with global ambitions. Petrov saw the intrigues of European monarchs against Russia as a malevolent plan to destroy the country's greatness. Although this cannot be called a genuine conspiracy theory since it lacks the crucial elements, it points to the origins of the phenomenon and the social level at which these concepts initially emerged. As with Western European countries, ideas about conspiracy in Russia initially emanated from intellectual and political elites who were well educated and who suffered the most from changes in the social and political environment (von Bieberstein, 2008).

Fears about masonic plots – one of the most popular and enduring of conspiracy theories, which first emerged in the mid eighteenth century – were also promulgated, for the most part, by people in the upper echelons of Russian society. As Smith (1999) demonstrates, suspicion of Freemasonry in Russia was based on rumours that its members had close ties to the devil, were atheists and indulged in sexual rituals. In this respect, Russia was no different to Europe. These fears about the Masonry appeared simultaneously in other European countries, with Freemasons accused, for example, of triggering the French revolution. A similar fear in Russia that Freemasons were plotting revolution led the Russian state to clamp down on them at the end of the eighteenth century, closing Freemason societies across the country and imprisoning the leader, Nikolai Novikov. All the same, fear of what was thought to be the omnipotent Masonry continued throughout the nineteenth and twentieth centuries as an important element in anti-Western conspiracy theories (Nilus, [1903] 2012; Platonov, 1996).

The anti-Western stance did not undergo any significant development until the mid nineteenth century. Even the famous debates between Slavophiles and the Westernizers, which began in the late eighteenth century, was less harsh at the beginning of the nineteenth century than it was at the end. Vera Tolz points out that the first round of debates between Westernizers and Slavophiles 'reflected the divide between cosmopolitans of the Enlightenment and (proto) nationalists' (2001, p. 65). In the late eighteenth and early nineteenth centuries the rapid development of the nation had not yet begun; this would not happen until the second half of the nineteenth century. Accordingly, a search for the dangerous 'Other', which would help to design the country's identity and clarify who was 'Us' and 'Them', was at a premature stage.

The watershed in the rapid development of conspiracy theories in Russia was the Crimean War (1853–6), which was triggered by the desire of Russia's rulers to gain control over the territories of the Ottoman Empire. The alliance of European governments supporting the Ottoman Empire was devastating for Russia, and resulted in her losing territory, influence in Europe, and the right to keep a fleet on the Black Sea. Many conservative thinkers in Russia had imagined her advancing into the Middle East and the Balkans as part of a messianic mission; these illusions of grandeur were now shattered (Duncan, 2005).

A new generation of Slavophiles emerged in the wake of the Crimean disaster, with more radical views about the West. Russia's humiliation in the Crimean War was not the only factor in the spread of anti-Western sentiment and conspiracy fears. The Slavophiles enjoyed the support of conservative groups in governing circles, especially during the reign of Aleksandr III, who promoted a counter-liberal agenda. Many elements of anti-Western conspiracy theories appeared in Russia at this time.

The proliferation of conspiracy fears in the Russian Empire in the late nineteenth century was the result of several factors. Aleksandr II introduced a series of reforms which liberalized Russia and set it on the path of rapid industrialization and modernization. The mass migration of people from villages to cities changed the social structure of Russian society, and helped spread rumours and fears (Fuller, 2006; Kolonitskii, 2010). In addition, Russians became better educated as a result of Aleksandr's educational reforms, and this was instrumental in helping to produce and disseminate conspiratorial ideas. As Hofstadter explains, conspiracy theorists aimed to present their ideas in an academic style, and this required a basic education and the ability to formulate ideas. Ironically, conspiracy theories became a mechanism by which conservative intellectual elites understood the liberal changes that were taking place in Russian society. Aleksandr's reforms, which allowed more freedom for both liberal and conservative groups, were perceived by the conservatives as a Western plan to corrupt and destroy Russia.

Among the first groups of intellectuals which openly endorsed conspiratorial notions to interpret domestic and foreign policies were the conservatives, that were called '*okhraniteli*' (defenders). Their clear anti-Western views were characteristic of conspiracy theories in late Imperial Russia. The idea that Russia had a special path (*teoriia osobogo puti*), an historic mission to save the world, rested on an idealized vision of the country as a repository of morality and of Christian Orthodoxy (Poe, 2000). The writer Dostoevsky became a driving force in disseminating the idea of Russia's global mission, both in the nineteenth century and for later generations of Russian conservatives. *The Diary of a Writer* became a manifesto for Russian conservatism, outlining the main tenets of Russia's 'special mission' (Dostoevsky, 1995). The dichotomy between the corrupt Catholic Church of the West and the pure and faithful Orthodox Church of the East framed the conflict between Russia and the West. The revolutionaries who emerged in post-Crimean Russia were in Dostoevsky's view, connected to Catholicism and hence a weapon being used by the West to destroy Russia from within.

The perceived need to extricate Russia from heretical Western influence was also an important issue for late Slavophiles. Aleksei Khomiakov, one of the early Slavophiles, had put forward the idea that Russia had become a virtual colony of the West because of Peter the Great's reforms. To shape a new national identity, Russians needed to rid themselves of Western influence and promote a spiritual rebirth (Khomiakov, 1982). Danilevskii, a prominent thinker of the late nineteenth century, went so far as to advocate the radical separation of Russia from Europe, insisting that Russia was an autonomous cultural-historical entity which must evolve independently from Europe (Danilevskii, 2013). Danilevskii's ideas have been widely adopted in the writings of post-Soviet conspiracy theorists and, as we will see, have often been used to explain supposed Western hatred towards Russia.

Nationalist movements reached their apotheosis in the period of Aleksandr II's reforms. Following the Polish uprising of 1863 and the rise of Ukrainian nationalists (Miller, 2012b), the term 'national' began to appear more frequently in the conservative press. The Poles and the Jews, who inhabited the Western territories of the Russian empire, were often depicted as Russia's main enemies. The Poles were considered particularly dangerous not only due to their religion but also because they had a strong and active nationalist movement which was thought to threaten the integrity of the Empire. The image of the conspiratorial Catholic Polish priest was central to these fears. The Imperial government was also suspicious about local anti-Russian Catholic activists who were thought to receive instructions from their foreign superiors on how to resist and overthrow the Tsar (Dolbilov, 2010).

Mikhail Katkov, a prominent writer and publisher in nineteenth-century Russia, was an iconic conservative conspiracy theorist of the late nineteenth century who focused on the supposed Western plot. He linked the threat to Russia by Polish revolutionaries directly to Western anti-Russian plotters. In his view, every Russian patriot had a duty to be loyal to the state in the same way that a soldier was loyal to his commander. A 'genuine Russian' had to be an Orthodox Christian, a committed monarchist and a loyal subject. If not, he would be considered an enemy of the nation (Katkov, 1863). Just as post-Soviet Russian conspiracy theorists claim that the opposition movement gets funding from the West, Katkov accused the Poles of funding bloodshed and revolution with money from abroad (Katkov, 1881). As is typical of conspiracy theorists, Katkov divided Russia into two groups, the national and anti-national. The nationalists rejected reforms which they considered to threaten Russia's very existence; they thought they were aimed at changing Russia's territorial integrity, and that this could only benefit Russia's enemies (Katkov, 1880). They believed that anti-Russian plotters in the West manipulated revolutionaries into threatening and destabilizing the Russian monarchy; they also tried to destroy Russia's reputation in the European press and wrote cynical lies portraying the country as backward (Katkov, 1865).

Katkov became the key intellectual in the promotion of the counter-reforms which began during the reign of Aleksandr III; his radical conservative views bolstered repressive legislation in schools, universities and the press (Riabov, 2010). The counter-revolutionary measures introduced by the government and the rise of radical Russian nationalism led to anti-Semitic conspiracy theories which became central to the conspiratorial discourse up to the October 1917 revolution and since then have been an important element in the conspiratorial discourse of Russia's far right movements (Shnirel'man, 2002; Rossman, 2002; Shnirel'man, 2012).

Savelii Dudakov *(1993)* undertook a detailed study of the anti-Jewish conspiratorial attitudes in Russian nineteenth-century fiction which provided the impetus for the dissemination of one of the most persistent anti-Jewish conspiratorial texts of all times, *The Protocols of the Elders of Zion*. This fabricated pamphlet was used as evidence of a global 'Jewish-Masonic conspiracy' to achieve world domination. Its impact on Russian society was enormous. Its origins are still not fully understood. It is likely that it stemmed from long-standing anti-Jewish sentiment, which increased considerably in the late nineteenth century. As Michael Hagemeister (2008) demonstrates, anti-Semitic conspiracy theories existed in Russia long before the *Protocols* appeared; they were just another iteration of the conspiracy myth.

Jacob Brafman's *The Book of the Kahal* could be considered a conceptual precursor of the *Protocols*. The Kahal was a traditional form of social organization of Eastern European Jews. The Russian authorities, together with enlightened and secularized Jews, attempted to dismantle the Kahal to assimilate Jews, who had hitherto lived in the pale of settlement, into mainstream Russian society. The state plan to take the Jews out of the Kahal was not well designed and was inconsistently applied, often leaving the newly assimilated Jews with, at best, very limited rights (Lowe, 1993). However, Brafman's interpretation of the persistence of the Kahal was influential. The author presented the Kahal as a 'state within the state' – a typical anti-Semitic image – which supposedly had tremendous power over its members, as well as tentacles which reached beyond its borders into the Russian Empire as a whole (Brafman, 2005). This portrayal of the Jewish organization added to concern on the part of Russian intellectuals from both sides of the political spectrum about the reforms in Russia. As Israel Bartal (2005) noted, the Jews were the 'convenient Other' for the left, who saw them as landowners and exploiters of peasants; while for the right they were subversive agents of Western modernization and hence represented mortal danger to the Russian nation.

The spread of popular political movements and the growth of the far-right movement in the run up to the 1905 revolution turned anti-

Jewish conspiracy theories into a powerful instrument for popular mobilization (Laquer, 1993). The 'Black Hundreds', a conglomerate of far right political movements in late Imperial Russia, were in the vanguard of the Russian conspiracy culture. They embraced anti-Semitic conspiracy theories, especially the *Protocols*, which won them substantial support. The anti-Jewish pogroms of the late nineteenth and early twentieth centuries, which were organized by the 'Black Hundreds', demonstrate the potentially destructive nature of conspiratorial ideas (Klier, 2014).

The rapidly changing socio-economic environment following Aleksandr II's reforms left many people vulnerable to the changing environment of everyday life, and this explains, to a certain extent, the wide acceptance of these ideas. There was a developing nationalist mood in Russia before and during the First World War, and this was used by the authorities to foster short-term social cohesion in support of the regime (Schimmelpenninck Van Der Oye, 2001; Lohr, 2003). As was usually the case, this mobilization was achieved by creating an image of a dangerous, conspiring 'Other', in the form of other nationalities. This alienated many ethnic groups, which in turn led to concern on the part of the authorities about potential treason.

Fears about rebellion within the Russian Empire demonstrate the pervasiveness of conspiracy theories among different social and political groups by the end of the Imperial period. Fuller (2006) argues that the pattern of conspiracy thinking, together with other social and political developments, prepared the intellectual platform for the February and October revolutions of 1917, and played a crucial role in undermining the position of the ruling elites. Fear of treason and conspiracy became accepted features of the interpretation of the political situation in late Imperial Russia, and contributed to the development of a conspiracy culture in the Soviet period.

The Soviet Period

While the political and intellectual elites of Imperial Russia occasionally utilized ideas of conspiracy to secure their positions, and justify the suspension of liberal reforms, in the Soviet period these ideas found a new purpose. The politics of large-scale social and economic modernization led to the instrumental deployment of conspiracy discourse in Soviet propaganda. The 'enemy of the people' (*vrag naroda*) is a particularly clear example of the Bolsheviks' binary view of the world (Bonnell, 1999), as is the discursive division of the world into the socialist and capitalist blocs. The search for internal and external enemies became a paradigm of Bolshevik rule after the 1917 revolution. The Bolshevik state had to protect itself from plots by capitalists and members of the ancien régime. The Emergency Committee (the notorious Cheka) and the Red Army fought against counter-revolutionaries who, in cahoots with their Western allies, had supposedly started the Civil War to reinstate the capitalist exploiters (Mints, 1979). This understanding of the Soviet Union as a besieged nation became a norm in Soviet life, especially in the 1930s when the active search for public enemies and 'wreckers' began. During the Great Terror, as Sheila Fitzpatrick (2000) has demonstrated, the pursuit of conspiracies affected millions of citizens in all walks of life. To the authorities' suspicious eye, friends and colleagues who created informal networks to help each other survive the hard times of post-revolutionary Russia looked like groups of plotters and spies.

The incredible number of deaths in the first post-revolutionary decades, as well as the devastated state of the economy, put additional burdens both on the party apparatus, and on ordinary people. The latter had to work in extreme conditions and under enormous pressure because of the state's single-minded focus on the country's economic development. The growth of Nazism and the threat of foreign invasion by the capitalist states meant that what had previously just been speculation about the possibility of conspiracy and 'wrecking' was now portrayed as fact. In 1937, an article in the *Pravda*, the Soviet main newspaper, stated: 'We know that engines do not stop by themselves, machine tools do not break down on their own, boilers do not explode on their own. Someone's hand is hidden behind these events' (quoted in Rittersporn, 2014, p. 34). This supposed certainty about the work of a malevolent hand enabled bureaucrats at all levels to explain away malfunctions in the economy and industry. In this environment of Stalinist repression, suspicion about conspiracies infiltrated all layers of Soviet life and even undermined the legitimacy of ruling elites.

The mass purges of the 1930s are often explained by reference to Stalin's paranoid personality (Robins and Post, 1987; Rhodes, 1997; Stal, 2013). This is an oversimplification although it is worth noting that constant power struggles did result in Stalin becoming suspicious. He dealt with internal opposition, as well as criticism from 'old Bolsheviks', with extreme post-revolutionary brutality, even though most of his victims swore allegiance to him (Khlevniuk, 2009). The battle for rapid industrialization resulted in a complete refusal to compromise and a demand for total loyalty. In the 1930s the intelligence service [OGPU] warned of imminent war on two fronts: with Japan and the Nazi Germany; this exacerbated the atmosphere of fear of subversion, which in turn reinforced Stalin's conviction that there were indeed malevolent plots. OGPU derived its 'evidence' of conspiracies by forcefully extracting the names of possible co-conspirators from people who had already been arrested. The apparent prevalence of 'enemies' was a further factor in spreading fear throughout the population, and reinforced Stalin's belief that there were malevolent plots against the country. Hence this use of fear was not a cynical ruse to gain greater control over the population; Stalin succumbed to it himself. In the view of the Soviet rulers, any relaxation of domestic policies, or the toning down of punishment for those who had not fulfilled the plan, could provide counter-revolutionaries with a reason for not adhering to the demands of the state (Harris, 2015). The notion that the country was under siege instrumentalized the conspiratorial discourse, turning it into an effective tool to secure absolute power.

Kratkii kurs VKPb (A Short Course of the All-Union Communist Party of the Bolsheviks), published in 1938, became the principal document outlining the ideological tenets of the Soviet regime and the reasons for the Bolshevik Party's success. It established the juxtaposition of the USSR and the forces of 'world imperialism', thereby justifying the belief in conspiratorial notions and the brutal punishments meted out to political opponents (Halfin, 2001). Stalin insisted that there would be an inevitable escalation in the conflict between the Bolsheviks and the bourgeoisie as socialism developed and this explained why internal enemies in the late 1930s had become so active. Article 58 of the Criminal Law of the RSFSR, introduced in the late 1920s, treated relations with a foreign state or its representatives as a serious crime against the Soviet Union, often punishable by death (Applebaum, 2004). In addition, the term 'agent of a foreign country' was used in the political discourse of the Stalin era as a synonym for a 'fifth column', a *spy (shpion)* or a *subversive element (podryvnoi element)* (Stalin, 1997). Public trials of 'enemies of the people' contributed to the atmosphere of suspicion. This was all linked back to the treachery of the capitalist countries. As we will see in the following chapters, these ideas have resurfaced in a specific form in Putin's Russia.

After the Second World War, despite the brief hopes of harmonious coexistence between the triumphant powers, the descending Iron Curtain and Stalin's growing suspicion of the Allies sparked the Cold War and caused a new wave of aggressive conspiratorial propaganda within the country. The Marshall Plan was rejected by the Soviet Union because it was viewed as a clandestine method on the part of the USA to destroy Communism by stealth by means of the economic control which the plan would initially impose on participants. The US nuclear tests pressurized the Soviet authorities into searching for an alternative path towards post-war recovery instead of cooperation with the Allies: the resources were drawn out from within the country. This led to further isolation from the West. The Soviet Union's plans for a rapid and independent recovery from the ravages of war resulted in a plummeting of citizens' living standards (Zubok, 2009). To justify this, another 'Other' had to be created. The foreign enemy was clear: the 'Anglo Saxon' world led by the United States and the United Kingdom. Citizens were ready to accept this latest standoff between the Soviet Union and the West because of rumours that an invasion by Western countries was, again, a distinct possibility (Johnston, 2011).

This apparent prospect of external invasion led to renewed fear of internal subversion and led to a new wave of repression. The victims were both ordinary citizens, and elite members of Stalin's inner circle (Gorlizki and Khlevniuk, 2004). A distinctive feature of these post-war conspiratorial witch-hunts was the focus on Jews as supposed agents of the West. From the late Stalin years, anti-Jewish and anti-Israeli conspiratorial rhetoric became a prominent part of official and informal discourse in the Soviet Union, right up to the country's collapse in 1991 (Korey, 2004; Kostyrchenko, 2010).

In the later stages of the Cold War, the principal protagonist in anti-Soviet conspiracy was supposedly the CIA, acting with the support of spies and dissidents within the USSR (Iakovlev, 1983). The CIA embodied the crucial features of conspiracy theories, and its intrigues even played a prominent role in late Soviet popular culture. Television series such as 'The Shield and the Sword' (1968), '17 Moments of Spring' (1973) and 'TASS is Authorized to Announce' (1984) made Soviet spies and intelligence officers role models for millions of young Soviet men. Fear of foreign subversion was, of course, not purely based on fiction; both the USA and the USSR were engaged in spy missions to gain access to military and political secrets with the view of destroying the other. The USA and the UK disseminated pamphlets, funded radio stations and waged propaganda campaigns to spread an alternative view of the news among the Soviet citizens and so subvert their trust in the regime.

Suspicion became part and parcel of the daily life of Soviet citizens. Living under the constant observation of neighbours and authorities in communal flats, attempting to keep secrets from them, and suspecting them of engaging in plots, served as a breeding ground for conspiratorial fears (Boym, 1994). As Ilya Utekhin has demonstrated, suspicion and paranoid assumptions about the people next door were central to the consciousness of the late Soviet citizen, and have survived the Soviet collapse (Utekhin, 2004).

The pervasive image of an internal, conspiring enemy had a deep effect on Russian national identity. In the post-war decades this identity was shaped by reference to the 'conspiring Western rival', and this became the ideological foundation of Russian nationalism (Brudny, 1998). Moreover, the notion of conspiracy was actively used to delegitimize political opponents, and to legitimize violence against various social groups. For example, during the Thaw era, when Khrushchev launched the de-Stalinization campaign, the modus of conspiratorial thinking was still very active and was used by Khrushchev's opponents to oppose dramatic changes in domestic politics (Dobson, 2009). On the other hand, the political persecution of different groups and the atmosphere of fear led to a suspicion towards authority, effectively laying the foundations for anti-government conspiracy thinking (Mitrokhin, 2003).

This short overview of Russian conspiracy theories before 1991 demonstrates that the Russian conspiratorial tradition is rich and multi-faceted, and to a large extent defines the conspiratorial thinking of the post-Soviet era. The legacy of both the Imperial period and, especially, the Soviet period of Russian history is evident in the common assumption that unpopular socio-economic and political changes are the result of conspiracy. Russian messianism and the insistence on Russian greatness underlie the popularity of conspiracy theories. At the same time, the constant purges of enemies of the regime in the Stalin era, and the spy battles – both real and fictional – during the Cold War contributed to the spread of conspiracy fears among the general population. Two hundred years of conspiracy mythmaking have been decisive in shaping the notion that the West is the ultimate enemy. The emergence and proliferation of anti-Western attitudes in the post-Soviet era have, then, a solid and well-developed foundation.

2
The Spectres of Conspiracy Mythmaking

Public intellectuals play an enormous role in the development and promotion of conspiracy theories.[1] To sound convincing, conspiratorial explanation must be well-executed, and the use of numerous references and conformity to pseudo-science are both features of conspiracy theory writing (Aaronovitch, 2009, pp. 9–14). A conspiracy theorist with high social status is also able to endow his or her interpretation with a certain academic credibility.

This is certainly the case with anti-Western conspiracy discourse in Russia. As mentioned in the previous chapter, Russian intellectuals in the nineteenth century started the mass dissemination of anti-Western conspiracy theories, and in the Soviet period prominent Soviet intellectuals, as well as various factions within the Soviet government, published conspiracy tracts in popular literary magazines (Brudny, 1998; Mitrokhin, 2003). Gorbachev's liberal reforms and the collapse of the Soviet Union created fertile ground for the dissemination of conspiracy myths, which were spread through books and political debates. The idea of the conspiring West, as articulated by national-patriotic forces, was added to the ideological arsenal of Yeltsin's opponents, and received the support of several prominent academics, writers and public figures such as high-profile historians Anatolii Utkin and Igor' Froianov. Through this collective intellectual effort, anti-Western conspiracy discourse was turned into one of the main lenses through which history and global politics were viewed by Russians after 1991.

---

[1] Given the fact that the phenomenon of the public intellectual attracted significant scholarly attention, for the purposes of this research I define a public intellectual as a renowned person whose activities are primarily aimed at the production and dissemination of knowledge among the public.

This chapter seeks to contextualize the role of public intellectuals in the production and dissemination of conspiracy theories within the broader anti-Western ideological movement in Russia. Previous works have focused more on concrete personalities and movements within the anti-Western intellectual camp (Shenfield, 2001; Umland, 2007; Laruelle, 2008), saying little about the conspiracy theories deployed by these individuals. This chapter goes beyond this approach and looks specifically at the conspiracy theories these people spread. The theories put forward by selected intellectuals are analysed within the context of their political and public careers; this will allow us to draw conclusions about the interplay of conspiracy discourse and official political discourse.

Hofstadter, analysing conspiracy theorists in the USA, saw them as adherents of the 'paranoid style' which had limited support in society as a whole; this meant that conspiracy views played a marginal role. Fenster, however (2008, p. 39), claimed that Hofstadter had been frightened by the rise of populist demagoguery in the 1950s, which he thought disrupted the usual border between the acceptable rationale of mainstream politics and extreme populist pronouncements. As a result, his reference to the 'paranoid style' was a way of excluding conspiracy theorists from mainstream politics. This exclusion and public criticism of individuals who promoted conspiracy theories took place despite the high social and academic status of those involved. For that reason, conspiratorial discourse in America now takes the form of an apparently anti-intellectual critique of political elites, and conspiracy theorists often present themselves as representatives of 'ordinary people', as challengers of the establishment. In contrast to the USA, conspiracy theorists in post-Soviet Russia often occupy high social and academic positions, which raises the profile of their ideas. Academic credentials and proximity to power have become key facilitators of the anti-Western conspiracy discourse.

The role of public intellectuals in disseminating anti-Western conspiracy theories can be analysed through the application of Michel Foucault's concept of the relationship between power and knowledge. In Foucault's view, knowledge is an integral part of any struggle for power, and hence the production of knowledge can reinforce power claims (Mills, 2003, p. 69). Intellectuals perform an important function in supporting a regime's claim to power and generating the concepts which structure society and its functions. A regime's stability is thus achieved, at least in part, by the production by intellectuals of a discourse that helps define true and false statements; Foucault described this as 'the regime of truth' (Foucault, 1980, pp. 131–2).

Accordingly, conspiracy theories become a type of knowledge produced by intellectuals to redistribute power between different political actors (Fenster, p. 89). Conspiracy discourses divide society into 'Us' and 'Them', thus reinforcing the claim for power by the group which is supported by their proponents.

It has been argued that Foucault's theories, which are rooted in analyses of Western European cultures, are not readily applicable to a study of power relations in Russia because of the transitional nature of Russian culture and its position on the threshold of East and West (Plamper, 2002). Laura Engelstein (1993) has gone further and argues that Foucault's theories cannot be applied to Russia at all because of its cultural and political backwardness in comparison to Western Europe. Although this study acknowledges the problems in applying Foucauldian methodology to this field, this branch of social history is so rich and complex that a careful selection of its elements can produce valid and insightful results (Koshar, 1993; Kotkin, 1995).

Hence, in accordance with Foucault's theory of power/knowledge, I argue that the main concepts of the supposed Western conspiracy against post-Soviet Russia were introduced and disseminated by intellectuals from the opposition movement, which helped them to reinforce their own claims for power. However, by the 2010s many of these intellectuals had become connected to the Kremlin and had begun using their status and popularity to strengthen and support the legitimacy of the political regime and its actions.

Gleb Pavlovskii: Conspiracy Theories as a Political Technology

In his study of post-Soviet Russian elections, Andrew Wilson (2005) devoted a chapter to the role of 'political technologists' in electoral politics. In his words, they 'apply whatever "technology" they can to the construction of politics as a whole. The manipulation of the media is central to their work, but by definition it extends beyond this' (p. 49). These political technologists have a particular interest in electoral campaigns and actively participate in all aspects of the political process. By the end of the 2000s, they had become an integral part of the Russian political landscape. Gleb Pavlovskii, a long-time adviser to the presidential administration and a pioneer of political technologies in Russia, was for two decades among the most influential intellectuals in Russian politics.

A political dissident during the Soviet period, Pavlovskii was arrested in 1982 for publishing the samizdat journal *Poiski* and spent five years in prison (Shargunov, 2011). Shortly after his release he opened a news agency, which later evolved into the first independent publishing house, *Kommersant*; and at the beginning of the 1990s he became involved in political consulting following the opening of the Foundation of Effective Politics (Morev, 2013). From the early 1990s, for almost two decades this foundation operated as a think tank developing the Kremlin's policies under Pavlovskii's guidance. His skill at political manoeuvring can be seen in his initial successes: the electoral campaign of the anti-Yeltsin nationalist party, *Kongress russkikh obshchin* (*The Congress of Russian Communities*) in 1995 where he served as a political strategist; and then the way in which he turned around Yeltsin's own campaign in 1996 to win a second term in office. At the start of this campaign, Yeltsin dramatically lagged behind all other major Presidential candidates and had only a 6 per cent public approval rating; but he went on to win the election with 53.8 per cent of the vote. Pavlovskii has acknowledged that this was the start of his cooperation with the presidential administration, and that this allowed him to increase his intellectual influence on the Kremlin (Shevchenko and Pavlovskii, 2012). In 2004, he was one of the advisers sent to Ukraine during the presidential elections to give support to the pro-Russian candidate Viktor Yanukovich. Yanukovich's failure at the polls triggered a massive campaign within Russia to ensure the smooth transfer of power from Putin to his successor in 2008. Pavlovskii, as a self-proclaimed expert on 'counter-revolutions', became one of the key intellectuals to shape the conceptual framework of Putin's political regime (Horvath, 2011, pp. 14–15).

Pavlovskii's views have been formed in the 1970s under the influence of Mikhail Gefter, a revisionist Soviet historian and philosopher who studied the history of the Bolshevik revolution, Russian intellectual thought and Stalinism. Gefter was ousted from the Institute of History at the Soviet Academy of Sciences in the 1970s after his more conservative colleagues criticized his works for being 'ideologically detrimental' to the regime (Kurnosov, 2006). He continued to work independently and became involved in the journal *Poiski,* where he met Pavlovskii. The latter has acknowledged that Gefter had a crucial influence on his personal development as a political technologist: 'Gefter picked me up and invented me (Gefter menia podobral i pridumal). I spent a lifetime in conversation with him. . . . All my "politics" is from Gefter' (Morozov, 2012).

Among the topics which Gefter's work addressed were the nature of Russian totalitarianism and the possibility of reconciliation with the Stalinist past. This was his major consideration in the 1980s and became even more significant when Gorbachev's reforms started the process of democratization. In Gefter's view, although Khrushchev began a process of national reconciliation in the 1950s in relation to the repressions of the Stalin era, the results were very limited. A lack of clarity in Khrushchev's discourse about the causes of the Great Terror allowed for the later expression of nostalgia for the supposed stability of the Stalin era and for the 'glorious past' when a strong leader ruled the country (Gefter, 2013). In Gefter's view, although there had been opportunities to debate these complicated feelings about the past during *perestroika*, no national consensus on the origins of the Stalinist repression had emerged.

Gefter thought that the Stalinist tradition of hunting out internal and external enemies could be reintroduced and used for political purposes. In his dialogue with Pavlovskii at the end of the 1980s, he stated that Stalin had only 'died yesterday' (Gefter, 1991), by which he meant that Soviet society had still not grasped the origins of the repressions and held some disconcertingly positive views about the totalitarian past. Gefter argued that late Soviet and post-Soviet political elites used certain aspects of Stalinist ideology in their political discourse, thereby reinforcing a positive attitude towards the totalitarian past and applying this to the current political situation. In Gefter's view, Yeltsin's desire to hold on to power resulted in him using totalitarian rhetoric against his political enemies (Pavlovskii, 2014, pp. 132–7, 218–23).

Yeltsin's signing of the Belovezha accords in December 1991 signified the collapse of the Soviet Union, which, in his own words, were a turning point in Pavlovskii's life (Pavlovskii and Filippov, 2013, p. 94). The political and intellectual crisis of the 1990s, which was accompanied by a crisis in national self-identification, led Pavlovskii to conclude that the state could be saved by the implementation of 'the intellectual mechanism which would help generate Russian power (vlast')' (Chudodeev, 2012). It is very likely that Pavlovskii was inspired by Gefter's ideas in his deployment of various narratives about the past in the Kremlin's political campaigns. He admitted that he knew more about the history of Stalin's totalitarian regime than any other period of Russian or Soviet history, which helped him employ narratives from the Stalin era in political campaigns of the 1990s and, most importantly, to strengthen Putin's regime after 2000 (Pavlovskii and Filippov, 2013, p. 106).

The ideological underpinnings of Putin's regime – which Pavlovskii played an important role in developing – were the representation of the Soviet collapse as the most tragic event in twentieth century history and the creation of a strong state which was supported by most Russian people. These two narratives framed many of Pavlovskii's arguments and, as we see later, were utilized by the political leadership to spread conspiracy fears. In Pavlovskii's view the Belovezha accords destroyed both the state and the nation while the Soviet Union's successor, the Russian Federation, was, throughout the 1990s, an artificial 'state formation' (*gosudarstvennoe obrazovanie*). In his essay *A Blind Spot* (*Slepoe piatno*) (Pavlovskii, 1995), Pavlovskii criticized Russian society for having a lack of national sentiment about the collapsed Soviet state, and described post-Soviet Russia as 'the Soviet Union dripping with blood'. In his view, the emergence of a new Russian nation would take place only when the state acquired power (vlast') and the nation recognized its past glory.

Following Putin's victory in the presidential elections of 2000, Pavlovskii contended that he was 'introducing a state' in Russia (*Putin vvodit v Rossii gosudarstvo*) after years of chaos, and uniting most of the Russian people (Pavlovskii, 2000). His use of the verb 'introduce' in relation to the state requires particular consideration. A law or a policy can be introduced; but 'introducing a state' has to be interpreted as a metaphor which aims to personalize political power. Similar metaphors were used in the past in relation to prominent political leaders such as Peter the Great. Hence it can be argued that Pavlovskii and other pro-Kremlin intellectuals were attempting to equate Putin to remarkable historical figures of the past to boost the popularity of the new president.

The stability of the regime from 2000 onwards was partly based on mass public support; around 70 per cent of the population supported Putin throughout the 2000s. This was a phenomenon that Pavlovskii described as 'Putin's majority' (Regnum, 2003). In their effort to bolster the image of Putin as a national leader, Pavlovskii and other public intellectuals used populist discourse to bring together highly diverse groups and ensure social cohesion. As Panizza noted (2005, pp. 12–13, 21), a populist leader emerges – an ordinary person to whom extraordinary abilities are attributed – when a nation suffers a collapse of political and social institutions, or when trust in existing political elites is destroyed because of widespread corruption. Putin's emergence as president in 2000 took place in just such a context, when Yeltsin's popularity was at its lowest level and people despaired of the future (Doktorov et al., 2002). As Pavlovskii stated in 2000:

> This is a breakthrough of the masses who were not represented on the political scene after 1991–1993. And Putin is their leader. ... Those who elected Putin perceive him to be a leader of the opposition, which has taken power in Russia. For Putin's majority, Putin is a leader of the party in opposition to the old regime. (Tregubova, 2000)

This populist juxtaposition of the new Russian president and the political elites of Yeltsin's Russia helped to discursively unite different social groups into 'the people', Putin supporters. Moreover, the notion that Putin had led the opposition to victory helped create the impression that his election had launched a new era of history, leaving Yeltsin's rule behind. The drama of the Soviet collapse, and exploitation of people's fears about the possibility of economic failure and of further territorial disintegration of the country formed the predominant discourse of this period, which was generated by the Kremlin and was aimed at building support for Putin's regime. Later, in the 2010s, Pavlovskii admitted that Putin's majority had indeed become a 'truncheon [to be used] against our political rivals' (Pavlovskii, 2012, p. 74). The Kremlin started to use this 'truncheon' in the 2000s to legitimize governmental policies and delegitimize its opponents. The division of society into Putin's majority and its enemies became a dominant political tactic.

Another trope in Pavlovskii's narrative was the comparison of the new Russian president with Stalin. Pavlovskii's interpretation of Stalinism, which he probably derived from conversations with Gefter, was used in the struggle against the oligarchs at the beginning of Putin's term in 2000. Two fugitive oligarchs, Boris Berezovskii and Vladimir Gusinskii, who were now perceived as Putin's opponents, were likened to Lev Kamenev and Grigorii Zinov'ev, leaders of the Bolshevik party who were executed during the Great Purge in the 1930s on charges of conspiracy against the state. As Pavlovskii described it, Putin's enemies acted against the will of the people and thus were not only Putin's enemies but were also hostile to society at large (Tregubova, 2000).

In the period between the Orange Revolution in Ukraine in 2004 and the presidential elections in Russia in 2008, Pavlovskii frequently used anti-Western conspiracy allegations in his commentaries and interviews, but, like many Russian politicians at that time, he did so with supreme caution. After returning from Ukraine in 2004, he portrayed the defeat of Yanukovich as the first stage in a Western plan 'to turn Ukraine into a huge testing area for anti-Russian technologies' (Tsenzor.net, 2004). He alleged that the West was not interested in

Ukraine *per se*, but that the real goal of the Orange Revolution was to set off revolution in Russia. His words resonated with the Kremlin elites, who feared that a transfer of power from Putin to a successor in 2008 might not go smoothly, and that Russia could repeat the example of its neighbour.

International criticism of Russia's foreign policy towards Ukraine and Georgia after the regime changes in those countries was attributed by Pavlovskii to the West's 'russophobia' and its determination to use Russia as a scapegoat in the event of a world economic crisis (Dymarskii and Pavlovskii, 2006). He repeated this paranoid interpretation of relations with the West on the eve of the parliamentary elections in Russia in 2007 depicting Russia, in a series of media interviews, as a country besieged by 'enemies' who despised Putin and were ready to take active measures against him (see, for example, Al'bats and Pavlovskii, 2007).

To provide ideological underpinning for Kremlin-initiated policies and spread anti-Western conspiracy theories, Pavlovskii created a loose framework of independent foundations, where academics, journalists and even graduates of the faculties of humanities produced ideas which would later be used for political purposes. Historian Alexei Miller noted (2009) that the authors of alternative discourses on Russian history included people employed by independent foundations connected with Pavlovskii and the presidential administration. Some of them were graduates of the Faculty of Philosophy at Moscow State University, and of other universities which produced students educated in the humanities (Ivangogh, 2011). Their accounts of Russian history, widely published in the 2000s with the support of Pavlovskii at *Evropa* Publishing house, put particular stress on external and internal enemies who strove to destroy the memory of the Great Patriotic War. The network of intellectuals set up by Pavlovskii and his aides in the 2000s was instrumental in the construction of an official political discourse that helped the Kremlin strengthen its influence over the country. By the end of the 2000s the authorities had almost total control over television, which remained the main source of information for most citizens. This enabled them to promote their desired agenda (Levada-tsentr, 2013c), often relying on conspiracy mythmaking to achieve both social polarization and social cohesion. Pavlovskii himself was the host of a weekly news show *The Real Politics* (Real'naia politika) on NTV, where he presented a Kremlin-centred narrative of global events which made conspiratorial allusions to both the West and the Russian opposition.

The political ideology elaborated by Pavlovskii and his team to reinforce the power of the Kremlin is a prime example of the impact public intellectuals can have on political development. Pavlovskii's knowledge of Soviet history, which he acquired during his collaboration with Gefter, was turned into a tool for wielding power. In turn, anti-Western conspiracy theories, which exploited unsettled issues in the recent past, were successfully used to delegitimize political rivals and divide society into 'the people' and the conspiring 'Other'. These views were successfully spread by many media personalities and public intellectuals, some of whom will be discussed next.

Aleksandr Dugin: The Eternal War of the Continents

No discussion of anti-Western conspiracy theories would be complete without an analysis of the works of Aleksandr Dugin, who made a crucial contribution to the debate about the relationship between Russia and the West in the post-Soviet period. Dugin is one of the few post-Soviet Russian public intellectuals whose work has figured prominently in Western scholarship, and whose philosophical concepts and political activity have received attention on the part of scholars working both on right-wing ideologies and Russian intellectual history (Shenfield, 2001, pp. 190–220; Bassin and Aksenov, 1999; Laruelle, 2008; Shnirel'man, 2016; Clover, 2016). Following the crisis in Ukraine, Dugin's ideas, to a large extent, came to define the strategy of the Kremlin, and some authors went so far as to dub him 'Putin's brain' (Barbashin and Thoburn, 2014). *Foreign Affairs* named Dugin the 'global thinker – 2014' for masterminding the separation of Crimea and the Donbass regions from Ukraine (Foreign Affairs, 2014). On the other hand, Dugin received the praises of American conspiracy theorists, such as Alex Jones (see Geopolitika, 2017). It is difficult to assess the full extent of the impact Dugin has had on Russian politics and the people who make them (acting politicians rarely admit to contacts with public intellectuals, but Dugin's books are quite popular and could have had an indirect impact on the development of views). Yet, it would be safe to argue that he has certainly played a large role in making anti-Western conspiracy popular in Russia.

In the late Soviet era, Dugin was involved with a group of dissidents, known as the Iuzhinskii circle, whose members were interested in mysticism and the occult. During *perestroika*, Dugin joined the far right nationalist organization *Pamiat'*, which was known for its crude anti-Semitic propaganda. However, he soon left the organization following disagreements with its leader, Dmitrii Vasil'ev (Umland, 2010). As the era of *perestroika* drew to an end, he travelled to Western Europe to take part n events organized by the groups comprising the European New Right; this led to close collaboration with the main figures in this movement (Shenfield, 2001, p. 194). It is likely that these people introduced Dugin to the various conspiracy theories popular among the European New Right and neo-fascist writers at that time (Shekhovtsov, 2015; Clover, 2016). He combined these with his existing body of ideas about esotericism and mysticism which he developed in the Iuzhinskii circle: together, these provided the basis for his conspiratorial notions. In 1991, Dugin joined the editorial board of Aleksandr Prokhanov's newspaper *Den'* (*The Day*), a flagship of the Russian nationalist movement, which gave him access to a wider public. At around the same time he set up a publishing house, *Arctogeia,* and a think tank, *The Centre for Special Meta-Strategic Studies*, both of which he used as platforms for the dissemination of his views (Umland, 2010, pp. 147, 149).

Dugin's ability to link a wide range of topics relating to politics, history, international relations and even popular culture with the mysterious world of secret societies resulted in him becoming a prominent figure on radio, television and in popular magazines during the 1990s. At the same time, his book, *Osnovy geopolitiki* (*The Foundations of Geopolitics*), published in 1997, established him as a prominent scholar; this reputation was enhanced by the fact that he also taught in the General Staff Academy (Umland, 2007, pp. 118–20; Clover, 2016, pp. 232–48) and was an adviser to the Speaker of the Duma, Gennadii Seleznev. *The Foundations* described global history as a permanent battle between two secret societies which represented 'The Land' and 'The Sea'. Dugin (2000) saw geopolitics as a kind of universal science: after grasping the principles of geopolitics, ordinary people would be able to independently analyse the history of humankind, understand the causes of events in the past and present, and hence uncover the true nature of things.

In a 1992 collection of essays with a telling title *Conspirology* (*Konspirologiia*) Dugin acknowledged the global popularity of conspiracy theories and presented his own reading of the phenomenon. He argued that they were the product of postmodernist culture, which treated reality as a single and complex self-referential concept. Dugin explained global popularity and relevance of conspiracy theories in terms of historical and social prerequisites rooted in the human subconscious. A belief in conspiracies was already part of the ancient human perception of the world, he argued, and the survival of this belief into the present day mentally connected modern people with their ancestors (2005, pp. 8–11).

While Dugin's justification for the popularity of this phenomenon might seem strange, it is actually not unusual for conspiracy theorists. The fact that people have believed in conspiracies for hundreds of years is in itself considered to be proof of the existence of secret plots. In turn, conspiracy theorists are doubtful that members of real secret societies are aware of the hidden workings of the world, and for this reason they pay to them particular attention (2005, p. 34). While such arguments convince Dugin that conspiracy theorists should be taken seriously, he still distances himself from them and calls himself a 'psychiatrist' who studies 'weird pictures of social delusions' (Dugin, 2010). Yet he contradicts himself: his collection of essays on conspiracy theories itself supports the idea of an anti-Russian plot.

Dugin contends that Russia is the Christian country which will save the world from the Apocalypse (Dugin, 2004, pp. 223, 229–32). He also sees her as the 'axis of the Eurasian civilization' which represents the powers of the Land, while the powers of the Sea are represented by the USA. This geopolitical standoff, he argues (2000), was one of the reasons for the collapse of the USSR; this was primarily the result of socio-economic factors, but the activities of internal enemies were a contributory factor. His acknowledgement that socio-economic factors were the primary cause of the Soviet Union's collapse is an indication that he wishes to position his work as an academic endeavour; it also shows his peculiar handling of conspiracy theories. In Dugin's view, the USA and the USSR represented two different models of society. The USSR was a society based on a tight cohesion of groups of people that was normally ruled by a single, 'spiritual leader', while the USA promoted individualistic aspirations and financial reward for its rulers (2005, pp. 191–2, 209–10). This division provides the framework for Dugin's interpretation of the current state of world politics. Dugin's reference to geopolitics was inspired by Halford Mackinder's theory of geopolitics, which introduced the concepts of the Sea and Land powers into world politics (Mackinder, 1904). However, as Bassin and Aksenov note (2006, p. 109), Dugin's interpretation of Mackinder's theory reflects a Cold War vision of world politics, in which the USA and Russia are the two antagonistic world superpowers.

Dugin reproduces the spirit of the Cold War in his description of how the USA has attempted to build the New World Order to Russia's detriment. The USA, or sometimes, more broadly, the Anglo-Saxon world (the USA and the UK), is presented as an undifferentiated West.

In turn, Western Europe is portrayed as Russia's ally in challenging US hegemony. This juxtaposition of Russia and the USA is one of the ideas which Dugin contributed to Eurasianism, a philosophy which emerged in the 1920s (Viderker, 2010). Eurasianism contrasted the Romano-Germanic world with the mixture of Slavic and Turkic cultures which were embodied in Russia (Laruelle, 2007). Dugin combined this understanding of geopolitics with Cold War thinking and with the body of anti-American literature popular among the European far right.

Among Dugin's most significant contributions to Russian anti-Western conspiracy discourse is his appropriation of ideas from both European and, paradoxically, American conspiracy theorists. His engagement with Western conspiratorial discourse began in the late 1980s, following his first meetings with European right-wing politicians. As Umland (2007, pp. 106–8) has demonstrated, the journal *Elementy: Evraziiskoe obozrenie* (*Elements: Eurasian Review*) was heavily influenced by Alain de Benoist, a French New Right intellectual. In its second issue, several articles were devoted to his description of the New World Order and its threat to Russia's security. These articles provided a detailed account of the ways in which internal and external conspirators had tailored the world in accordance with US ambitions. The editorial article in this issue briefly outlined the main aspects of the New World Order – world government led by the Trilateral Commission, market liberalism, the merging of different ethnic groups – which threatened to destroy the cultural uniqueness of nations (Dugin, 1992).

It is worth noting that narratives about the New World Order, which had allegedly started in the USA in the 1970s, reappeared in the USA as well as Russia at the beginning of the 1990s. This theory claimed that there was a single overarching organization that aimed to seize global power. As Michael Barkun notes (2003, pp. 62–4), the New World Order conspiracy emerged in the USA in the 1990s as a replacement for the image of the conspiring Other that had earlier been personified by the Soviet Union. The Soviet collapse in 1991 had left a vacuum in conspiratorial theorizing, which was filled by a new overarching concept of a single world government.

Dugin's adoption of the New World Order theory, while it was simultaneously being embraced by his Western European and American counterparts, demonstrates his close engagement with foreign counter-cultural life. As Barkun noted (p. 64), the New World Order concept included every facet of the domestic and international agenda; it was this all-encompassing nature that made it virtually unfalsifiable. Dugin used this to the full. He merged his occult knowledge, his understanding of Eurasianist concepts and his work on geopolitics into an overarching theory of a Manichean divide between Russia and the USA. Dugin's *Foundations,* which became popular among Russian political and academic elites in the 1990s, facilitated the development of a conspiratorial perception of global politics at the highest political level.

John Dunlop (2004, p. 49) and Charles Clover (2016, pp. 254, 260) suggest that Pavlovskii helped Dugin gain access to the Presidential Administration in the 1990s and the 2000s. In 2001, Dugin established a political movement, *Eurasia,* whose executive board included several high-ranking politicians, academics and journalists (Umland, 2009, pp. 133–5). In 2008 Dugin was appointed head of the Centre for Conservative Studies in the Faculty of Sociology at Moscow State University (Umland, 2011), despite not having the necessary academic qualifications. This appointment was the summit of his pseudo-academic career, reflecting the prominence of his ideas among the Russian political and intellectual elites. In 2014, he was removed from this position, however, and allegedly lost the support of the Presidential Administration, because of his critical comments on Putin's actions in Ukraine (Filipenok, 2014). All the same, in 2016 he was instrumental in solving the crisis between the Russian and Turkish governments (Meyer and Ant, 2017).

Dugin's conspiratorial ideas had an immense influence on Russian anti-Western discourse and were very much in evidence in popular television talk shows and programmes. At the beginning of the 2000s Mikhail Leont'ev, a prominent pro-Kremlin journalist and, from 2014, vice-president of Russia's biggest oil company Rosneft and a member of Dugin's *Eurasia* movement, helped Dugin gain access to television shows which were broadcast on the main state-aligned channels (Clover, 2016, p. 271). He replaced liberal-minded journalists and speakers who were gradually being squeezed out by the Kremlin. For Leont'ev, whose programmes were often called 'five minutes of hate' (Pomerantsev, 2013), Dugin was a great choice. In 2007 Leont'ev broadcast a television series entitled *Bol'shaia igra* (*The Great Game*) on Channel One (*Bol'shaia igra,* 2007). Broadcast two months before the parliamentary elections, its eight episodes presented a conspiratorial outline of the struggle between Russia and the West, as represented by Britain and the USA, for world dominance, in terms which echoed Dugin's philosophy. This notion of a standoff between Russia and the West was openly linked to Dugin's theory of geopolitics and, at the same time, articulated one of the main narratives of the parliamentary campaign in 2007: resistance to an attack by the West against Russian statehood.

All the same, Dugin is very receptive to changes in the political sphere and successfully engages with mainstream political discourse. This is especially evident at times of tension between Russia and the USA. During the Russo-Georgian war in 2008, Dugin was among the first public intellectuals to claim that Ossetians had become victims of 'the Georgian genocide' in which allegedly the USA was involved (Ganapol'skii and Dugin, 2008). In fact, accusations of genocide were first made by the Ossetian political elite (Marzoeva, 2008). A few days later, they were reiterated by then President Medvedev, who hinted at the West's possible interest in the conflict (Simonyan and Medvedev, 2008). Dugin's involvement could be seen as an attempt to give a high media profile to an extremely controversial allegation, which the Kremlin was ready to use in its official discourse because it legitimized its invasion of Georgia.

Dugin's *Foundations* was seen as a highly influential academic work, but in fact it sought to erect a scientific-sounding framework for an anti-Western outlook that could explain the collapse of the Soviet Union in 1991. Paradoxically, it achieved this goal largely by adopting US and Western European conspiracy theories. Adapting Western conspiracy theories to the Russian context helped Dugin weave together diverse narratives about the threat to Russia from the West and turn them into mainstream political thought.

Nataliia Narochnitskaia: Orthodox Russia vs. the Spiritless West

Dugin's rise as a prominent intellectual with reputedly academic credentials, but whose public career was mainly based on conspiracy mythmaking, was not unique. Nataliia Narochnitskaia occupies a significant place among the pro-Kremlin public intellectuals specializing in a particular interpretation of history for the purpose of nation-building. She often takes part in television discussions on various aspects of Russian history and publishes books and articles concerning the bravery of Russians which, she holds, has saved the world from global catastrophe. Her work deals with both the tragic and glorious moments in Russian history, and emphasizes the disparity between Russia's heroic past and bleak present (Krotkov, 2007).

Narochnitskaia constantly reminds her readers and viewers about her academic status and her previous successful careers as a diplomat in the 1980s and a Duma deputy in the 2000s. These credentials serve to enhance her public profile and her status as an expert in global politics. Her father was a prominent scholar of diplomatic history in the Soviet era, and she sees him as the source of her academic and political views. Narochnitskaia claims that her father had uncovered possible strategies which the West then took over and used against Russia, and that this knowledge has helped her decipher global politics and, accordingly, protect Russia from the West (Narochnitskaia.ru, 2007b). She uses her own successful career to add weight to her pronouncements. In 2004, she established *Fond istoricheskoi perspektivy* (*The Historical Perspective Foundation*), whose official aim is to carry out research projects on Russian history which can be used to promote patriotism. By the end of the 2000s she had acquired the status of expert in Russian history and from 2009–12 was a member of the notorious Presidential Commission to Counter Attempts to Falsify History to the Detriment of Russia's Interests (Sherlock, 2011).

Narochnitskaia's argument is that Russia's past territorial and geopolitical achievements cannot be dismissed today since they form the basis of the country's greatness. These achievements were not realized by state rulers, but by ordinary Russians who sacrificed their lives in defence of their country. In Narochnitskaia's view, the Russian nation differs from other countries because of its spiritual life, interethnic tolerance and social justice (Chernov, 2013). Her eulogy to Russian culture is interlaced with comparisons with foreign countries, primarily Europe and the USA, which invariably lag behind Russia in political and spiritual achievements. This, she argues, is why the West is determined to undermine Russia.

In Narochnitskaia's view a nation state is a gift from God to its people, in order to aid their moral and patriotic development (Chernov, 2013). By contrast, supra-national institutions like the EU and the UN are created by the Freemasonry and seek to achieve global domination by erasing the borders between nations (Narochnitskaia, 2003, p. 252). This is another cross reference to the American conspiracy culture. According to Narochnitskaia, Russians have high moral standards and a sincere tolerance towards people of different cultures and races (Popova, 2007). By contrast, cosmopolitan societies – which, she argues, are under the control of foreign elites – introduce artificial concepts such as political correctness, which do not require citizens to love their own country (Chernov, 2013). The Western type of patriotism, Narochnitskaia argues, is based on the idea that the Motherland is 'where taxes are low' (Politcom.ru, 2007).

Another crucial difference between Russia and the West, according to Narochnitskaia, is the role played by religion. She argues that religion defines national culture, and that Orthodox Christianity forms the basis of Russian identity. It has helped the Russian nation avoid the obsessive pursuit of wealth, which is so central to Western culture, and it has peacefully integrated a range of ethnic and religious groups within one state. However, Narochnitskaia is not completely consistent. On the one hand, she contends that Christianity unites Russia with Europe because the value of human life originates from the word of Jesus (Pozner and Narochnitskaia, 2007); this could form the basis for the pursuit of common goals and mutually beneficial policies. However, she also claims that all the major denominations of West European Christianity hate Russia and desire its destruction. Narochnitskaia sees the Vatican as Russia's permanent adversary since it has always wanted to colonize Russian territory. There is, she argues, a 'fifth column of liberals' linked to the Vatican, who criticize the Russian Church in an attempt to undermine what she sees as the foundation of the Russian nation (2002). Hence, she links this to the anti-Catholic fears of subversion and of Polish conspiracy which were widely prevalent among Russian conservative thinkers in the aftermath of the Polish uprising of 1863.

Narochnitskaia is equally hostile to Protestantism. She contends that Anglo-Saxon Calvinism has traditionally been indifferent to other nations, regarding them solely as a source of profit. She also alleges that Calvinists were involved in South Africa's apartheid, British colonialism and the oppression of native Americans in the USA, each of which was rooted in the religious principles of Protestantism (2003, pp. 67–70). She sees US domination of global politics as a hallmark of Calvinist philosophy; this eventually evolved into messianic neo-liberalism, which aimed at restructuring the world into a single atheistic country (2003, pp. 80–3).

Narochnitskaia's philosophy, like Dugin's, includes elements of anti-globalist conspiracy theory, with the building of the New World Order the ultimate goal of the conspirators. Influenced, perhaps, by her father's work, Narochnitskaia adapts Soviet anti-Western propaganda to current conspiracy thinking. For example, she divides the world into ordinary people and the small but powerful group of Western countries that calls itself the 'world community' (*mirovoe soobshchestvo*), whose elites, whom she calls the 'world elite' (*mirovaia elita*), are supposedly bent on controlling the world (Narochnitskaia, 2001).

This discursive division is used to stress two important ideas which are central to her work. Firstly, it accentuates the ultimate threat of US domination over Russia, and the possible consequences if Russia falls under the influence of the West. Secondly, loyalty to the USA and the Westernized 'world elite' helps Narochnitskaia identify an internal group of conspirators within Russia.

In her speeches Narochnitskaia has described pro-Western liberals as a group of internal conspirators who have nothing in common with the Russian nation and who are doing untold harm to Russia's memory of its great past (Narochnitskaia.ru, 2007a). She compares the intellectual and political elites of the present day with those of the past and praises Soviet intellectuals and Russian immigrants who fled from Russia after the revolution in 1917 but remained patriots (Narochnitskaia.ru, 2008). In this way, she promotes a national cohesion of different social and political groups, despite the differences in their political views. Even the nineteenth-century debate between Westernizers and Slavophiles is presented as a dispute between two equally patriotic groups of intellectuals who emphasized Russia's unique position in the world (Narochnitskaia.ru, 2007c). In contrast to the political and intellectual elites of the past, current pro-Western liberal elites are described as people who neither love their own country, nor comprehend the intellectual legacy of European intellectual thought. As Narochnitskaia puts it, they hate the Russian people and Orthodoxy, and the only thing that they hold sacred is the bank accounts they have in the West (Narochnitskaia.ru, 2007d). This derogatory description is usually applied to people who oppose the Kremlin and is used to delegitimize any statements critical of Putin's policies.

Narochnitskaia claims that the fact that the liberal opposition in Russia is Western-oriented is used by conspirators from the West to undermine Russia's greatness from within. Referring to the collapse of the Soviet Union, Narochnitskaia claims that under the influence of external forces, 'liberals threw away and trampled upon three hundred years of Russian history' (Narochnitskaia.ru, 2007b). She sees critical remarks about the Soviet past, and in particular attempts on the part of some Russian (and Western) historians to downplay Russia's role in the Second World War, as an act of conspiracy that seeks to delegitimize the Soviet Union's post-1945 territorial possessions. She fears that this could lead to Russia's expulsion from international organizations and the loss of its post-war territorial possessions on the Baltic Sea, Black Sea and Pacific Ocean; this, in turn, would diminish Russia's status as a great global power (Narochnitskaia.ru, 2009).

It can be argued that Narochnitskaia's ideas have had a significant influence on the politics of nation-building in Russia. It is not possible to trace any direct connection between them and the Kremlin's official nation-building policies, but her access to the presidential administration and the fact that she has held leading positions in major Kremlin-sponsored think tanks puts her in a very strong position. For instance, Narochnitskaia's approach to Russian history stresses that all periods and events have been important for the nation: 'We should not omit a single page from the history of the Fatherland, even those which we do not want to repeat' (Krotkov, 2007). When Putin suggested that a single history textbook be adopted by all schools in 2013, he argued, in similar vein, that it should show respect for all 'the pages of Russian history' (Putin, 2013).

Narochnitskaia's views crucially influenced the First World War commemoration held at the end of the 2000s. In her speeches and interviews, she praised the heroism of the Russian soldiers who had saved Europe, complaining that their deeds had been either forgotten or obscured both by Bolshevik propaganda and the West. She argued that Russian action in the First World War must be returned to its place in the pantheon of heroic deeds: this would link contemporary Russia with the glory of Imperial times. She insisted that subversive forces within the country and abroad were intent on destroying people's understanding of the war as this would undermine Russia by depriving Russians of their patriotism and their trust in the Fatherland (Pleshakova and Narochnitskaia, 2009). As Vera Tolz has noted (2014), Narochnitskaia has been at the centre of commemorative events devoted to the First World War since 2009, and has attracted much attention on the part of leading politicians. In 2013, at a meeting of the Russian Military-Historical Society, Putin agreed to the creation of a monument commemorating the First World War. This led to a fully-fledged state-sponsored campaign to commemorate Russia's role in the war. The main narratives articulated by its participants were based on concepts outlined by Narochnitskaia in the preceding years (Radio Ekho Moskvy, 2013).

Narochnitskaia's access to the media and her academic status have allowed her to play the role of prominent spokesperson for Russian patriotic groups and to defend Russian political interests in debates with the opposition. Her case demonstrates how anti-Western conspiracy theories become an instrument of national reconciliation because they shift the blame for the breakdown of the Soviet Union from Russians themselves onto conspiring foreign enemies. This is a trick that is widely used by the Kremlin, as we shall see later.

Maksim Shevchenko:
The Battle Against Western Neo-Liberalism

Since the mid 2000s, Maksim Shevchenko has been one of the most outspoken figures in the anti-Western conspiracy discourse. Shevchenko began his media career as a journalist with *Nezavisimaia gazeta*, covering issues relating to religion. He also published articles about the military conflict in the North Caucasus in the 1990s and the conflict in Afghanistan at the beginning of the 2000s. From 2006, he hosted a television talk show, *Judge for Yourself* (*Sudite sami*) on Channel One, which began his television career and helped to establish his public profile as one of the main commentators on interethnic and interreligious relations in Russia. Twice, in 2008 and 2010, he was selected by then President Medvedev to be a member of the Public Chamber, which was created by the Kremlin in the mid 2000s to function as a forum for the discussion of issues pertaining to Russia's 'civil society'. Shevchenko's participation was primarily focused on interethnic relations, and as a result he became one of the principal spokespersons for matters connected with the North Caucasus in the Russian press. In 2012, he became editor-in-chief of the website *Kavkazskaia politika* (*The Politics of the Caucasus*), an open forum for the discussion of issues relating to the Caucasus. Shevchenko has built a profile for himself as a leading expert in interethnic relations; this allows him to promote his views on various television talk shows and radio programmes.

Like Dugin and Narochnitskaia, Shevchenko describes Russia as a great world power, which brought European methods of administration and cultural development to new territories during the Imperial and Soviet periods. Ethnic Russians served in this process as a 'frame for the nation' (*kostiak natsii*) (Shevchenko, 2010). He sees the prerequisite for Russian greatness as a combination of the three ethno-religious groups: Orthodox Russians, the Turkic Muslims who inhabit large areas of Siberia, and the various ethno-religious groups of the North Caucasus (Zatulin and Shevchenko, 2012). Shevchenko insists that if any of these groups were to disappear it would destroy Russian nationhood and Russians would fall under the control of the West. Accordingly, he offers a theoretical framework for the national cohesion of the Russian Federation, which centres on the idea of territorial unity. He considers that Russia's superiority over the nation-states of Europe is rooted in its composite quality, the inclusion of several 'civilizations' in one nation. This guarantees social justice and interethnic tolerance. The Caucasus itself represents a model of interethnic dialogue because it incorporates various religious and ethnic groups.

Shevchenko has a two-fold goal when he points to the Caucasus's unique role in the process of Russian nation-building. On the one hand, he delegitimizes the arguments of isolationist Russian nationalists, whose idea of separation from the Caucasus has gained popularity since the mid 2000s (Markedonov, 2013). In his view, calls for separation come from the same 'fifth column' within Russia which devastated the great country in 1991. According to this logic, Russian nationalists who advocate the separation of the Northern Caucasus from the Russian Federation cannot be Russian patriots as they support the aims of Russia's enemies. On the other hand, Shevchenko's admiration for the uniqueness of the Caucasus boosts his popularity among the elites of the North Caucasian region. When addressing these elites, Shevchenko stresses their region's great past and the fact that most of the cultures in the North Caucasus are descended from ancient civilizations (Shevchenko, 2013b).

As Shnirel'man (2006) notes, the idea of ancient ancestry played a key role in shaping the nationalist discourse of the North Caucasian republics as far back as the Soviet period and has been actively developed by local intellectual elites since the Soviet collapse. By supporting this approach, Shevchenko can reinforce the notion of Russia's greatness and claim that the great histories of individual nations within Russia combine to strengthen Russian statehood. Regarding the situation in the North Caucasus, Shevchenko utilizes conspiratorial notions and emphasizes the West's key role in inciting interethnic conflicts. As he puts it: 'All attempts to present the Chechen conflict as a conflict between the Chechens and the Russians, between Chechnia and Russia, originate from Russia's mortal enemies, who wish for [Russia's] collapse and destruction. . . This is my sincere conviction' (Samsonova and Shevchenko, 2009).

The attempt to explain interethnic unrest in post-Soviet Russia in terms of conspiracy is a recurring pattern in Shevchenko's works. Because of his reputation as an expert on interethnic issues, Shevchenko is approached by the media every time an interethnic conflict in Russia breaks out. This allows him to promote a conspiratorial reading of the event to the public and to shape public perception of the conflict's causes. For instance, when, in July 2013, social unrest in Pugachev was triggered by a domestic fight between two men, one of whom was of Chechen origin, Shevchenko represented the conflict as part of a broader campaign to destroy Putin's regime and bring down Russia. In his view, the event had been planned and carried out conjointly by opposition politicians, the media and sociologists who were allied to them; the sociologists apparently confirmed to journalists the existence of strong public support for the idea of separating the North Caucasus from Russia just after the conflict flared up and thus provided a basis for the anti-Caucasian rhetoric (Fel'gengauėr and Shevchenko, 2013).

Despite his use of conspiracy notions in his public speeches, Shevchenko attempts to tailor his arguments to the real social and political challenges that confront post-Soviet Russian society; this means that he positions himself at the centre, rather than the margins, of political discourse. His populist conspiratorial utterances refer to anonymous groups and individuals allegedly responsible for Russia's social problems. In his description of the socio-economic environment in the North Caucasus, Shevchenko refers to the rampant corruption and violence of the law enforcement agencies against residents of the region. Similarly, he traces the sources of interethnic conflicts in other regions of Russia back to the criminal character of political elites, whom he regularly accuses of corruption (Shevchenko, 2013a).

Quite often, Shevchenko refuses to name the exact members of the political elite whom he accuses of conspiracy, and changes his opinion whenever he feels the situation requires this. He presents himself as an opponent of the government by means of critical remarks about its policies in the North Caucasian region. However, he was a member of the Presidential Council for Interethnic Relations, established in 2012 and hosted personally by Putin. Moreover, Shevchenko played an active part in the coalition of pro-Putin forces during the 2012 presidential elections and supported the Moscow Mayor, Sergei Sobianin, during his electoral campaign in 2013 (Azar and Shevchenko, 2013), even though the mayor's campaign was framed by anti-migrant narratives, including statements levelled against the North Caucasus (Arkhipov and Kravchenko, 2013).

Shevchenko also regularly criticizes the Russian opposition and its alleged supporters abroad. He has argued that in the 1990s the USA established a semi-colonial regime in Russia (Pozner and Shevchenko, 2009), and that the signing of the Belovezha Accords in 1991, that destroyed the USSR, provided the means to set up an 'oligarchic tyranny' supported by corrupt journalists and politicians working closely with the West (Shevchenko, 2011a). Shevchenko contrasts the comparative socio-economic stability of the Putin regime with the oligarchic regime of the 1990s. In Shevchenko's view, Putin's regime symbolizes a return to independent decision-making in domestic and foreign policy, which makes it possible for the greatness of the lost empire and its economic stability to be restored (Shevchenko, 2011b).

Shevchenko depicts the West as a unified entity in which many citizens embrace neoliberal views which he describes as 'criminal in nature'. It should be noted that his perception of the West has changed since he emerged as a public intellectual in the mid 2000s. Perhaps this relates to the changing focus of the Kremlin's political discourse in this period. In 2004, in response to interventionist US policies in the Middle East, Shevchenko called for a union with Europe against US domination (Buntman and Shevchenko, 2004). However, by the end of the 2000s in his speeches he was portraying the West as a single hostile entity. In support of Putin's turn away from the USA and Western Europe during his third presidential term, Shevchenko published an article with the telling title *We are not Europe? And thank God!* (*My ne Evropa? I Slava Bogu!*), in which he drew a clear distinction between Russia and the West: 'There is a growing feeling that most Western people belong to a different humanoid race from us' (Shevchenko, 2013c). Shevchenko insisted that Russia had to defend herself from the corrupt spirit of neoliberal thought, which was focused solely on consumption and sexual promiscuity; in contrast, Russia's adherence to traditional values would save the world.

Like Narochnitskaia, then, Shevchenko combined demonization of the USA with the negative image of a so-called 'liberal opposition' alien to the Russian nation. This opposition, funded by the USA, was relentless in its attempt to create numerous nation-states on the territory of Russia. US policies were allegedly carried out by disloyal 'fifth columnists' in Russia, who possessed dual citizenship and lacked a sense of national identity (Shevchenko, 2012a). The reference to dual citizenship serves as another marker of the otherness of the opposition. Shevchenko's attempt to divide the world in this way was strengthened by reference to anti-Semitic conspiracy theories which were popular in the Imperial and, even more, in Soviet times, and which encouraged fear of a small but powerful group of people within the state.

This use of anti-Jewish attitudes in his speeches and articles marks Shevchenko out from other public intellectuals who are involved in the dissemination of conspiracy discourse and loyal to the Kremlin. As a self-proclaimed spokesperson for Muslims in Russia, Shevchenko provides his audience with a particular interpretation of the Middle East conflict which paints Israel as a 'fascist state' committing genocide against the Palestinians. In trying to promote solidarity between Muslims in Russia and in the Middle East based on a common hatred of Jews, Shevchenko utilizes the narratives traditional to anti-Zionist conspiracy discourse which is popular in the Middle East (Pipes, 1998; Gray, 2010). For example, he depicts Israel as 'a purely virtual state' which was created by the USA with the sole purpose of achieving global domination in the Middle East (Shevchenko, 2012c).

However, Shevchenko's anti-Israeli conspiracy mythmaking has a peculiar rhetorical twist aimed at the Russian domestic audience. He depicts the Russian-speaking community in Israel both as the most vitriolic in its attitudes towards the Palestinians, and the most mercantile. He contends that Jews left the Soviet Union when times were hard, and went to Israel in search of the good life. Settling in Israel, they criticized interethnic relations in Russia and made clear their hatred of the country's Muslims, thus challenging the possibility of peace between nationalities in Russia (Shevchenko, 2012b). Shevchenko maintains that Russian Jews who oppose Putin are responsible for triggering interethnic conflicts between radical Islamists and Russian nationalists in the south of Russia. He also asserts that the Israelis will soon cause the disintegration of Russia and will build a new state on its territory to replace Israel in case the latter collapses (Goncharova and Shevchenko, 2012).

Shevchenko's use of anti-Jewish conspiracy theories is an important development both in the nation's discourse, and in its interethnic relations. Drawing on the extensive corpus of anti-Israeli and anti-Jewish writings, Shevchenko turns the Jews into the conspiring 'Other', determined to hinder the development of interethnic peace in Russia and to instigate conflicts in the North Caucasus. The connection between Israel and the USA allows Shevchenko to embed anti-Jewish discourse within the body of anti-Western conspiracy theories.

Shevchenko's use of anti-Western and anti-Jewish narratives in a discourse about national cohesion is an interesting case of how conspiracy theories could be applied. By addressing his speeches to ethnic and religious minorities who are suffering from the growth in xenophobic attitudes on the part of the general Russian public, Shevchenko incorporates various minorities into the category of 'the people' who supposedly share a common 'glorious past' with the ethnic Russian majority. The promotion of conspiracy theories thus helps explain the growth in interethnic tension; they point to supposedly treasonable actions on the part of the opposition, corrupt authorities and external powers, while at the same time distancing the Kremlin from the conflicts. Shevchenko's charisma and rhetorical skills, together with the support of the Kremlin, enable him to act as an efficient agent of conspiracy mythmaking and a contributor to the official political discourse.

Conclusion

This chapter has demonstrated the significant role performed by public intellectuals in spreading anti-Western conspiracy theories in Russia. The intellectuals' efforts to develop their own conspiracy theories or borrow them from foreign sources has played an important part in strengthening anti-Western attitudes in the country. The fact that they focus so much on Russia's geopolitical domination as a superpower in the past demonstrates how strongly they resent their country's loss of international influence in the 1990s. The political elites' inability to cope with the changing system of international relations after the Soviet collapse has, paradoxically, stimulated, rather than constrained, this 'great power' mentality (Lo, 2003, p. 74).

The popularity of anti-Western conspiracy theories explaining Russia's loss of superpower status and the uncontested domination of the USA could be interpreted as a manifestation of the inequality in relations between Russia and the USA after 1991. Public intellectuals' criticism of the West, as expressed through conspiracy theories, helps to present a more positive image of Russia. Despite socio-economic upheavals, public intellectuals have managed to portray the country as a great multi-ethnic state, which resists the West's attempts to control the world and take over Russian territories and resources.

What distinguishes Russian from US conspiracy mythmaking is the engagement of public intellectuals in the politics of the ruling elites. The anti-elitism of conspiracy theorists in the USA indicates that they belong to 'the people' (Kay, 2011) and strengthens the populist aspect of their rhetoric. It is likely that US conspiracy theorists aspire to becoming part of the political elite and influencing the political agenda, but this is not how they represent themselves. Furthermore, in the USA, unlike in Russia, public consensus regarding the boundaries and rules of permissible types of political rhetoric significantly reduces the chances of conspiracy theorists gaining high social and academic standing. Even if they do, they generally do not remain in office for long.

Unlike their counterparts in the USA, some Russian authors of anti-Western conspiracy theories are ranked among the most influential public intellectuals; they publish books and have access to the mainstream media, particularly those controlled by the state. The articulation of even the most bizarre conspiratorial ideas does not lead to exclusion from mainstream politics. Indeed, as early as the late 1990s, the ruling elite of Russia understood that anti-Western conspiracy discourse could lead to the achievement of social cohesion. This has allowed top-ranking officials to put the work of conspiracy theorists to use for both domestic and international purposes.

Producers of knowledge – in this case, public intellectuals – have made their own attempts to gain power by becoming part of the political hierarchy. The Foucauldian concept of power/knowledge, as applied to conspiracy discourse in Russia, highlights the dependence of public intellectuals on the power institutions in the state. At the same time, the political elites are dependent on producers of such knowledge for their ability to provide intellectual support to the political regime.

Pavlovskii's attempts to use public intellectuals to create a political discourse favourable to the Kremlin were successful; they took the form of a range of Kremlin-connected think tanks and foundations which praised Putin and criticized his opponents. The intellectuals affiliated with these organizations spread anti-Western conspiracy theories among ordinary Russians through the media, claiming to reveal the 'genuine' causes of domestic and international events. The Kremlin's control of major information sources, particularly television, has offered loyal intellectuals a unique opportunity to articulate populist conspiratorial notions effectively. Accordingly, public intellectuals have become important producers of conspiratorial discourse, which has been aimed, to use Foucault's theory, at establishing a particular regime of truth.

Each of the intellectuals discussed in this chapter has contributed to the promotion of a conspiratorial perception of the West by publishing books, hosting talk shows, and supplying highly ranked politicians with ideas which the intellectuals adopted from the West. The public careers of Dugin, Narochnitskaia and Shevchenko reveal that anti-Western conspiracy theories are among the most popular instruments of social cohesion used by the political elites to maintain control over the country. Opposition to the Kremlin is the usual target of the otherwise different populist discourses articulated by these intellectuals, each of which has the aim of constructing an 'Other' within the nation. None of the intellectuals openly acknowledges his or her affiliation with the authorities and at times even stresses that their activities are oppositional. Yet they all support Putin's role as the single political leader of the country. In line with Pavlovskii's political projects, the anti-Western conspiracy theories expounded by public intellectuals have become a populist tool; this serves to legitimize the authoritarian rule of the president and delegitimize his opponents.

3
In Search of the 'Agents of Perestroika'

The attempted coup of 19–21 August 1991 was an important turning point in Russian history. The crumbling economy, ethnic conflicts in the republics and the chance to adopt a new Union treaty, which could have turned the Soviet Union into a confederation, prompted the conservative bloc in the Soviet government to set up the State Committee of the State of Emergency (*GKChP*) and introduce a State of Emergency on 19 August. However, this failed; the opposition to Communist Party rule, led by the President of the Russian Federation, Boris Yeltsin, defeated the coup, marking the victory of democratic forces in the country. The Russian Federation authorities decreed that these days would henceforth be commemorated as the starting point of a new, democratic state.

In anti-Western conspiracy discourse, however, the events of August 1991 have been interpreted as a prime example of the West's success in challenging Russia's greatness. Because of the breakdown of the Soviet state which followed the attempted coup, the West succeeded in imposing its rule on Russia. The remarkable failure of the *GKChP* to suppress a relatively small opposition fed suspicions that the coup had been staged and that treachery was at work in the highest ranks of the Soviet ruling elite. In the 1990s, various factions among the Russian conservatives disseminated these versions of the August coup and accused Yeltsin of pursuing an anti-national policy.

In the first decade of the twenty-first century, several influential members of Putin's political elite put forward an interpretation of the August 1991 coup which stressed the conspiratorial nature of the events. The combined efforts of the state-aligned media, book publishers and pro-Kremlin politicians resulted in a reinterpretation of the events of that summer and their aftermath. By the mid

2010s, Russians had come to perceive them as a tragic episode in the country's history and the result of a conflict within the political leadership (Levada-tsentr, 2013a). Largely thanks to the conspiratorial allegations surrounding it, the initial symbolism concerning the coup's failure – that it marked a victory of democracy in Russia – was now rejected.

This chapter will discuss conspiratorial interpretations of Mikhail Gorbachev's *perestroika* and the collapse of the Soviet Union in 1991, and the deployment of these interpretations in the political struggles of post-Soviet Russia. The August 1991 coup appears to be a foundational moment in the history of the new Russian state, thus triggering heated debates about its causes. In these debates, specific interpretations of the coup are often linked to particular conceptions of Russian identity. Throughout the post-Soviet era, interpreting the Soviet collapse through the prism of conspiracy theory has played a powerful role in redistributing power between the Kremlin and the opposition. In the 1990s it served as an ideological platform on which the forces of opposition against the Yeltsin regime were able to unite, and the notion of an engineered collapse of the USSR was used to delegitimize the president. After an unsuccessful attempt to impeach Yeltsin in 1999, which was largely based on conspiratorial interpretations of the Soviet collapse, Kremlin officials realized the value of this idea for the purposes of nation-building and delegitimizing political opponents. Thus, state-sponsored conspiratorial discourse about the Soviet collapse, shared and developed by numerous public intellectuals, facilitated the promotion of a national unity based on the memory of both the Soviet past and the dramatic experiences of the first post-Soviet years. As a result, in the 2000s attitudes towards the Soviet collapse were used by the ruling elites as a key marker distinguishing 'the truly Russian people' from the conspiring, alienated minority.

Language of the Intelligence Services

A common feature of conspiracy theories relating to the collapse of the Soviet Union is the notion of 'agents of *perestroika*' (*agenty perestroiki*) who allegedly worked in close collaboration with Western intelligence to corrupt Soviet institutions and ideology. This idea is especially popular among authors with a background in Soviet intelligence, who associate the break-up of the Soviet Union with pro-Western 'agents of influence' (*agenty vliianiia*). The term 'agents of influence' is itself part of the lexicon of intelligence services. Viacheslav Shironin, a KGB general and author of three books about the conspiratorial causes of the Soviet collapse, sees the destruction of the USSR as a top-priority goal which shaped American politics for decades, and argues that *perestroika* was planned from abroad to aggravate the Soviet Union's economic problems (Shironin, 2010). Another ex-KGB officer, Igor' Panarin, claims that in 1943 the United States and the United Kingdom started the 'First Information War' against the Soviet Union. He argues that the Committee of 300, the Trilateral Commission and the Council on Foreign Relations waged this war by organizing subversive campaigns against the USSR. He also holds that 'subversive agents' in the Soviet Union, controlled by the United States, were actually discovered by the KGB, but were not 'neutralized' due to their connections with top-ranking Soviet leaders; for example, General Secretary Nikita Khrushchev supposedly supported them (Panarin, 2010, pp. 154, 176–81). It should be noted that two of these organizations, the Trilateral Commission and the Council on Foreign Relations, both of which are important US non-governmental and non-partisan organizations, and think tanks, also occupy an important position in conspiracy theories in the United States and Europe (Marrs, 2000).

Shironin's and Panarin's works do have significant conceptual differences. Shironin's ideas are mainly concerned with subversive US activities aimed at global domination. He portrays Russia as a key adversary of the USA, with the latter attempting to undermine the former through a highly-sophisticated combination of intelligence operations. Shironin's analysis is thus reminiscent of Soviet propaganda and its main features can be traced back to the popular culture of the Cold War period.

Panarin's work, which was published thirteen years after Shironin's, is clearly influenced by foreign literature on conspiracy theories available in Russia at that time, and could even be said to function as a Russian guide to Western conspiracy theories. It is likely that his concept of Western conspiracy was shaped by ideas about global conspiracy which were popular in Western Europe and the USA, and that he then reinterpreted them as exclusively anti-Russian. For instance, he identified an American banker, David Rockefeller, as a key mastermind behind the Soviet collapse. Rockefeller can be found at the centre of numerous conspiracy theories in the USA that involve the Trilateral Commission and Council on Foreign Relations (Cooper, 1991; Keith, 1995). Panarin also depicted The Committee of 300, the Council on Foreign Relations and the Trilateral Commission as the main centres of anti-Russian conspiracy in the West (Panarin, 2010, pp. 154–5). However, while these organizations do play major roles in Western conspiratorial literature, they are concerned with the creation of the New World Order, and do not specifically mention Russia.

In texts about the Soviet collapse, subversive 'agents' of the West are blamed for kindling nationalist movements in the Soviet republics which destroyed the multinational Soviet state. Many authors, including Panarin and Shironin, emphasize the role here of Aleksandr Iakovlev, one of Gorbachev's closest political advisers and the mastermind of *perestroika*. According to the former head of the KGB, Vladimir Kriuchkov, Iakovlev was an American spy recruited in the 1950s during an internship at Columbia University (Kriuchkov, 2003, p. 324). Echoing this theory, Igor' Froianov, a highly controversial Russian historian who was, nonetheless, dean of the History Faculty at St Petersburg State University, concluded (2009, pp. 222–4) that Iakovlev acted in agreement with Gorbachev to approve the military repressions in 1991 in Vilnius which triggered the separation of the Baltic states from the Soviet Union, a key milestone in the Soviet collapse (Suny, 1993, pp. 145–52).

The idea of 'subversive agents' intent on destroying the Soviet Union is one of the most popular conspiratorial notions. The search for a scapegoat in the form of a 'foreign agent' draws on a large body of publications and stories concerning treason against Russia. This concern about 'foreign agents' can be traced back to fear of German subversion before and during the First World War, the show trials accompanying the Great Purge in the 1930s, and a veritable spy mania on the part of the elites in the Soviet era. The concept of a 'subversive agency' can be a convenient and powerful tool. Authors of conspiracy theories merge real historical facts with imagined stories of treason, thus bringing into doubt former and current politicians' loyalty to the state and, by doing so, undermining their reputations.

'Westernized' Intelligentsia Against Motherland

While Panarin and Kriuchkov are concerned with 'agents of influence', Sergei Kurginian, political consultant and former theatre director, has focused on the social factors relating to the Soviet collapse. Yet, it is rumoured that Kurginian was a political consultant to the leaders of *GKChP*, trying to arrange lucrative business under the government's protection and later, in the 2010s, advised the controversial Moscow mayor Iurii Luzhkov, known for the corruption of the Moscow property market (Minkin, 2012; Belkovskii, 2016).

Kurginian blames the liberal intelligentsia and pro-Western political elites for selling the interests of the country in 1991 and ruining its historical mission. He uses the term *anti-elite* to describe what he sees as a union of the pro-Western political elites with the Russian liberal intelligentsia, who, together, corrupted Soviet politics during *perestroika* and 'robbed' the Soviet Union of its greatness (Chernykh, 2011). This *anti-elite* consisted of top-ranking figures in the Communist Party and the KGB. They initiated the August coup to cover up their destructive policies. Kurginian explains the dramatic decline in Russians' standard of living as the result of pro-Western intellectuals making alliances with 'shadowy business', whose representatives eventually destabilized the Communist Party and became oligarchs, while the intelligentsia had to survive as best it could (Legostaev, 2002). The American 'plan' for Soviet destruction included producing a corpus of anti-Soviet historical research which corrupted Soviet ideology and demonstrated the supremacy of Western capitalism. During *perestroika,* as Kurginian (n.d.) argues, Russians were told that they should not dream about the glorious Communist future; 'only the interests of the individual were important'.

Kurginian's rhetoric about treacherous, pro-Western elites was interlaced with references to the socio-economic and ideological problems which emerged with the collapse of the Soviet state. His populist appeal, which involved laying the blame on the 'anti-elite' for the destruction of the state, was targeted primarily at educated Russians, the so-called intelligentsia, who suffered enormously under the economic reforms of the 1990s. Exploiting the grievances of this group, Kurginian further boosted his popularity by becoming a frequent guest on television talk shows. By the end of the 2000s he was hosting his own show, *Istoricheskii protsess* (*The Historical Process*), on the state-owned television channel Rossiia; this was dedicated to the discussion of various historical topics closely connected with contemporary political issues. Being the host of a television show provided him with an effective vehicle for disseminating conspiratorial ideas about the Soviet collapse. His popularity, in turn, helped him to gain a position in Putin's presidential campaign of 2012 (discussed in Chapter 6); this clearly indicates the close ties he has with the Kremlin.

The Manipulation of Consciousness

The Russian chemist and writer Sergei Kara-Murza has presented another conspiratorial conceptualization of the Soviet collapse. This is based on the idea that a small group of people in the Soviet Union, with 'external' partners, and by means of manipulation, convinced the entire Soviet nation to destroy the country and abandon its ambitions to build Communism: 'A certain influential and organized part of humankind (into which some of our compatriots have been accepted) . . . has convinced our society to act according to a programme which has brought enormous benefits to this group at enormous cost to ourselves' (Kara-Murza, n.d.). He sees the consciousness of the Soviet people as a combination of 'rationality (mind) and common ethics (heart)' which allows them to grasp the world in its complexity, unlike the 'technocratic Europeans' who only have a restricted view of the world. He explains that a positive perception of the West first became popular among so-called anti-Soviet intellectuals; they distorted the meaning of Soviet symbols and institutions such as the Motherland, the State and the Army, all of which were crucial for the nation (Kara-Murza, 2009).

Kara-Murza's writings have a strong focus on manipulation of public persuasion. This accords with an idea which was particularly popular in Russia at the beginning of the new millennium, that 'social programming' could replace genuine public engagement in politics (Gusev et al., 2006). This idea is linked to the successful deployment of the crude propaganda campaign which took place during the presidential elections in 1996, when within six months Yeltsin had gone from being at the bottom of the list of candidates to winning the election (Shevtsova, 1999, p. 156).

Kara-Murza's focus on the use of manipulative technologies, and the relative popularity of this explanatory framework during the 2000s, can be compared to the American conspiracy theories devoted to brainwashing technologies which emerged during the Cold War. As Melley (2008, pp. 149, 162–4) suggests, conspiracy narratives about brainwashing are an attempt to theorize social and ideological influences on American society. For instance, the changing role of women and other progressive social changes in the 1960s were regarded by some American conspiracy theorists to be the result of Communist brainwashing tactics which endangered the ultimate virtue of American culture, individualism. According to this view, brainwashing corrupted liberal individualism, turning rational agents into brainwashed subjects under the control of an external, Communist mastermind.

The Russian version of the brainwashing theory echoes American fears of a less autonomous society, but places more concern on the possibility of a 'thinking nation' being replaced by a mob (Kara-Murza uses the term 'mob-creation', or *tolpoobrazovanie*). According to Kara-Murza, the populations of West European countries, under the influence of television and popular culture, have been 'transformed into a huge virtual mob always ready to sanction the policies of the leaders' (Kara-Murza, n.d.).

In addition, Kara-Murza echoes American fears about threatened individuality. He states that 'Western manipulators' pose a threat to the 'traditional Russian idea of the common cause' that has always bonded individuals to society and thus strengthened the state. 'Western society' lacks 'the core of ethical values' which characterize Russia because of the unprecedented atomization of Western society which stems from the fact that it values individual rights and private ethics above all else (Kara-Murza, 2011, p. 170).

We can see from this that proponents of the brainwashing conspiratorial concepts in both the USA and post-Soviet Russia had a similar anxiety about social influences. The changing nature of Russian society, its transition to a market economy and the increasing value placed on individual rights evoke fears of an 'evil-minded manipulation' carried out by the West to destroy the 'uniqueness' of Russian society. According to this interpretation, the ease of the Soviet collapse in 1991 resulted from the persistent brainwashing of the Soviet people by Mikhail Gorbachev and the political elites loyal to him (Kara-Murza, 2002).

1917–1991: Nikolai Starikov's Interpretation of the Soviet Collapse

In the huge body of Russian conspiracy theories of the 2000s, the works of Nikolai Starikov occupy a particularly important place due to the popularity of the writer and to his insistence that the West is actually engaged in a war with Russia. By 2017 he had sold over a quarter of a million copies of his books. He regularly travels round Russia giving lectures and book presentations, and he takes part in television shows. In 2011, he became actively involved, together with Kurginian, in Russian political life: he is now a leader of the movement *Profsoiuz grazhdan Rossii* (the trade-union of Russian citizens) and the head of the *Great Fatherland* party (Partiia 'Velikoe Otechestvo').

Starikov's method of studying Russian history is typical for a conspiracy theorist: 'Many things in our history become clearer if you try to look behind the curtains of world politics. The aspirations of states and nations are always similar – nothing changes in the geopolitical causes of conflicts and wars. You only need to catch the correct logic of events and then you can easily understand both the past and the future' (Starikov, 2009, pp. 9–10). This is how Starikov discovered the Anglo-Saxon conspiracy against Russia that caused the revolutions both of 1917 and 1991:

> When I understood that the February and October revolutions were both part of the British intelligence to [bring about the] collapse [of] its geopolitical rival, the signs of repetition of the same scenario at the end of the twentieth century became obvious to me. It has become especially evident during the August events of 1917 and 1991 . . . (2011e)

In Starikov's view, the USA and the UK have always been engaged in a war against Russia because of its vast territory and abundant natural resources. He considers (2010a) that Russian revolutionaries represented the geopolitical interests of Russia's enemies and undermined Russia's greatness and political stability purely for financial gain. The events that took place in the CIS countries in the 2000s were an extension of the model which was implemented by the West both in 1917 and 1991:

> We witness all sorts of velvet, rose, and orange revolutions . . . [Behind] the curtains of unrest in 1917 [in Russia] stood foreign intelligence services. Strikers also need to eat something and it means that someone must pay for that. Those who are interested [in Russia's collapse] will pay. This is a simple idea and something that historians and politicians make wrong conclusions about although they initially might have correct assumptions . . . The answer to the question 'Who was the historical and geopolitical enemy of the Russian empire?' is the answer to the question about the mysterious author of our revolution. (Starikov, 2009, p. 48)

Just as in 1917, the Soviet collapse was supposedly the result of the global operation of British and American intelligence, together with a mass betrayal of Russia by top-ranking Soviet officials. In 1985, almost at the same time that Gorbachev was appointed General Secretary of the CPSU, Saudi Arabia increased its petroleum production and dramatically brought down oil prices which caused enormous economic problems for the Soviet Union. Saudi Arabia engaged in this financially unprofitable action to gain economic advantages from the

United States (Starikov, 2010b). The reference to the oil price is key: indeed, the drop in the oil price, as well as the agreement between the USA and Saudi Arabia, played important roles in the Soviet collapse (Gaidar, 2007).

Yet Starikov's rant against Gorbachev emphasizes that some members of the political elite might also be dangerous for Russian statehood. The Soviet collapse was possible only when the US leadership realized that the new Soviet leader, Mikhail Gorbachev, could destroy the country he was leading (210b, p. 80). By the end of 1991, due to his destructive actions, the USSR was on the brink of total collapse because it had lost almost all sovereignty. Diplomatic sovereignty was replaced by friendship with the West; military sovereignty was lost when Gorbachev destroyed the Soviet army; economic sovereignty was demolished by selling out Soviet industrial potential; and cultural sovereignty was exchanged for 'alien' Western values (2011c, pp.16–17).

Mikhail Gorbachev as a Favourite Scapegoat

Starikov's attack on Gorbachev is not unique; the first and last Soviet President is seen by many commentators as someone who consciously contributed to the collapse of the Soviet Union. In the early 1990s the Soviet writer and political émigré Aleksandr Zinoviev wrote that Gorbachev started the epoch of 'great treason' by visiting Queen Elizabeth II at Windsor Castle in 1985 instead of paying his respects at the grave of the founder of Communist ideology, Karl Marx, in Highgate cemetery (Zinov'ev, 1995). This 'treason' label was attached to Gorbachev in all the conspiracy writings about the Soviet collapse. While acknowledging that the economic situation in the USSR had not been good, various authors (including those who were Gorbachev's closest aides) claimed that he had deliberately destroyed Soviet military strength and got rid of political rivals in exchange for the support of the West. Anatolii Luk'ianov, Chairman of the Supreme Soviet of the USSR, wrote that there were no 'objective prerequisites' for the demise of the USSR, but this happened because of a struggle between irresponsible politicians, with Gorbachev playing one of the leading roles (Luk'ianov, 2010). Russian historian Anatolii Utkin asserted that Gorbachev committed a crime against the Motherland by allowing Ukraine to declare its independence, which destroyed forever any hope of Russia regaining its imperial greatness. Gorbachev agreed to everything that his American partners suggested, Utkin argued, thereby betraying the geopolitical interests of Russia (Utkin, 2009, pp. 30–2, 199).

In November 1991, Viktor Iliukhin, a top-ranking official in the USSR General Attorney's office, filed a lawsuit against Gorbachev accusing him of high treason, planning the collapse of the state at the behest of the USA, and signing decrees that contravened the Soviet Constitution and state laws (Iliukhin, 2011). Iliukhin did not win the case and was dismissed from his post. At the end of 2011, however, Starikov filed another lawsuit against Gorbachev, charging him with the collapse of the Soviet Union, the disappearance of the country's gold reserves, the destruction of the army and the pauperization of the population.

Starikov's attack against Gorbachev was a response to the fact that Gorbachev criticized Kremlin policies under Putin (Telen', 2009). He argued that since Gorbachev did not repent of his sin of destroying Russia in 1991, he had no right to criticize Putin and other 'patriotic' politicians (2011b). It is important to note that Starikov's words were later reiterated by the Kremlin spokesmen. Amidst the protests in Moscow in 2011–12 by opponents of Putin and the *United Russia* party, Gorbachev criticized Putin and the fact that he was running again for president (Dymarskii et al., 2011). Putin's spokesman Dmitrii Peskov replied that 'the former head of the huge country, who basically destroyed it, suggests to another man, who managed to save Russia from the same fate, to resign' (Russkaia sluzhba BBC, 2011). More recently, in April 2014, several deputies of the State Duma asked the General Prosecutor of the Russian Federation to open the case against Gorbachev which charged him with triggering the collapse of the Soviet Union (Runkevich and Malai, 2014).

Gorbachev's role in the collapse of the USSR is really hard to underestimate. The reforms he launched in 1985 were key steps in the process of democratization and, in many ways, undermined the legitimacy of many symbols that held the Soviet regime together (Gill, 2013). However, despite the revolutionary nature of his reforms, many commentators argue that it was not his intention to dismantle the Soviet Union. On the contrary, he did his best to preserve it (Brown, 2011; Plokhy, 2014).

Yet Russian public opinion, and the Russian media's coverage of Gorbachev's role in these events, is largely negative (Vanhala-Aniszewski and Siilin, 2013). This, in many ways, reinforces conspiracy allegations and makes Gorbachev a perfect scapegoat for the Soviet collapse. Many Russians have a negative attitude towards him, accusing him of political weakness and of turning a blind eye to the erosion of the country in the late 1980s. According to an opinion poll taken in 2001, Gorbachev was seen as the main cause of the Soviet Union's collapse. The two most common reasons given for the break-up of the country were that it was a result of the disorder created by *perestroika* (55 per cent), and the conflict between Gorbachev and Yeltsin (28 per cent) (Dubin, 2011). Another poll conducted in 2016 by the *Levada-Centre* found that 67 per cent of respondents had negative attitudes towards the last Soviet ruler (Aleksandrov, 2016).

Forgeries as Main Argument

Claims about Gorbachev's involvement in the 'Western plan' to destroy the Soviet Union rest on several documents that supposedly provide evidence of an anti-Russian plot. The first thing that puzzles some conspiracy theorists is how Iurii Andropov, one of the most powerful men in the Soviet Union – ex-chief of the KGB and leader of the country following Brezhnev's death – could promote a person whose policies would cause the dissolution of the Soviet state a few years later. Since Andropov did indeed support Gorbachev (Brown, 1996; Galeotti, 1997), some Russian nationalist writers contended that Andropov himself was one of those 'agents of influence' who destroyed the Soviet Union:

> All these human rights campaigners, 'antisovetchiks', are an element in the 'Golgotha' plan. This is exactly the legion that will control the minds of the befuddled masses in the period of global perestroika. Andropov was intimately acquainted with the fact that in Russia martyrs are loved and trusted. The first democratic elections proved the accuracy of Andropov's plan, elaborated [together] with the CIA and Mossad. (Perin, 2001)

The author of this source refers to one of the conspiratorial forgeries which were popular in the 1990s and whose origins are to be found in the spoof novel '*Operatsiia Golgofa': sekretnyi plan perestroiki* ('*Operation Golgotha': The Secret Plan of Perestroika*), written by Mikhail Liubimov (1995), himself a Soviet spy. The story shows a dying Andropov hatching a plan to plunge the Soviet Union into political chaos and 'wild capitalism' to renew Russian society without the need for mass purges. The plan describes *perestroika*, the August coup and Yeltsin's reforms in such detail that the novel triggered a parliamentary investigation into whether it was actually authentic (Sid, 2004). Although law-enforcement agencies repudiated the claims made in the novel, it still resulted in conspiracy theories becoming part of popular culture. In November 2012, an article about Andropov's planned reforms was the main feature of the magazine *Russkii Reporter*. Based on mostly anonymous interviews with former officers of the KGB, the author claimed that Putin's own reforms could be seen as a follow-up to Andropov's plan and its successful results (Kartsev, 2012).

The most important and influential forgery about the Soviet collapse is the so-called *Plan Dallesa* (*The Dulles Plan*), which purports to be a US National Security Council directive about a strategy to bring about the moral and cultural corruption of the Soviet people. The informal style of the text and some bits that have been copied from the Soviet spy novels makes it unlikely to have been an official governmental document (Deich, 2005):

> People's brains and consciousness are subject to change. By disseminating chaos there we shall surreptitiously replace their values with fake ones and we shall force them to believe in these values. How? We shall find like-minded persons in Russia ... Impudence and insolence, lies and deception, drunkenness and drug dependence, bodily fear of each other and barefacedness, treachery, nationalism and national conflicts, pre-eminent hostility and anger towards the Russian people – all this we shall cunningly foster. (Dalles, n.d.)

The *Dulles Plan* places the conspiracy conceptualization of the Soviet collapse within a particular time-frame. Post-Soviet Russia's socio-economic, interethnic and cultural problems are traced back to the past and connected with the Western plan for destruction. In contrast to Andropov's plan, the aim of which was to reform the stagnating Soviet Union, the *Dulles Plan* saw the destruction of the USSR as the ultimate goal of the US political elites. Like the conspiratorial notion of 'agents of influence' which is popular among ex-KGB officers, the *Dulles Plan* has been taken up by former intelligence service employees who treat it as a springboard for various subversive operations (Khlobystov, n.d.). As Julia Fedor (2011) writes, the notion that the West destroyed the once great Soviet Union by means of moral corruption and brainwashing is an ideal reason to denounce it as a diabolical enemy. To a certain extent, the logic of the Cold War was shaped by the possibility of mutual nuclear destruction and the two camps had various projects planning how to destroy its ideological contender (Gaddis, 2005; Young, 2007). However, the supposed plans by US intelligence to defeat the USSR, which can be found in various Cold War sources, are too confusing to serve as genuine narratives of conspiracy theories. In addition, they constantly emphasize the moral superiority of the USA as the country of freedom and democracy, and this works against the image of the Soviet Union as an innocent victim of the West's plans (Fedor, 2011, p. 849).

The *Dulles Plan* held a popular position in post-Soviet Russian culture and is often cited by film directors, actors and politicians. In 2012 NTV released a four-episode 'mockumentary' called 'Russia: The Full Eclipse', which explored various conspiracy theories popular in Russia today. One of these was that the Russian spies arrested in the USA in 2010 had discovered evidence that the *Dulles Plan* existed and passed it on to Russian journalists (Constantine26rus, 2012). The *Dulles Plan* framed each episode and was discussed by famous actors and presenters, who, according to the filmmakers, sincerely believed in the existence of this plan (Afanas'eva et al., 2012). Moreover, the film's author, Andrei Loshak, admitted that rating of the film was high and the channel's management praised his work (Malkina, 2012). However, it is not clear whether the audience treated the film as a mockery or as another conspiracy theory (Staryi televizor, 2012).

Belief in the *Dulles Plan* is not limited to celebrities and often is mentioned by mainstream politicians. Andrei Savel'ev, former MP and leader of the *Great Russia* party, stated: 'There are few people who doubt the authenticity of this text [*The Dulles Plan*], because it utterly and completely reflects both the policy of the US towards the USSR and the achieved results of this policy – the breakdown of self-awareness of our people and the destruction of our country' (Savel'ev, 2007). Nikolai Merkushkin, the then governor of Samara region, reiterated Savel'ev's view in 2016 and accused Russian opposition leader Aleksei Navalny of fulfilling the aims of the *Dulles Plan*. Navalny, according to the ex-governor, brainwashes people and creates chaos in the country, and this will help the USA to destroy Russia and divide it into 32 puppet states (Nastoiashchee vremia, 2016). Savel'ev and Merkushkin, then, prominent politicians, use this proven forgery in an argument to delegitimize the positions of pro-Western proponents.

Some forgeries which support the supposed existence of conspiracy against Russia are used to denounce individuals who were supposedly interested in bringing about the collapse of the Soviet Union. One of these is a speech supposedly delivered by Gorbachev at the American University in Turkey in 1999, and published in the Slovakian newspaper *Ušvit*: *Tsel'iu moei zhizni bylo unichtozhenie kommunizma* (*The aim of my life was the destruction of Communism*) (Gorbachev, n.d.). Russian translations of this document always refer to this issue of the Slovakian newspaper, and often to its subsequent publication in the

Russian newspaper *Sovetskaia Rossiia*. Another forgery is a speech supposedly delivered in November 1991 by Margaret Thatcher, in Houston, at a meeting of the American Petroleum Institute, entitled *Sovetskii Soiuz nuzhno bylo razrushit'* (*The Soviet Union had to be destroyed*). The third is a report allegedly delivered by the US President Bill Clinton at a meeting of the Joint Chiefs of Staff in 1995, which supposedly confirms US involvement in the Soviet collapse (Amerikanskie politiki o budushchem Rossii, n.d.).

A preliminary analysis of these documents demonstrates that the speeches were neither delivered, nor published as claimed. There was no article about Gorbachev's speech in the Slovakian newspaper *Ušvit*. Although the newspaper did exist, it had a very limited circulation even among Slovakian Communists and it is unlikely that it was known in Russia. It was, however, published in the conservative, Communist party newspaper *Sovetskaia Rossiia*. Margaret Thatcher did not give a speech at the meeting of the American Petroleum Institute; indeed, the supposed speech was on a topic which would have been completely irrelevant to that conference. Her official website lists the speeches she has given, and there is no suggestion that she even participated in this meeting (Margaret Thatcher Foundation, n.d.). Bill Clinton's supposed speech, in terms of content and linguistic details, resembles *The Dulles Plan*, and has also never been published anywhere but in post-Soviet conspiratorial literature.

Russian politicians and conspiracy theorists continue to refer to these documents to demonstrate the evil intentions of Western politicians towards Russia (Kazintsev, 2001), and to undermine the decisions of acting political leaders. In the 1990s, Yeltsin's opponents often used a negative image of the Russian president to delegitimize his policies and gain the support of both the national patriotic and Communist electorate (March, 2002). The claim that there were real political leaders – both Russian and foreign – who were proponents of anti-Russian conspiracy was the main feature of this use of forged documents. These forgeries helped to attract supporters by appealing to their emotions; naming real politicians instead of expressing generalized hatred towards the West is more effective as it helps to make conspiratorial claims sound more persuasive (Fedor, p. 849).

Competing Interpretations of the August Coup

There are two different conspiratorial interpretations of the August 1991 coup which have competed throughout the post-Soviet period.

The first was disseminated by Yeltsin's administration as the official explanation of the events. It treats the attempted coup as a plot by conservative forces in the Soviet government against the democratically elected authorities of Russia and an attempt to nullify the democratic achievements of *perestroika*. In contrast, the citizens of Moscow, who came to the Supreme Soviet building on 19 August and helped defend it from the *GKChP*, were members of civil society and were fighting for freedom and democracy.

From the start of the coup, Yeltsin referred to *GKChP* members as 'plotters'. This word was subsequently used by Gorbachev and by those who participated in the events, whose accounts were published during the investigation of the coup (Gorbachev, 1991; Stepankov and Lisov, 1992; Yeltsin, 1994). Soon after the coup's failure, members of the *GKChP* were arrested and charged with treason. Later, another charge was levelled at them: conspiracy aimed at the seizure of power. The labelling of the *GKChP* as conspirators allowed pro-Kremlin speakers to divide Soviet society at the time of the coup into 'the people' and the powerful 'Other' – the conservative bloc in the Communist Party and the Soviet government. The victory of Yeltsin's supporters over the alleged 'conspirators' provided Yeltsin's team with arguments to justify their actions during and after the coup.

This official version of events presents a coherent narrative; a conspiratorial reading of the coup helps lay the foundations of national cohesion by depicting this moment of history as the birth of the new democratic Russian state. On the first anniversary of the coup, Yeltsin praised Muscovites for having resisted the *GKChP* and congratulated 'the new Russia ... that could overcome its old instinct of resigned submissiveness' (quoted in Smith, 2002, p. 33). Gennadii Burbulis, then Secretary of State, drew a clear line between the new, progressive Russians and the plotting retrogressive minority:

> I stand in awe of and admire those who demonstrated ... an uncompromising devotion to freedom, and, thus, gave support to the president and to all of us, and [I feel] appalling sadness and am grossly insulted ... by those who acted according to their repressive ... worldview in such a fascist, conspiring manner. (Kommersant-Vlast, 1992)

This pro-Yeltsin version of the August coup is challenged by an alternative version in which it is presented as the last stage in the 'Western plan' to destroy the greatness of the Soviet state and put it under the control of foreign governments who wish to plunder its wealth. Foreign conspirators were acting in league with Gorbachev to influence the liberal intelligentsia in the Soviet Union and turn them into a 'fifth column' aimed at corrupting Soviet ideology during *perestroika* (Legostaev, 2002).

Other explanations for the August events were published in the following years. They vary significantly in accordance both with the ideological views and beliefs of the authors, and the extent of their involvement in present-day politics. Many of them are members of the *GKChP*, or the conservative opposition of the 1990s, and are supporters of Communism. Not withstanding their differences, most of the authors consider the August coup to have been a response to *perestroika;* at the same time, it created an interlude before the onset of Yeltsin's reforms. *Perestroika,* the August coup and the radical economic reforms of the 1990s hence merged into a single narrative of an anti-Russian plot masterminded in the West. This interpretation served as a powerful tool to win over Russian voters, most of whom found the economic reforms extremely painful.

In fact, even before the coup took place, the grounds for an alternative reading of it had already been set out. The idea that foreign powers were plotting to destroy the Soviet Union had surfaced early in 1991. Vladimir Kriuchkov, head of the KGB, stated several times that CIA agents abounded in the USSR and were working hard to push the country towards catastrophe (Shved, 2013). In February 1991, Valentin Pavlov, the last Soviet Prime Minister, claimed that he was introducing financial reforms in order to prevent Western banks subverting the Soviet economy. According to Pavlov, these banks were aiming to cause hyperinflation by pouring seven to eight billion roubles into the Russian economy (Golovachev, 2012). Later, during a meeting with West European businessmen, Pavlov apologized for these words and emphasized that he did not mean to file claims against 'solid businessmen'. However, he did insist that 'improper businessmen had ambitions to undermine *perestroika*' (Kommersant, 1991).

Pavlov, a member of the *GKChP*, was arrested after the failure of the coup. In 1993, he published his own account of the events, in which he claimed that in mid 1991 the *GKChP* had been created by Gorbachev, Yeltsin and Gavriil Popov, then mayor of Moscow, to enable them to retain their power over the state; it was coordinated by the US president, George Bush (Pavlov, 1993, pp. 67, 79). Pavlov contended that the official version of events, which was actively promoted by Gorbachev and Yeltsin, was a cover for the real reason behind the attempted coup: these men's lust for power. Pavlov's account was published in 1993, soon after the shelling of the parliament building in October which led to many civilian deaths. He referred again to Yeltsin's lust for power, accusing him of disregarding the interests and the lives of ordinary Russians:

> Members of the *GKChP* by no means contemplated restoring dictatorship and repression. Moreover, the main thing for us ... was the prevention of bloodshed, the unleashing of civil war and mass purges. Power was not my personal goal for which I would be ready to sacrifice the lives and blood of innocent civilians. ... [Yeltsin] was ready to sacrifice thousands of lives to keep the office ... (p. 70)

The attack on parliament gave some credence to Pavlov's claim that Yeltsin's regime was even more brutal than the *GKChP*. Taken together with his conspiratorial description of the August coup, the argument about Yeltsin's brutality and the alleged backing of the United States became a powerful tool which could be used by the opposition to delegitimize the president.

Pavlov's book is a particularly important element in the establishment of a conspiratorial interpretation of the coup. Pavlov was the first active member of the *GKChP* to offer an analysis of the coup; this ensured that there was an alternative reading of the event almost immediately. His insider's view and elaborate arguments supplied the opposition with the necessary 'factual' basis for questioning Yeltsin's legitimacy. The publication of his book in 1993 was also timely, since there was a significant growth in anti-Yeltsin feeling after the October atrocities. The conspiratorial interpretation of his actions during the 1991 coup helped to lay the grounds for an attempt to impeach him in 1998–9, and played an important part in transforming conspiracy theories into an instrument of mainstream politics.

Yeltsin's Impeachment (1998–1999)

Yeltsin became the victim of conspiracy theories soon after becoming president in 1991. The opposition accused him of bringing about the demise of the USSR by signing the Belovezha accords, and of a 'genocide of the Russian people' by means of his economic reforms. The forces opposed to his government formed a loose coalition that was sometimes referred to as a 'revanchist party'; in the first half of the 1990s, this brought together the Communists (Gennadii Ziuganov), national patriots (Vladimir Zhirinovskii and Aleksandr Prokhanov) and Russian fascists (Aleksandr Barkashov), all of whom subscribed to the notion of a war waged by the West against Russia (Yanov, 2010, pp. 192–4).

IN SEARCH OF THE 'AGENTS OF PERESTROIKA'

Gennadii Zyuganov, the leader of the newly formed Communist party of the Russian Federation, had seriously reconsidered the old Communist corpus of ideas to attract new supporters. He claimed that 1991 was the start of the New World Order which required the destruction of the United States' major rival, the Soviet Union. In his view the Bilderberg club, the Trilateral Commission and the American Council for International Relations were building the new global order and were using the territories of Eurasia to put an end to Russia's statehood and Orthodox Christianity (Zyuganov, 1997). As David Remnick notes (1998, p. 314), at the meetings in Washington with the US Ambassador to Moscow, or at the summits in Davos to which Zyuganov was often invited in the 1990s, Zyuganov kept quiet about his ideas. Yet inside Russia, at meetings with supporters or on television, he repeated them constantly.

After the parliamentary elections in December 1993, a considerable number of representatives of the 'revanchist party' were elected to the State Duma where they had the opportunity to legitimately use anti-Western conspiratorial rhetoric in political struggles against Yeltsin's government. The zenith of these struggles was an attempt, in May 1999, to impeach the president; this was initiated by Iliukhin, who had unsuccessfully tried to put Gorbachev on trial for the same reasons in November 1991. The parliamentary commission, headed by Vadim Filimonov, a deputy from the Communist Party, levelled five charges at Yeltsin: the demise of the USSR, the shelling of the parliament building in October 1993, the war in Chechnia, the deterioration of national military defence and the genocide of the Russian people. At least four of the five charges contained elements of a conspiracy theory about an attack being carried out by Yeltsin, the Western European countries and the USA against the Russian people.

According to those trying to bring about the impeachment, the signing of the Belovezha accords by Yeltsin should have been treated as high treason; this was an organized conspiracy to seize power in the USSR and change the constitution. The accords were signed despite the results of a national referendum, which was conducted on 17 March 1991, which supported the preservation of the Soviet Union. The Belovezha accords impacted on Russia's defence potential, and Yeltsin's policies fit the geopolitical interests of the USA and were 'rendering help to foreign countries to the detriment of the external security of the Russian Federation' (Kommersant, 1999c).

It is important to stress that the accusation of treason made against Yeltsin was based on the notion that technically the President of

Russia did not have the right to sign the Belovezha accords, and by doing so he had breached Soviet law; this meant that he had forfeited his right to rule. Both the dissolution of the USSR and the shelling of the parliament building in 1993 violated article 64 of the Criminal Law of the USSR:

> The actions of B. N. Yeltsin in the organization of conspiracy, aimed at the seizure of power in the Union, had a conscious, purposeful character. As part of the preparation for the destruction of the USSR, B. N. Yeltsin issued several decrees, which overreached the bounds of his constitutional authority and aimed at the usurpation of Union power. (Kommersant, 1999c)

This claim cast doubt on Yeltsin's legitimacy and emphasized his 'otherness' in relation to 'the people' of Russia. Iliukhin, as the initiator of the impeachment, based his speech on the corpus of conspiracy theories about the Soviet collapse which had been developed in the 1990s. As he put it:

> The Soviet Union collapsed not because of natural processes, not as a result of the August 1991 events, but as a result of political conspiracy on the part of the 'fifth column,' with the connivance, and at times with the participation, of the president of the USSR M. Gorbachev and leaders of several Union ministries and agencies, and as a result of a conspiracy headed by B. Yeltsin. (Iliukhin, 1999)

It is certainly the case that the signing of the Belovezha accords was not entirely legal. As Lilia Shevtsova has observed, the Soviet Union was dissolved by the decision of a handful of political leaders who 'were not concerned about the legality of their actions' (Shevtsova, 1999, p. 14). This circumvention of the law helped reinforce the opposition's claims about the 'alien' nature of Yeltsin in relation to the 'Russian people', whose desire to save the Soviet Union had been betrayed. Moreover, the fact that the US President Bush was the first person Yeltsin called after signing the agreement (Colton, 2008, p. 206) provided additional 'evidence' of a conspiracy between the Russian and US Presidents.

> The will of the majority was expressed in the All-Union referendum on 17 March 1991, and the state leaders of the USSR and Russia, provided they were patriots, with the fondest love of the Motherland, rather than creeping accomplices (*kholuistvuiuschie prispeshniki*) of the USA, should have realized the people's will. (Iliukhin, 1999)

The shelling of the parliament building in 1993, which eventually resulted in Yeltsin having more power, also enabled the opposition to argue that his rule was illegitimate. In the words of some of the deputies, the president had been involved in a conspiracy to turn Russia from a parliamentary into a presidential republic. Indeed, as Vladimir Gel'man notes, the 1993 adoption of the new constitution turned Yeltsin into the country's 'boss' (Gel'man, 2015, p. 55). Operating on the basis that he could do anything that the law did not expressly prohibit, Yeltsin placed himself at the very top of the power structure. The opposition tried to challenge him by means of another powerful tool – conspiracy theories.

The last of the charges against Yeltsin was that of the premeditated genocide of the Russian people. This was carried out by means of the liberalization of prices and the privatization of state property, which deprived the majority of Russians of jobs, financial assets and social guarantees. Iliukhin argued that 'the clan', consisting of between two hundred and three hundred families, became the main beneficiary of this privatization and usurpation of state power. To erase the memory of the previous social system and of Soviet patriotism, Yeltsin supposedly planned to eliminate pensioners and the intelligentsia – that is, those who could pass on knowledge about the glorious Soviet past to younger generations (Iliukhin, 1999). Despite the attempts of patriots like Iliukhin to prevent any further destruction of Russia, Yeltsin allegedly confirmed, in a letter to President Clinton on 18 September 1998, that there would be 'no turning back, the reforms will continue' (*Kommersant*, 1999c).

Iliukhin implicitly likened Yeltsin's genocidal social policies to Nazi policies against the Slavic nations during the Second World War. Since the memory of the Great Patriotic War is so vital in post-Soviet Russia and serves as the foundation for national cohesion, this helped Yeltsin's opponents to label his policies anti-Russian. In addition, as Bernard Harrison (2006, p. 68) has demonstrated, applying the 'Nazi' label in a public speech to a specific group or movement automatically stigmatizes it and implies that nothing can be said in its favour. Likening Yeltsin and his team to the Nazis helped to strengthen the populist dimension of anti-Yeltsin arguments. However, the notion of genocide against the Russian people proved to be more problematic.

An accusation of genocide, used as a political instrument, can have a powerful resonance: it can strengthen the moral and legal pretentions of a group which claims to be the victim of genocide. As Evgeny Finkel (2010) has demonstrated, in the post-Soviet world, the accusation of genocide gained popularity because it supplied the political elites of the newly founded states with a powerful tool for national cohesion. When Russian nationalists accused Yeltsin of conspiring to destroy the Russian nation, they were bringing the notion of genocide into the official political language.

However, an accusation of genocide can backfire. By claiming that elements in the government were responsible for an anti-Russian conspiracy, the parliamentary opposition divided Russian society into 'the people' and the Yeltsin-led 'occupational government' (*okkupatsionnoe pravitel'stvo*). Filimonov quoted Albert Camus: 'If you don't fight injustice – you cooperate with it'. The journalist of the pro-Communist newspaper *Zavtra*, who covered the debates in the Duma, added: 'In other words, it will not be possible for other deputies to stand aside. You cannot have it both ways' (Brezhnev et al., 1999).

The deputies did not grasp the fact that if an accusation of genocide is made, the alleged target of this genocide is required to acknowledge its status as defenceless victim. As Finkel noted, in Russia, 'the dominant historical myth of military strength, superpower status and victory in the Second World War is difficult to reconcile with the powerless victimhood embedded in the claims of genocide' (p. 57). Russian nationalist ideology stumbled at this point. It came into conflict with a key element in the profile of a victim of genocide: it required an acknowledgement of weakness. In the context of post-Soviet Russian politics, this was unlikely. It is telling that of all accusations levelled at Yeltsin in the attempted impeachment, it was the genocide of the Russian people that attracted the lowest number of votes (Kommersant, 1999b).

None of the five charges against the president succeeded in gaining the 300 votes required for an impeachment (Kamyshev, 1999). However, since it rested on the claim that Yeltsin had been involved in a conspiracy against the Russian people, it still enabled the accusation of conspiracy to become a legitimate political strategy; it was this notion that united highly diverse opposition forces (from the Communists of *KPRF* to liberal politicians represented by *Yabloko*) and pro-Yeltsin forces (*Kommersant*, 1999a).

The liberal forces which opposed Yeltsin used the impeachment procedure as a way of returning to power that they have lost after the August 1998 financial crisis. On 17 August 1998, the Russian government defaulted on its debts to a degree that seriously undermined the positions of deputies from liberal parties in the Duma. So, by supporting the impeachment, they sought to dissociate themselves from their friends and political allies in Yeltsin's government and gain the support of those voters who were also dissatisfied with Yeltsin. In turn, the Communists and various representatives of the 'revanchist' bloc in the Duma attempted to exploit the conflict between Prime

Minister Evgenii Primakov and Yeltsin by strengthening their alliance with Primakov, who was at the time widely considered to be a potential future president, and get the support of Russian voters before the parliamentary elections in December 1999 (Zhukov and Samoilova, 1999). The impeachment also coincided with the rise of anti-Western sentiment in Russia which was related to the NATO operation in Serbia in 1999; this too was used by the opposition to win voters' support.

The impeachment gave rise to concern in the Kremlin about the outcome of the forthcoming presidential elections. The rise of Evgeny Primakov – a former head of the Russian intelligence services, and Russian Prime Minister from 1998–9 – as an independent and powerful politician took place at the same time as the impeachment. The Communists' support for Primakov and their attempt to impeach Yeltsin by putting forward populist conspiratorial allegations caused major concern among liberal politicians. The image of an aggressive nationalist attempting to challenge executive power by mobilizing the people against the government, and in particular by means of conspiracy allegations, pushed liberal reformers to support the Kremlin's candidate, who advocated a strong super-presidential model that eventually paved the way for a further shift towards authoritarianism (Shevtsova, 2005, pp. 20–1).

Fenster has pointed out (p. 90) that conspiracy theory as a mode of populist logic is a feature of many political systems, incuding democracies; it can be used to mount a significant challenge to the political order while at the same time highlighting structural inequalities in society. An impeachment of Yeltsin based on conspiracy theories posed a challenge to the post-Soviet Russian political system. The populist conspiratorial rhetoric of the conservatives was bolstered by the social and economic problems that emerged after 1991, which were hugely aggravated by the economic crisis of 1998. Under these circumstances, the government dropped the idea of fostering national consensus and further democratic developments to achieve a compromise with the opposition; instead it focused on creating a consensus among the elites as to who would be a suitable presidential candidate in 2000, so that they could successfully compete with the Communist challenge. As Shevtsova noted (2005, p. 20), those who called themselves liberals in the 1990s were caught in a historical trap, fearful of growing populism and suspicious of the deputies. The political elites were unable to cope with the populist challenge expressed in conspiratorial rhetoric: this was one of the many reasons behind the authoritarian turn in the 2000s. From the moment Putin came to power there have been conspiracy theories about the Soviet collapse, though they have acquired new forms and are now employed by the Kremlin and its leaders.

The Narratives of the Soviet Collapse in Putin's Russia

In the twenty-first century, the government-sponsored nation-building project included intense speculation about the causes of the Soviet collapse, and fear that it was primarily due to the malign activities of Western plotters who were becoming increasingly prominent in politics. Putin summed up the official attitude towards the collapse in 2005 in his opening address to the Federal Assembly, when he described it as 'the major geopolitical disaster of the century' (Putin, 2005). This view, which had some public support at the beginning of the 2000s, was widely disseminated by pro-Kremlin politicians and loyal public intellectuals in the years which followed, and helped foster nostalgia about Soviet times (Dubin, 2011).

Putin's view of the Soviet collapse capitalized on a particular socio-cultural position, which Serguei Oushakine (2009b) described as 'the patriotism of despair'. Feelings of regret about the demise of the great country, supported by the conviction that this was the result of a conspiracy by 'Western enemies', encouraged national cohesion and made it seem as though the political leadership was in tune with the people. Putin placed much emphasis on the socio-economic and political inequalities which Russians suffered in the wake of the Soviet collapse. In this way he was able to foster a positive attitude towards a lost past, which he contrasted so significantly with the post-Soviet situation; hence it served as an important tool with which to identify 'the people' as a pan-national 'community of loss', in opposition to the collective 'Other' which was formed of those who shared no such nostalgia for the Soviet past (Oushakine, 2009a, p. 114). Members of this collective 'Other' generally consisted of the most 'Westernized' part of Russian society. This made it possible to portray them in the emerging official discourse as 'agents' of foreign influence. As we shall see, this rested, once again, on conspiracy narratives.

Putin's opening remarks to the Federal Assembly outlined the events of the previous decade, and included several elements which make it clear how popular the conspiracy discourse about the Soviet collapse had become in the 2000s and 2010s. The first, and most crucial, part of Putin's speech referred to the most dramatic issues of the post-1991 era:

Tens of millions of our co-citizens and compatriots found themselves outside Russian territory. Moreover, the epidemic of disintegration infected Russia itself. Individual savings depreciated and old ideals were destroyed. Many institutions were disbanded or reformed carelessly. Terrorist intervention and the Khasavyurt capitulation that followed damaged the country's integrity. Oligarchic groups – possessing absolute control over information channels – served exclusively their own corporate interests. Mass poverty began to be seen as the norm. And all this was happening against the backdrop of a dramatic economic downturn, unstable finances, and the paralysis of the social sphere. (Putin, 2005)

This focus on social trauma indicates the populist approach taken by the ruling political elites to unite a highly-divided society on the basis of common negative experiences. Reference to 'the oligarchic groups' immediately after the mention of mass poverty and severe economic hardship appealed to the masses, who contrasted the current situation with the relative economic stability of the 2000s (Shcherbal', 2010). At the same time, an emphasis on 'oligarchical rule' helped identify the 'Other' to whom they could direct their anger.

As Oushakine's analysis has demonstrated (2009a, p. 75), 'post-Soviet uneasiness about the increasing social role of capital is translated into stories about universal lies and deceptions. The perceived exposure to foreign values and capital is often counterbalanced with ideas of an enclosed national community and unmediated values.' By referring to socio-economic problems, Putin attempted to expose inequality in post-Soviet society and demonstrate his concern about improving the situation. His address served as an important springboard for public debate, and for public intellectuals to find a suitable approach to national development. These intellectuals drew on conspiracy allegations about the Soviet collapse and socio-economic hardships to identify the plotting 'Other', who had initiated the collapse of the Soviet Union and then profited from it themselves while the majority of the population suffered. It is important to note that top-ranking officials interpreted the Soviet collapse as a tragedy; this allowed them to shift the symbolic potential of this notion from the opposition parties and movements who had used it in the 1990s, into mainstream political discourse.

Interpreting Putin's speech as solely rhetorical is incorrect; as the national leader, he could not denigrate the institutions that allowed him to become president. Hence alongside the depiction of the Soviet collapse as a tragic event, Putin included in his address a few rather less tragic consequences. In his words, the misfortunes of the 1990s were accompanied by 'significant' progress in some areas:

> In those difficult years, the people of Russia had to both uphold their state sovereignty and make a correct choice in selecting a new vector of development in their thousand-year-old history. They had to accomplish the most difficult task: how to safeguard their own values, not to squander undeniable achievements, and confirm the viability of Russian democracy. We had to find our own path in order to build a democratic, free and just society and state. (Putin, 2005)

This 'positive' reading of the recent past urged the audience to recognize the socio-economic and political progress which had been made after the Soviet collapse. It was impossible for the regime and its ruling elites to totally disavow the complex post-Soviet heritage; this would have seriously undermined their own legitimacy. Selective memory was the watchword. Referring to post-Soviet progress in this strategically important political text demonstrates the ways in which the notion of the Soviet collapse was deployed in Russian politics during the Putin era.

As a key event in Russian political life, the President's address offers the main official interpretation of events and authoritatively addresses major political and socio-economic issues. Its opening part included two different concepts, both of which related to important features in Russia's national history. The first conveyed the idea that the collapse of the Soviet state had been a dreadful event, but this, nevertheless, created the foundation for a positive reading of Soviet history. Given the growth of positive attitudes towards the Soviet past at the beginning of the 2000s, this dramatic interpretation of the Soviet Union's collapse received public support and converted nostalgic feelings about a common past into a powerful political resource.

According to the *Levada-Centre*, throughout the 2000s most Russians regretted the dissolution of the Soviet Union, although this number has been gradually decreasing, from 75 per cent in 2000 to 59 per cent in 2017 (Vedomosti, 2016; Masci, 2017). The second concept emphasized the importance of the post-Soviet period in constructing the institutions of a democratic society. This was used to support the argument that the Russian government and political establishment sustained good relations with the West and viewed Russia as part of European culture. These two concepts were aimed at gaining the support of different groups within Russia, promoting bonding within society as a whole. The combination of these two rather contradictory ideas has become characteristic of Putin's approach to national cohesion.

The perception of the Soviet collapse as tragic, and the myth that it was deliberately destroyed by political elites in conjunction with the West, has become a tool of political strategy. The political establishment of the 2000s used this idea firstly, to increase national cohesion, and, secondly, to delegitimize political opponents. The narrative of the lost country served as a unifying principle for the creation of a national community. Using this dramatic reading of the Soviet collapse in such a key political speech legitimized further reference to it in subsequent official discourse. The collapse of the Soviet Union became a symbolic construction which defined the borders of the nation and simultaneously marked out its 'Other', those who supposedly welcomed the destruction of the Soviet Union and facilitated Russia's economic and political collapse in the 1990s. In this context, anti-Western conspiracy theories about the origins of the Soviet collapse justified the internal division of society and allowed political opponents to be identified with 'Western conspirators', thereby raising concern about their loyalty to the country and their legitimacy as political actors.

Putin's announcement of the annexation of Crimea in 2014 and Russia's involvement into the Ukraine crisis can be seen as a case-in-point. The primary point in his address is the tragic loss of Crimea because of the Soviet collapse:

> I heard residents of Crimea say that back in 1991 they were handed over like a sack of potatoes. This is hard to disagree with. And what about the Russian state? ... It humbly accepted the situation. This country was going through such hard times then that realistically it was incapable of protecting its interests. However, the people could not reconcile themselves to this outrageous historical injustice. (Putin, 2014)

This statement is key to understanding the events behind the annexation of Crimea and the war in Eastern Ukraine. The dramatic and almost overnight fall of the Soviet state in 1991 served as a legitimate reason to annexe the Crimean Peninsula. According to Putin, the return of the territories that had been stolen by the Soviet political elites restores dignity to ordinary Russians who had no say in the process of dissolving the Soviet Union. The will of the Russian leadership to protect the country's great power status, even at considerable cost to the nation, triggered the war in Ukraine. At the same time, the possibility of a NATO invasion and the threat to Russia's military presence in the region intensified the fear of war with the West. As the final chapter demonstrates, the idea of a fifth column conspiring against the majority of Russians who supported the Crimean annexation was not only a major tool of social mobilization in the midst of this international crisis but served to promote the new legislative amendments. Fear of the possibility of the state collapsing again (a re-run of what happened in 1991), and the assumption that only malign forces could bring this about, are in many ways crucial for understanding Russia's political development after 2000.

Conclusion

From the very first days of the Russian Federation's independence, the notion that the Soviet Union's collapse had been brought about by the intrigues of the West served, on the one hand, as a unifying platform for patriotic groups, and on the other, as a political concept for different forces in the political establishment. The events of August 1991 possessed a uniquely symbolic potential to become a fundamental element in the foundation of the new state; they could show that totalitarianism had been transformed into democracy thanks to the joint efforts of popular politicians and ordinary Russians. Yet as Kathleen Smith has argued (2002, p. 55), Yeltsin and his team failed to ensure that a commemoration of the August events was central in the collective memory of post-Communist Russia. This fell instead to the Communists and national patriots, who 'recognized the value of investing organizational resources in spreading their version of events' using the courtroom, the floor of the legislature, and the streets to propagate an alternative reading of the August 1991 events.

The use of conspiracy theories enhanced the opposition's criticism of Yeltsin's policies and facilitated their promotion in the public space, especially against the background of socio-economic difficulties of the 1990s. Despite attempts by Kremlin officials to define the *GKChP* as 'plotters', the alternative reading of the attempted coup – as a staged part of 'the Western plan' to destroy the USSR – turned out to be more effective as a political strategy; it generated a sense of solidarity among the people, and delegitimized Yeltsin's regime.

In the 2000s, the Kremlin reassessed its approach to the events of 1991. The value of a conspiratorial reading of the August coup for political purposes began to be used against the Kremlin's opponents. The fact of the Soviet collapse, and confusion about why it happened so rapidly, formed the basis of powerful political concepts which were aimed at achieving social and national cohesion. We shall see in the next chapters that widespread belief in the pre-planned collapse of the USSR has been used by the political establishment of Putin's Russia to solve several domestic political issues. First, the political establishment of the 2000s exploited the lack of public consensus about the August 1991 events; it overdramatized the Soviet collapse, turning the spotlight on the unreliable elites who tolerated the country's dissolution. This supplied the establishment with a range of populist demands calling for power to be returned to the Russian people so that they could enjoy sovereignty over their own country. The idea of Russia as a 'sovereign democracy', which was introduced in the mid 2000s as a mainstream nation-building strategy, charged the Russian political elites and society in general with the task of maintaining independence and rejecting foreign influence.

Second, the use of conspiratorial narratives – shaped, in particular, by the language of the intelligence services, and replicating espionage narratives of the Soviet period – introduces the notion of a 'subversive agency' into the daily language of post-Soviet Russia. This operated as a formula which could endow the developments of the present day with familiar meaning. As Oushakine puts it, the Soviet past became 'an object of purposeful commodification and a product of active post-Soviet cultural consumption' (Oushakine, 2000, p. 999). The sense of a common experience was transmitted to the masses through the promotion of nostalgia about the Soviet past, generated by means of various symbolic models. This experience was associated with the bond between 'agents', 'Western subversion' and the collapse of the Soviet Union and served to provide a simplistic but powerful instrument to distinguish 'the people' from the 'Other'. The model was also sufficiently flexible to be extended to fit different situations, so that the Other could be NGOs, political parties or particular politicians.

The official narrative of the August coup, as disseminated through the media and the public speeches of intellectuals and politicians, merged nostalgia about the lost Soviet Union with the idea that Russia has been besieged by countries interested in the acquisition of its abundant natural resources and vast territory. This reading of the August events closely linked the Soviet collapse to the loss of national identity and unambiguously marked it as a tragic landmark in the history of Russia. The Russian authorities used charges of conspiracy against political opponents to blame them for plotting against independent Russian statehood, which had already been destroyed once before, in 1991. This established a precedent for several significant political reforms in the 2000s which substantially curtailed public liberties. The authorities also used positive public attitudes towards the

Soviet Union as a means for creating national cohesion. According to the polls regularly conducted by the *Levada-Centre*, it would seem that this perception of the August coup found a positive response in Russian society. Around one-third of Russians see the coup as 'a tragic event which had sinister consequences for the country', while another third perceive it, sceptically, as a struggle for power (Levada-tsentr, 2016a). This disillusionment makes it easier to use the notion of conspiracy in relation to the August coup in political strategies, something which is constantly happening under Putin's reign.

4
Sovereign Democracy and its Enemies

After the collapse of the Soviet Union, the search for a new national identity became a serious challenge both for intellectuals and political elites. Various groups of intellectuals developed different approaches to the post-Soviet Russian nation, but many of them were based on the works of pre-revolutionary authors and did not fully correspond to the realities of the post-1991 world. Yeltsin's government opted for a civic model of nation-building, introducing the notion of *rossiiane* (Russians). This model was based on the idea of a community of all citizens of the Russian Federation regardless of their ethnic or religious origins. However, it was challenged by other models which perceived the Russian nation as a community of Eastern Slavs, Russian speakers, ethnic Russians and Russians as an Imperial nation. This was reminiscent of the Soviet model of nation-building (Tolz, 2001, pp. 236–51, 267). Commitment to the building of a civic national identity was fairly constant throughout the Yeltsin era, but in order to attract voters, Yeltsin's government also tried to depict the Russian nation in other ways, such as an Imperial nation or as part of the Eastern Slavic community.

When Putin came to power, this did not fundamentally change the approach towards nation-building, and the model of Russia as a civic nation continued to predominate. Both Putin and his supporters emphasized that Russia was a multi-ethnic country whose multi-cultural diversity provided stability for political development and for the maintenance of peace. This idea is enshrined in governmental policy (Prezident Rossii, 2012). However, during Putin's years in the Kremlin, policies regarding nation-building have acquired two important new attributes. First, as Oxana Shevel (2011) demonstrated, the political leadership of post-Soviet Russia has been deliberately ambiguous when defining the nation-building agenda.

This has allowed the political leadership to operate pragmatically, even opportunistically, to pursue its goals by shifting the terms of official discourse pertaining to geographical boundaries and to membership of the Russian nation. Second, debates about Russian national identity have become an efficient political tool, utilized in the pursuit of aims which were not always directly connected with nation-building issues.

The cynical deployment of conspiracy theories by political elites for the purpose of national cohesion can be dated back to 2004, when the Kremlin was faced with two serious challenges: the Beslan terrorist attack in 2004 that took the lives of 333 people, including 186 children, and the 'colour revolution' in Ukraine. First, the domestic threat posed by North Caucasian separatism was used to limit the power of regional governors and assert the Kremlin's control over the regions. Explaining why there was no longer direct election of governors after Beslan, First Deputy of the Presidential Administration, Vladislav Surkov, stated that 'unity of executive power' was achieved through unity of the nation, and justified the political changes by reference to domestic threats:

> We should all recognize that the enemy is at the gates. The frontline goes through every city, every street, every house ... in a besieged country the fifth column of left- and right-wing radicals has emerged ... Fake liberals and real Nazis have a lot in common. [They have] common sponsors from abroad. [They have] common hatred towards Putin's Russia, as they describe it. In reality [it is a hatred towards] Russia as such. (Surkov, cited in Kaftan, 2004)

At the same time, the defeat of the pro-Russian candidate Viktor Yanukovich in Ukraine in 2004 caused concern that the transfer of power to Putin's successor in 2008 might not be as smooth as was hoped. Describing the thoughts of the Russian political establishment in the aftermath of Ukraine's 'Orange Revolution' in 2005, Pavlovskii noted: 'There was a feeling that somewhere around these people [those protesting against the results of the presidential elections], those regiments (*polki*) are gathering to take to the streets of Moscow' (Pavlovskii, cited in *Putin, Russia and the West*, 2012).

These events triggered a wave of conspiracy theories, which were aimed at mobilizing Russians in support of Putin's leadership and against the purported threat of domestic subversion. This mobilization was achieved largely by stirring up debate about Russian national identity and the new Russian ideology (Finkel and Brudny, 2013), with conspiracy theories playing a crucial role in this process. Defined by Surkov as a *sovereign democracy*, Russia, in official discourse, started to be juxtaposed to the West in terms of political, national and religious differences. In the view of pro-Kremlin intellectuals, Russian greatness and the country's history of determining the agenda of global politics were constantly being challenged by European and American governments in an attempt to undermine and split the country into numerous 'puppet' states. Thomas Ambrosio noted (2009, pp. 71–9) that Surkov's *sovereign democracy* was one of the major discursive instruments invented by the Kremlin to insulate Russia from democratization and to facilitate an authoritarian backlash in the 2000s. The conspiratorial nature of the concept was aimed not only at achieving obvious political outcomes for the Kremlin, but also at the promotion of the new nation-building project.

In this chapter, it will be argued that since the mid 2000s the political elites of post-Soviet Russia, including top-ranking politicians, have been making more use of the notion of the West as the conspiring 'Other' for the purpose of nation-building. The ambiguity of the nation-building agenda has enabled the Kremlin to pursue pragmatic political goals, often aimed at the suppression of political opposition. In this context, dividing society into 'the people' and the 'Other', by using conspiracy theories to facilitate social cohesion, appear designed to meet the Kremlin's goals: to boost national cohesion in support of the regime and to suppress opposition. However, Putin's return to the presidency in 2012 marked a significant change in official discourse on national identity. As the controversy around the Pussy Riot performance demonstrates, at times which are considered critical for the Kremlin, Russia's political leadership and the state-aligned media promote a less ambiguous image of the Russian nation: it is now Orthodox and conservative.

Theorizing the New Russian Identity

Vladislav Surkov is one of the most intriguing and ingenious Russian politicians of the post-Soviet era. He began his career as Mikhail Khodorkovsky's bodyguard in the turbulent period of Gorbachev's *perestroika*, but quickly evolved into highly ranked manager responsible for public relations in Khodorkovsky's company, MENATEP. In 1999, he joined the Presidential Administration and for twelve years was its deputy head, sharing responsibility for domestic politics. An amateur writer and fan of American hip-hop (Wikileaks, 2010), Surkov's initiatives in many ways defined Putin's regime: the fear that the state would collapse without the strong hand of a leader like Putin is among the central ideas of the 2000s (Surkov, quoted in Voronin, 2013). More than a decade in the Kremlin before his unexpected departure against the background of the street protests of 2011, Surkov was something of a court philosopher and chief designer of the ideological concepts behind Russia's authoritarian turn (Sakwa, 2011). The idea of Russia as 'sovereign democracy' is his favourite creation, though many Russia observers criticize the concept for helping to preserve the worst aspects of Putin's Russia: isolationism, corruption and propaganda (Judah, 2013).

On 17 May 2005, Surkov gave a speech at a closed session of *Delovaia Rossiia* (*Business Russia*), a public association of Russian businessmen, in which he identified Russia's current priority as the creation of a sovereign democracy and 'a truly national elite'. The then-head of *Delovaia Rossiia*, Boris Titov, later held that the version of the speech which was disseminated by the press distorted what Surkov had actually said (Stanovaia, 2005). All the same, the issues raised in this version of the speech have not officially been denied. Hence Surkov's speech, at least in the form that leaked to the press, offered an intellectual framework for subsequent public debates on national identity. Furthermore, it was delivered only a few weeks after Putin identified the collapse of the Soviet Union as a 'major geopolitical disaster'. The articulation of these two ideas in such a short space of time demonstrates growing concern among political elites at this time about social cohesion, something which was considered essential for the future stability of the regime.

In particular, Surkov was worried both about Russia's territorial integrity, and the colour revolutions in the CIS countries. He considered concerns raised by the European Union, Finland and Estonia about the supposed suppression of the cultural heritage of the Finno-Ugric nationalities living in the Russian Federation as a threat to Russia. Noting that the territories where these ethnic groups lived were rich in oil, Surkov observed: 'I am not a supporter of conspiracy theories. However, it is obvious that this is a planned action' (Surkov, 2005). This remark served to encourage the mobilization of political and business elites in support of the government. At the same time, Surkov pointed to a lack of loyal elites in Russia who could contribute to Russia's development and resist Western influence. He compared this to the political situation in the last years of the Soviet Union:

> Unfortunately, an enormous part of our bureaucracy views [the vertical structures of power] with neither understanding nor comprehension of

the processes which are currently taking place [in the country]. This is a problem of education and the backwardness of [our] political culture. This was the reason why the Soviet Union collapsed. This could become the cause of Russia's collapse. Whereas the Soviet Union collapsed with majesty – it was a catastrophe worthy of a film – we shall decay silently and that will be the end. (Surkov, 2005)

Reference to the Soviet collapse in both Putin's and Surkov's texts demonstrates the centrality of this event in the elite's interpretation of affairs. It seems that the Kremlin's leaders realized the hidden potential of the Soviet collapse as a symbol. These two speeches, although they both evoked the notion of the Soviet collapse, were addressed to different audiences and aimed to shape perceptions of the demise of the Soviet Union among different social groups and to demonstrate its impact on post-1991 national identity. The absence of public consensus about the Soviet collapse left a vacuum that the political establishment could fill as it wished, a space in which to shape a favourable identity discourse.

Surkov's notion of Russian identity included a definition of the West as Russia's competitor rather than its enemy. This was a major shift in thinking. In an interview with *Der Spiegel*, Surkov said: 'The people have attained a new sense of sobriety. The romantic days are gone. We no longer have the feeling of being surrounded by enemies, but rather by competitors' (Klussmann and Mayr, 2005). No longer seeing Russia as a besieged nation, but as one which could now engage in acts of political pragmatism with the West, opened up a new space for the populist expression of Russia's inequality in relation to 'the foreign Other'; this would prove vital for further conspiratorial mythmaking. That Surkov's statement was made in an interview with a leading European periodical was a way of suggesting to the West that by the mid 2000s the Russian political elite, and society at large, had developed greater open-mindedness and was now interested in building relations with other countries because of mutual economic interests.

Yet Surkov had a different, more conspiratorial message for his domestic audience. In a speech addressed to activists of the United Russia party, Surkov again put forward his pragmatic approach, but this time he explicitly identified the Western protagonists who, in his view, were interested in exploiting Russia's natural resources:

If we are not going to rule ourselves, but entrust everything ... to transnational companies, to powerful nongovernmental charitable organizations that dream of ways to bring us charity. ... Then I think they will leave us just what they consider essential for us to live on, rather than what we would have kept for ourselves. ... That does not mean they are enemies. No, they are competitors. ... It is nothing personal. (Surkov, 2010, pp. 102–3)

It is this shift in the perception of the West – from enemy to shrewd competitor – which helped to relocate anti-Western conspiracy theories from the margins of Russian political discourse to its centre. From now on, the idea of economic and political competition with the West could be used by mainstream politicians and supported by factual evidence taken, selectively, from the global political agenda. With that reconceptualization of Russian–Western relations, the language of anti-Western conspiracy became an inherent part of mainstream political discourse.

Surkov's comparison of Russia and Europe, as made in a range of texts on sovereign democracy, had two important particularities. First, he admitted that Russia was a European country, despite attempts by some Russian nationalists to see it as something separate. In an article entitled *Natsionalizatsiia budushchego (The Nationalization of the Future)*, Surkov stressed the importance of pragmatism in establishing relations with other European countries:

> We should note again that the people living to the West of Russia vary in their attitudes: there are those who want to subjugate her [Russia] and those who are counting on a mutually beneficial partnership. To the former, our democracy can show its determination to maintain its sovereignty, and to the latter it can show openness, flexibility and productive cooperation. Not falling out with Europe and keeping close to the West are essential elements in the construction (*konstruirovaniia*) of Russia. (Surkov, 2006a)

On the one hand, this strategy of improving relations with European countries by depicting them as a complex conglomerate of opinions could provide a basis for Russia's integration into European and global institutions. Russia's future is inherently connected with that of Europe, and this seems to be one of the pillars on which Surkov's political philosophy is built (Mäkinen, 2011). On the other hand, Surkov's emphasis on the groups which, he alleges, stand to gain from Russia's collapse, for economic and political reasons, became the basis for the dissemination of his anti-Western conspiratorial discourse. Indeed, as Andrey Tsygankov demonstrates, some political circles inside the USA do have anti-Russian views, regularly take a critical stance on developments in the post-Soviet space, and urge the US government to enact harsher policies towards Russia (Tsygankov,

2009). The dichotomy in Surkov's representation of the West has challenged a dominant perception of the West as a single, undifferentiated entity. However, an analysis of domestic and international events put forward by public intellectuals (which we shall discuss later) focused in particular on groups with an economic or political interest in Russia's collapse. As a result, the public was provided with what at first seemed like a sophisticated description of global events, but which once again turned into a one-dimensional picture of Russia under threat from the malign activities of powerful political groups in the West.

The supposed equality of Russia and the West as actors on the global political stage was another important factor in the dissemination of conspiracy theories in Russia. According to Laclau, in populist movements 'the people' identify with each other because of the contrasting image of 'the Other'. It is imperative that these two actors – 'the people' and 'the Other' – be seen as equals: this is what creates social frontiers and distinguishes 'the people' from their enemy, 'the Other', which prevents them from achieving their demands. This maintenance of the social environment is achieved by means of a popular, universal demand, what Laclau defines as 'the elementary form of building-up of the social link' (2005b, p. 35). In this case, the Kremlin's demand was the creation of a new national identity of *sovereign Russians*, which was hard to achieve because of Western resistance. Using a populist form of discourse, Surkov expressed the division of the social sphere into 'the power', embodied by the West as a whole, and 'an underdog', represented by a sovereign and democratic Russia. In this context, the term 'sovereignty' became the empty signifier through which all the demands of the Russian people could be expressed (Laclau, 2005a, pp. 97–9). No matter what the problem, and whether it was experienced by an individual or by a social group in Russia, it would be solved once the nation became *sovereign* and self-sufficient. It should be noted that Laclau's theory treated populism as a manifestation of anti-elitist attitudes on the part of ordinary people, who seek to challenge the ruling elites. The case of Surkov's sovereign democracy proves that populist rhetoric can be used successfully by the elites themselves to reinforce their claim to power.

In fact, Russia's status as 'an underdog' in relation to Europe was further reinforced by Surkov's critical portrayal of Russia as 'a badly illuminated outskirt of Europe, but not Europe yet' (Surkov, 2005). Surkov managed to transform 'a simple request' from both political elites and the Russian people for a clear understanding of Russian identity into, to use Laclau's term, the 'fighting demand' of the Russian people to become a nation. He did this by exploiting the belief that certain aspects of Russia were underdeveloped when compared with Europe (Laclau, 2005b, p. 38). The ability to compete with the West in global politics required social mobilization and national unity, which were expressed in Surkov's concept of a sovereign democracy.

The basis for this 'demand' was the notion of Russian greatness and her ability to determine a political agenda in the world, in contrast to the lesser ability of certain other countries in the post-Soviet space to do so:

> Russians, the people of Russia, have been a people with a state for 500 years. We are a nation that is used to statehood. Unlike many of our friends from the Soviet Union and plenty of other countries, we always had the idea of the state. ...[1] They were provinces of one country, they will become provinces of another. I cannot imagine Russians, people from Russia, who would think like this: 'Now we shall meld with someone else, we shall run off to them, and they will cuddle us and comfort us and rule over us'. And we have got no one to blame but ourselves for what has happened to us. And we have got nowhere to run, except back home. Here is another – and for me, actually, the most important – reason why Russia should be a self-reliant state that influences world politics. (2010, pp. 103–4)

Pointing at the countries which underwent regime change after the colour revolutions, Surkov inadvertently exposed the neo-imperial character of his model of nation-building. By making European integration a key issue in their political agendas, the leaders of Georgia and Ukraine had posed a serious challenge to Russian dominance in the post-Soviet space. The new political elites of these countries articulated their ambition to join the EU and NATO, which, in turn, for certain sections of the Russian elite, meant the decline of their own influence and an end to plans to restore Russia's former glory (Tolz, 2001, pp. 238–40). In the 2005 speech, Surkov expressed more bluntly the idea that the former Soviet republics had been dependent on Russia and her policies: 'They were drawn on the maps by Russian politicians of the past. ... We were in the co-creative process, co-working with the world powers to re-arrange the world' (Surkov, 2005).

The idea of Russian greatness was amplified by the notion that the

---

[1] By 'many friends from the Soviet Union' Surkov most probably meant political elites of non-Russian states of the former Soviet Union whose state structures were created during the Soviet period under decrees of the Central Committee of the Communist Party.

Russian people were 'the tireless masters' of their own fate. Surkov saw ethnic Russians as the core of the nation; they were inherently tolerant and had created a 'special Russian political culture' which was aiming at interethnic peace (Surkov, 2006a). Again, this points to the imperial roots of the Russian nation-building model and reiterates some of the ideas developed by the Slavophiles in the nineteenth century. Against this backdrop, the tragedy of the Soviet collapse, which also destroyed the imperial foundations of Russian statehood, could be given even more emphasis. In fact, the Soviet collapse acquired an important function in defining the political 'Other' in domestic politics. The rise of Russian ethnic nationalism in the 2000s (Verkhovsky, 2016) was described by Surkov as a 'nationalist-isolationist' issue and an internal threat to Russian territorial integrity. The break-up of the Soviet Union had also been the result of a resurgence of Russian nationalism during Gorbachev's *perestroika*:

> There was a time when we were told that the Kazakhs, Ukrainians and other comrades were a mill-stone round Russia's neck. . . . What was the result? We lost half of the country [in 1991], half of the population, half of the economy, and so forth. And if we believe that today these guys or those guys are to blame for everything, then we shall lose another half of the country and another half of the economy. (Surkov, 2006b)

Surkov was particularly critical of the demand by ethnic Russian nationalists that part of the North Caucasus be separated from the Russian Federation. Linking this to the Soviet collapse gave the political establishment and pro-government intellectuals a powerful tool with which to delegitimize the ideology of the Russian nationalists, who often attacked Putin's policies as anti-Russian. Nationalists were depicted as a 'fifth column' funded by foreign sponsors. The existence of an internal enemy served as one of the main pillars of Surkov's schema (Surkov, quoted in Kaftan, 2004).

Oligarchs in cahoots with liberals, who were alleged to be working with foreign sponsors, constituted another 'subversive group'. Labelled as 'radicals', who would normally inhabit 'the fringes of democracy', this group was portrayed as the second main threat to the democratic development of Russia (Surkov, 2006a). The main danger of these critics was their 'malign corruption' of national values; they achieved this by depicting Russia as an inefficient state; this caused internal conflict and opened the way for a 'soft takeover' (*miagkoe pogloshchenie*) by foreign countries:

> The methods of the Orange Revolution show that very clearly. I cannot say that this is no longer an issue, because if they managed to do it in four countries, then why not in a fifth? I do not think these attempts will be limited to 2007 and 2008. Our *foreign* friends could somehow try to repeat them in the future. . . . There is one real medicine here – to create a nationally-oriented class in Russian society. (Surkov, 2010, p. 108)

The various internal and external political actors referred to in Surkov's speeches were used to form the category of the 'Other', who was involved in conspiracy against the Russian nation. The use of the word 'foreign' (*inozemnyi*) in the above quotation served to further alienate the West in Russians' eyes. This argument, as we shall see, provided pro-Putin politicians and intellectuals with a tool with which to neutralize opposing political views.

The notion of Russia as a sovereign democracy makes it possible to juxtapose the subversive 'Other' to the sovereign Russian nation (*rossiiskaia natsiia*), and to emphasize its absolute supremacy in determining domestic policy. In his definition of 'the people', Surkov paid tribute to their civic character and quoted the Russian constitution: 'The bearer of sovereignty and the only source of power in the Russian Federation shall be its multinational people' (Surkov, 2006a). The democratically elected president Putin, who represented the majority of the people and their historical greatness, provided the basis for this sovereignty (Orlov, 2006, p. 6).

According to Surkov, in contrast to the 1990s, when Russia's future was decided from Washington, it was Putin who now provided the Russian people with democratic elections, enabling the majority to decide on the nation's future. In this way Surkov was claiming that the popular demand for real democracy was realized by Putin in the 2000s (Surkov, 2010, p. 98). The majority of the population had voted for him, and he had then turned Russian dreams into reality: to turn Russia into a sovereign nation and reinstate the Law and the Constitution. Hence 'Putin's majority' rule the country in accordance with the principles of democracy, and any attempt to undermine this situation, from within the country or from abroad, is illegitimate and threatens the country's stability.

Any parties or individuals who expressed criticism of Putin's regime were automatically perceived as a potential threat to the legitimacy of the Kremlin. When describing the opposition, Surkov's adviser, Pavlovskii, clearly stated that 'existing Russian opposition parties may be working with outside forces to engineer a Ukrainian-style revolution against Putin. That would rob Russian rule of legitimacy, while the decision-making centre would shift to another force – one outside Russia' (Pavlovskii, quoted in Weir, 2005). The national elite's concern with Russian sovereignty and the lack of national unity generated a range of intellectual projects to facilitate national cohesion. These projects contributed to the public promotion of the idea of Russian greatness as a key factor in the development of Russian national identity.

The United States as Russia's 'Other'

In the mid 2000s, the role of Russia's main 'conspiring Other' was assigned to the USA, whose active foreign policy in several regions, which the Kremlin regarded as part of Russia's sphere of influence, caused major concern among the Russian political establishment. Immediately after 1991, when Russia and the West were enjoying a period of friendship and cooperation, a chain of events (the expansion of NATO, a lack of cooperation during the crisis in Yugoslavia, US criticism of the Chechen war) ensured that Russian elites became disillusioned with the West, and this led them to reconsider the Kremlin's foreign policy agenda (Trenin, 2011). US attempts to dominate in post-Soviet space triggered fear in the Kremlin that Russia could lose its dominant position in post-Soviet space and, with it, any chance of re-establishing itself as a global power. This triggered conspiracy theories about attempts on the part of the US government to undermine Russian integrity and destroy the country's economic potential by intervening in its neighbouring states. The search for Russian identity thus became closely related to issues on the global political agenda; Russian policies were constantly juxtaposed with US attempts to achieve global domination by means of Russia's destruction.

In Surkov's view, Russia's primary goal was to defend her own sovereignty and identity by resisting the efforts of certain governments to gain global supremacy, with the help of bands of terrorists and criminal gangs. Sustaining sovereign democracy in Russia, according to Surkov, would guarantee a prosperous future for the nation and enable her to make great historical achievements (Surkov, 2006a). It should be noted that Surkov never provided any explicit conspiratorial analysis of US policies regarding Russia.[2] On the contrary, according to Wikileaks cables from the US embassy in Moscow, Surkov considered himself an Anglophile and admired the US as

---

[2] The only example of a blatant allusion to the anti-Russian conspiracy appeared in a secret speech in 2005; these ideas did not appear in subsequent public texts.

a 'generous and humane country, a model for Russia' (Wikileaks, 2010). However, despite Surkov's positive view of Western culture, his conceptual framework provided pro-Kremlin intellectuals and journalists with the intellectual means to engage in unfettered anti-Western conspiratorial mythmaking.

In contrast to Surkov's representation of the West as a complex and pluralistic community, Russian political elites became actively involved in producing and spreading conspiracy theories about Russia and the West that amalgamated images of the USA and West European countries to create a single political actor hostile to Russia. As a former Moscow mayor put it, historically, the West hated Russia because of its political and religious, as well as ethical, differences. Unlike the West, the Russian nation was not focused on financial profits, and maintained its old traditions – primarily Orthodox Christianity and the collective spirit (Luzhkov, 2007). The dominance of the USA in global politics was presented as evidence of an anti-Russian conspiracy; this became particularly clear in relation to US international policies after the Cold War. The head of the Russian Constitutional Court, Valerii Zor'kin, contended that the very sovereignty of nation states was under threat from American politicians and ideologues of the New World Order who promoted the process of globalization (Zor'kin, 2006). Zor'kin's remark suggests that by the mid 2000s, Russian political elites had internalized conspiracy theories which were traditionally popular in the USA and European countries.

The range of ideas used in anti-Western conspiracy discourse has increased in accordance with the introduction of new terms into the mainstream political discourse, such as *vashingtonskii obkom* (*The Washington Regional Party Committee*) and *rukovodiashchie krugi SShA* (*ruling circles of the USA*). These terms are derived from Soviet propaganda and constitute an example of how post-Soviet political discourse assimilates the symbolic constructions of the Soviet past. Moreover, prominent media and government representatives have facilitated the entry of these notions into mainstream political discourse by actively using them in public.

The first term, *vashingtonskii obkom*, identifies the US government in Washington as the centre of anti-Russian conspiracy. Originally, this term was used by Russian nationalists to infer that the US administration was having an influence on the policies of Yeltsin's government. It was then gradually transferred to mainstream political discourse and became an important political symbol (Maslov, 2007). Dmitrii Rogozin, who has served as Deputy Prime Minister, Russian ambassador to NATO and Duma deputy, described public protests in the aftermath of the Russian parliamentary elections in December 2011 as '*vashingtonskii obkom* in action' (Regional'nyi sait Kostanaiskoi oblasti, 2011). After his appointment as Deputy Prime Minister in January 2012, Rogozin developed this idea and claimed that Putin was defending the Russian people from the hegemony of the *vashingtonskii obkom* (Rogozin, 2012). Putin's economic adviser Sergei Glaz'ev repeated this idea of a '*vashingtonskii obkom*' in relation to the crisis in Ukraine (Glaz'ev, 2014), while Putin himself suggested that the '*vashingtonskii obkom*' did not allow US politicians to attend the Victory Day ceremony in Moscow in 2015 (Putin, 2015).

The other term, *rukovodiashchie krugi SShA*, has been used in anti-Western conspiratorial discourse to describe groups of American and European politicians who are critical of Russia's policies. It has also been linked to the language of Soviet propaganda about the 'managing circles of the imperialistic bourgeoisie of the USA and England' (*rukovodiashchie krugi imperialisticheskoi burzhuazii SShA i Anglii*). For example, Aleksei Pushkov, a prominent journalist and, since 2011, deputy in the state Duma, wrote in the aftermath of the Russo-Georgian war in 2008 that 'the managing circles of the USA will not come to terms with the existence of an independent Russia any time soon. If we intend to assert our right to independence, we shall have to fight for it' (Pushkov, 2009, p. 225).

Another important aspect of anti-American conspiratorial discourse is the perception that American politicians are fearful of Russia's growing power (Gorianin, 2009). Veronika Krasheninnikova, Director General of the Institute for Foreign Policy Research and Initiatives, wrote (2007, p. 306) that the American neoconservatives' hatred of Russia originated in Russia's unique ability to challenge the United States' liberal global messianism. This was particularly evident during the Cold War, when there was competition between the two different ideologies. Following the general narrative of Surkov's speeches, Krasheninnikova claimed that the USA held a variety of perceptions of Russia. However, she concluded (p. 383), without providing any references, that: 'As some historians have said, other countries have to be either America's colonies or its enemies'. Hence despite claiming to provide a balanced analysis of American policies in relation to Russia, her arguments supported the idea of a US conspiracy against Russia.

One of the important trends in the development of anti-American conspiratorial narratives during the 2000s was their gradual absorption into official political discourse. In fact, the state leadership implicitly supported certain conspiratorial claims, thus legitimizing their existence in the public space. For example, in December 2006 the government's daily newspaper, *Rossiiskaia gazeta,* published an interview with Boris Ratnikov, the former general of the Federal Guard Service, who seemed to think he could read the mind of the former US Secretary of State, Madeleine Albright:

> In the thoughts of Madam Albright we discovered a pathological hatred of the Slavs. She was outraged by the fact that Russia possessed the biggest mineral reserves in the world. According to her, in future Russia's resources should be administered not by one country, but by humankind, under the control of the US, of course. (Ptichkin, 2006)

This idea was further developed a year later during a presidential press conference, when Putin was asked by Aleksandr Sibert, a worker from Novosibirsk, about Albright's thoughts on the redistribution of Siberian resources. Putin admitted that he did not know about this, but that he was aware that such ideas existed in the heads of 'certain politicians' (Putin, 2007a). This remark became a reference point for anti-Western propaganda during the parliamentary elections of 2007; it was then used to strengthen the image of a 'conspiring America' and its allies within Russia (Smolchenko, 2007). However, in 2014, when the reference to Albright's statement was reiterated again by Putin, both Ratnikov and Sibert refused to accept that Albright had actually stated these words. In fact, Ratnikov stated that he never met the US Secretary of State (Krechetnikov, 2015).

This episode illustrates the process of the development and dissemination of anti-Western conspiracy theories in the public space, and the role played by top-ranking politicians in this process. Firstly, the claim about Albright appeared in an article in an official, state-funded newspaper as part of a far-reaching conspiracy theory. It subsequently appeared on several news websites (Noskov, 2007; Trukhachev, 2008), and this helped to spread the theory among various audiences which were not made up only of conspiracy theorists and their fans. Putin's television interview was a major political event and led to further dissemination of the idea. In these press conferences, the questions addressed to the president are often chosen because they tackle important current issues and make it possible for the president to express the desired interpretation of these issues, or they bring up other issues which are important for the Kremlin (Kozlov et al., 2017). Accordingly, it is possible that the question about Albright's views was selected by Putin's political advisers for strategic reasons: to encourage alarmist views of the West's threat to Russian national resources, and to personify the plotter, as had been done in other conspiracy hoaxes. Although Putin claimed to be unfamiliar with the statement which Albright never made (Krechetnikov, 2015), it is likely that he played a key role in legitimizing this allegation in the public sphere.

'Nashi': The Creation of Anti-Western National Elites

The activities of the youth movement *Nashi* (*Ours*) constitute one of the most significant examples of how anti-Western conspiracy theories have been used to establish greater social cohesion among young Russians and to use a particular version of nation-building discourse in support of the Kremlin's policies. The movement was often presented by pro-Kremlin speakers as a career path for young people in Putin's Russia but its real aim was to prevent possible street unrest during the forthcoming elections.

Pro-Kremlin political elites were shaken by the participation of youth groups in the revolutions in Ukraine and Georgia (Finkel and Brudny, 2012, p. 18). These groups had shown that they were effective at street action; they were a constituency that the Kremlin would ignore at its peril in the 2007–8 elections. In the post-Soviet period, neither pro-Kremlin political parties nor opposition organizations managed to create a well-functioning movement which could mobilize large groups of young people. The main impediment was perhaps the complete lack of any conceptual framework which could unite this highly disparate and fragmented social stratum. Accordingly, high on the Kremlin's agenda was the need to create a political identity for young Russians who were supportive of the regime, and perhaps, in the long term, to turn this movement into a successful example of civil society (Hemment, 2012).

Nashi first appeared on the political scene in February 2005, defining themselves as a 'Youth Democratic Anti-fascist Movement' with the goal of 'making Russia a global leader for the twenty-first century' (Manifest, n.d.). However, the journalists who attended the movement's first meetings described its main goal as resisting the threat of 'the external control of the country' (Kashin, 2005b). The very name of the movement, *Nashi* (*Ours*), was a linguistic symbol distinguishing 'Us' from 'Them'. The community of young Russians united under its banner attacked opposition activists, criticized political elites, and accused international foundations of representing interests and values foreign to Russian society (Blomfield, 2006). Although scholars, not without reason, tend to see the movement as a form of civil activism (see Atwal, 2009), we will focus here on a single ideological aspect of *Nashi*'s activities – nation-building.

The name *Nashi* was originally used by a controversial nationalist reporter and former Duma deputy, Aleksandr Nevzorov, for his own movement. This was established in November 1991 as a reaction to the failure of the August 1991 coup. Its members called for Yeltsin's removal from power and for the restoration of the Soviet state. Nevzorov claimed in 1991 that: 'Every proper citizen of Russia, deep in his soul, dreams about the *GKChP*, because in reality the country is occupied by the enemy' (Zakharov, 2011). This conspiratorial narrative of foreign occupation, which became a commonplace in nationalist opposition ideology throughout the post-Soviet period, helped Nevzorov to mobilize supporters and become a parliamentary deputy. However, he later admitted that in the 2000s Surkov had personally asked him to 'donate' the name to his youth project (Levkovich, 2012). This is another demonstration of the fact that the conspiratorial rhetoric concerning the Soviet collapse, which possessed such strong potential for social mobilization in the 1990s, was, in the 2000s, relocated from the nationalist margins to mainstream political discourse and became a political tool for the development of social cohesion.

By the time the main principles of a sovereign democracy were formulated, *Nashi* had already organized two events, both of which related to the memory of the Second World War and the Russian resistance to fascism. On 15 May 2005, *Nashi* organized a demonstration in the centre of Moscow of some sixty thousand young people who, according to the movement's leader, Vasilii Iakemenko, 'took up the torch from war veterans [and took it] to the struggle for Russia's independence' (Korobov, 2005). These actions, which were extensively covered by the state-aligned television channels, were aimed at creating the impression of a large mass of young people concerned about the country's future.

Conspiratorial rhetoric was at the centre of *Nashi*'s ideology; this was supposedly a community of 'the people' who were resisting the West in their struggle to ensure Russia's survival. In his address to participants of the movement's first summer camp, held in 2005, Pavlovskii followed the main thrusts of Surkov's ideology:

> European civilization has a different mentality; it always needs an enemy, especially in periods when everything is good. It happened with the Jews at the end of the nineteenth and the beginning of the twentieth

centuries. Now it is happening with the Russians. Nowadays, for the West, the Russians are – let us face it – the main outcasts, no matter how good we are. (Kashin, 2005a)

Nashi's nation-building rhetoric adopted two main positions. First, it appealed to the memory of the Second World War, which was the most uncontestable and powerful narrative in post-Soviet Russia public consciousness. Second, it emphasized the anti-fascist views of its members, and that Russia's multi-culturalism was the key to the country's prosperity. As stated in its manifesto:

> The clash of civilizations can kill Russia, as it has already killed the Soviet Union. Our aim is to prevent the expansion of the ideas of fascism, aggressive nationalism, religious intolerance and separatism, which threaten the unity and territorial integrity of Russia. (Manifest, n.d.)

Supporting a multi-cultural Russia served as a positive element in social cohesion and community building. *Nashi* articulated a civic model of national cohesion: a prosperous Russia could be built if Russian youth shared the idea of racial, religious and cultural solidarity. This could account for the fact that *Nashi*'s manifesto contained only the civic term, *rossiiskii*, and made no reference to the ethnically-associated term, *russkii*.

The intention was to share this ideology of Russian multi-culturalism with the majority of Russian youth who, according to the manifesto's authors, would replace the 'defeatist generation of the 1980s' (*pokolenie porazhentsev*) which had destroyed the Soviet Union. These 'defeatists' consisted of so-called oligarchs and radical nationalists (or 'fascists') who were both allegedly under the control of the West. These groups were considered to be the main threat to the country's stability. *Nashi* defined them as 'the unnatural union of liberals and fascists, Westernizers and ultranationalists, international funds and international terrorists', who, despite their differences, were united by their common hatred of Putin (Manifest, n.d.).

Nashi's call for the current elites to be replaced was supposed to serve as another factor in political cohesion among young Russians. Defining the ruling class as 'defeatists' backed by oligarchs and international foundations, *Nashi* was at the same time attempting to valorize the civic, state-framed model of Russian nation-building and promote it as something worth defending from international conspiracy. Building its ideology based on anti-fascism and the memory of the war, it served to promote patriotic ideas and bind them together with notions about conspiracy.

The nation-building strategies of *Nashi* were mainly aimed at the development of a civic model of Russian nationhood by attracting potential members by the anti-fascist rhetoric. Still, since it was largely based on conspiratorial notions, *Nashi*'s ideology mainly served as a Kremlin's political tool with which to suppress those opposing the political establishment on the eve of the 2007 parliamentary elections. As Maya Atwal and Edwin Bacon noted (2012, p. 265), *Nashi* was able to engage in contentious politics which United Russia could not do because of the constraints imposed on the formal political arena. *Nashi*'s failure to prevent the opposition rallies in 2011–12 resulted in the decline of the movement, and many of its former leaders then embarked upon political or business careers. However, the Kremlin experimented with other conspiratorial concepts in its attempt to define the Russian nation, and disseminated them through campaigns publicized on the state-aligned television channels. Most of the ideas put forward during these campaigns would be used whenever the regime was challenged by waves of protest, especially after 2012.

'The Fall of an Empire: The Lesson of Byzantium'

From the beginning of the 1990s, pseudo-historical books explaining how the origins of contemporary events could be traced back to conspiracies in the past became bestsellers (Sheiko and Brown, 2014). As Laruelle (2012, p. 580) notes, the conspiratorial interpretation of the past, which in the post-Soviet period created a large corpus of books on an alternative Russian history, is a powerful promoter of national cohesion. Ideas about the greatness of the Russian imperial order and the malevolent intrigues behind the Soviet collapse created a comfortable intellectual environment for these ideas to become popular. By the late 2000s, pro-Kremlin public intellectuals had realized the value of biased historical accounts in constructing a national identity. Politicians and public intellectuals employed a range of historical 'facts' in books and television programmes to convey a political message and turn conspiracy theories into a legitimate element of popular discourse. For instance, Russian minister of culture Vladimir Medinskii has, by means of a series of books on the myths about Russia and anti-Russian plots, made a successful career as a writer and high-profile bureaucrat (Parfitt, 2017).

One of the most obvious cases was the film *Gibel' Imperii: Vizantiiskii urok* (*The Fall of an Empire: The Lesson of Byzantium*) which was broadcast on 30 January 2008 on the state television channel Rossiia. The presenter of the film, Archimandrite Tikhon (Shevkunov), was the Superior of Moscow's Sretensky Monastery, and apparently has close relations with Putin (Korobov, 2008; Clover, 2013). In the film, Tikhon narrates his version of the collapse of the Byzantine Empire. Supported by a dynamic promotional campaign and praised after its screening by the pro-government press, the film produced a heated media debate among Russian intellectuals about parallels between Russian and Byzantine history (Borodina, 2008).

In Tikhon's view, the collapse of the Byzantine Empire was largely due to the West, whose economic and political interests were represented by Byzantine intellectuals and unfaithful oligarchs. Supposedly the West had stolen from Byzantium in order to create the conditions for its own economic prosperity, which, in turn, helped transform the then-barbarous European states into civilized countries. In the words of Tikhon, one of the greatest Byzantine rulers, Emperor Basyl II,

> took tough measures to enforce a vertical power structure, quelled all separatist movements in the outlying territories, and suppressed rebellious governors and oligarchs, who were preparing to dismember the empire. Then he 'purged' the government and confiscated huge sums of stolen money. (Archimandrite Tikhon (Shevkunov), 2008)

However, Basyl II's legacy was soon squandered by his corrupt and weak successors, who, most importantly, allowed the emergence of a 'national question' in this multi-ethnic empire. Hence one of the most important issues in the film is the collapse of the Byzantine empire due to a foreign conspiracy. Apparently, this has been taken by the film's authors as a covert reference to the Soviet collapse.

According to Tikhon, the multi-ethnic people of the Byzantine Empire lived in harmony, unified by Orthodox Christianity. The West, which he depicted as rude and greedy, despised this attachment to Orthodox Christianity and wanted to break the empire up into nation states. Its promotion of the idea of the nation state convinced the Greeks, 'the state-forming nation', that they should claim independence from other nations. As a result, the Balkan region became a battleground of different religious groups, whose calls for independence were supported by the West.

This portrayal of the ethnic situation in the Byzantine Empire is accompanied in the film by impressive pictures which connects the events of the Byzantine past with post-Soviet history. In one episode, a map of the empire shows an independent Serbia and Bulgaria respectively coloured yellow and blue, which implicitly makes reference to the Ukrainian national flag. At the same time, the concept of 'enmity' within the empire is visually reinforced by images of people fighting, of oranges falling on the street, and of a man calmly walking along with his face covered by a Venetian carnival mask – a clear reference to the Americans in the post-Soviet countries. Moreover, to emphasize the comparison with the USA, Tikhon describes Venice as the 'New York of the 13th century' (Archimandrite Tikhon (Shevkunov), 2008).

This interpretation of the Byzantine collapse makes implicit reference to both the Soviet collapse as described by Surkov, and to current political developments in the CIS. It should also be noted that Tikhon depicted the West as a single entity, a competitor which was 'only pursuing its own interests' (Archimandrite Tikhon (Shevkunov), 2008). This narrative thread, repeated several times throughout the film, has its origins in Surkov's conceptualization. This use of anti-Western conspiracy theories in a prime-time television programme was again aimed at moving the anti-Western conspiracy narrative into the mainstream of Russian political discourse.

The film departed from Surkov's approach in one respect, however. This was its emphasis on Orthodox Christianity as the foundation of Byzantine and, by association, Russian identity. It was the growth and domination of pro-Western views among Byzantine intellectuals that supposedly destroyed their community cohesion. For this reason, the Turks were able to conquer the empire, while the West offered it no help in resisting them. The visual background to this point was a painting depicting Judas kissing Jesus. According to the film, the legitimacy of the imperial heritage and Byzantine greatness were transferred to Russia through Orthodox Christianity. Hence Tikhon explicitly refers to 'Moscow [as] the Third Rome', stressing Russia's messianic role in world history. To make this point, he draws on a large body of pre-revolutionary ideas which were largely based on Orthodox beliefs, and which have been sporadically disseminated in popular literature and post-Soviet pseudo-historic research. Using some of Surkov's concepts allowed Tikhon to depict Orthodox Christianity as a necessary, but just one, marker of national identification.

Most of the public speakers – intellectuals and media professionals – who expressed support to Tikhon's film emphasized the political, cultural and spiritual similarities between Russia and the Byzantine Empire, noting his references to the impact of the 'Byzantine heritage' on Russian history. Narochnitskaia – an active participant in discussions about the film – claimed that Byzantium was Russia's foremother. She referred to Arnold Toynbee's essay, *Russia's Byzantine*

Heritage (1947, pp. 82–95), in which he argued that Russians as well as Byzantines always had to try to protect themselves from the Western conqueror, Narochnitskaia maintained that Toynbee, an acknowledged Western historian, had discovered the cause of the West's contempt for Russia. The Byzantine heritage made Russia a powerful actor in global politics and the centre of a significant non-Western civilization. The debates about the film, in Narochnitskaia's view, demonstrated the timeliness of defining Russia's national idea (Narochnitskaia, 2008).

Tikhon's film was shown again on 9 February 2008 on the talk show *Natsional'nyi interes* (*The National Interest*) on the channel Rossiia; it was hosted by Dmitrii Kiselev, who would soon become the mouthpiece of state-produced conspiracy theories. The film was followed by an organized discussion in which both Tikhon and Narochnitskaia took part. Narochnitskaia emphasized that the Russians were a particularly spiritual people in comparison to those in the West, and this had led them to think about their nation's world mission as soon as the 'famine' (*golod*) of the 1990s had been resolved. Tikhon argued that liberal freedoms became an instrument of suppression in Russia, and that the West used them to pursue its economic goals in relation to the country (*Natsional'nyi interes*, 2008). Four of the five guests agreed that the way to build a strong nation was to recreate the Russian empire; only this could tie the Russian nation together.

Tikhon's film and the subsequent discussion were examples of the instrumental use of Christianity in shaping the vision of the Russian nation. While we cannot know for sure because such information is not in the public domain, it is likely that the Kremlin exploited Russians' trust in the Orthodox Church to promote its political agenda. Sociological research carried out in 2008 demonstrated that approximately 65 per cent of the population trusted the Church, and that this was seen by the Kremlin as an attractive resource which it could utilize (Gudkov et al., 2008, pp. 28–9). Having a priest as the film's narrator served to indicate that Orthodoxy was one of the crucial markers of Russian national identity. However, the religious components of national identity, as identified both in the film and in the discussion, were overlaid with the ideas circulating in current politics. In the talk show, there was virtually no discussion of the impact of Orthodoxy on the Russian identity; the guests were more concerned with criticizing the Russian opposition and the West. The appeal to Orthodoxy hence appears to have been another element in the Kremlin's somewhat ambiguous nation-building agenda; it was using public trust in the Church to help develop social cohesion.

It is worth noting that the attempt to promote the Kremln's model of nation-building was articulated through anti-Western conspiracy theories and broadcast prime-time on the major state television channel. This Kremlin approach to developing social cohesion, as we shall see, was even more evident during the campaign against Pussy Riot in 2012.

Pussy Riot: Making a Nation of the 'Soviet Orthodox People'

Using the narrative of conspiracy in relation to the Orthodox religion became an important trope at the time of the 2012 presidential campaign. Patriarch Kirill stated, in his address on 7 January 2012, that the Russians' strong faith caused their enemies and ill-wishers to hate them (Revenko, 2012). This address made it clear that Kirill was actively involved in Putin's campaign; this made him the butt of much criticism, with the performance by the band *Pussy Riot* dealing the most controversial attack.

On 21 February 2012, six women from the all-female band *Pussy Riot* performed a so-called 'punk-prayer' at the Cathedral of Christ the Saviour in Moscow, in which they called on the Mother of God to drive Putin away. Almost two weeks later three members of the band were arrested. This incident garnered more publicity than all of the scandals which had emerged in the spring of 2012 in relation to the head of the Russian Orthodox Church. One of these concerned a lawsuit which revealed that Kirill owned an expensive flat in the centre of Moscow; Kirill wanted his neighbour, Iurii Shevchenko, to pay compensation of approximately £400,000 because of dust which had entered his apartment during the renovation of Shevchenko's apartment. Later, it was revealed by bloggers that Kirill owned an extremely expensive watch – a gold Breguet, worth around £19,000.00 – when an attempt to airbrush it from his photo on the official Church website failed because its reflection could be seen in the polished table he was sitting at (Weaver, 2012). The authorities initially treated the Pussy Riot performance as 'hooliganism'; however, soon the case against them escalated into something much more significant. According to the state-aligned media, their critique of the Church posed a major threat to Russian statehood.

Numerous television programmes, as well as interviews given by politicians and pro-Kremlin intellectuals, had begun to depict Orthodoxy as the key element in both Russian identity and the Russian state, and the foundation of Russian greatness (*V Kontekste:*

Chto stoit za aktsiei 'Pussy Riot' v Khrame Khrista Spasitelia, 2012; Gavrov, 2012). Accordingly, by April 2012, the Pussy Riot incident, and, in particular, their attack on the Church, had acquired a distinctive conspiratorial character. This approach was actively disseminated in the media. On 3 April, Kirill stated that the Russian Orthodox Church had become the victim of an 'information war' (*informatsionnaia voina*) (Sopova, 2012). This date was the turning point in a media campaign against Pussy Riot.

From April 2012, the notion of a war against the Orthodox Church dominated the speeches of pro-Kremlin intellectuals and Church representatives, who interpreted public criticism of the Church as part of the West's conspiracy against the Russian nation. The Patriarch himself insisted that the Church was the essential element of national identity and for that reason had always been the first target of Russia's enemies and invaders (Rossiia-1, 2012). Commenting on the Pussy Riot affair, Sergei Markov, a prominent pro-Kremlin spin doctor, stated that there were powerful forces at work both inside and outside the country which wished to deprive the Russian people of their mission in global history and which sought to destroy the Church as 'a depository of Russian national identity' (Nadezhdina, 2012).

In the state-aligned media the Pussy Riot incident was framed as a latter-day version of the anti-religious campaigns of the Bolsheviks, in which many priests were persecuted and churches were closed. Arkadii Mamontov, a high-profile journalist with the Rossiia television channel and an active defender of the Church in the Pussy Riot scandal, called their actions a 'relapse into neo-Bolshevism', implicitly raising the possibility of new anti-Church pogroms (Kashin, 2012b).

These allusions surfaced repeatedly in television programmes and news reports on the state-aligned channels throughout the period of the trial, which ran from April to October 2013. To encourage widespread support for the Church, the Moscow Patriarchate decreed that prayer services be held in defence of 'desecrated relics' in the Cathedral of Christ the Saviour; some 30 icons, according to the clerics, had been recently attacked by vandals (Rozhkov, 2012). On 22 April these services were held in all major Russian cities, and served to demonstrate that the great majority of Russian people stood behind the Church in the face of a hostile minority who aimed to destroy the unity of the nation. In his address before the start of the Moscow service, the Patriarch evoked the unique multi-cultural spirit of Russia, and claimed that the attack on the Orthodox Church threatened the unity of the entire nation (Patriarkh Kirill, 2012a).

These prayers, widely covered by the major television channels, were portrayed by the state-aligned media as an embodiment of 'the people', who shared the Orthodox faith and supported the Patriarch as well as the federal authorities. Supporters of the Church were described as pious, loyal to the government, and not involved in recent political activities. The Russians in television coverage of the Pussy Riot case were generally depicted as a homogenous, Orthodox community, and any opinions which differed from the norm were downplayed (Hutchings and Tolz, 2015, pp. 194–221). However, Russian television's approach was very far from reality (Kashin, 2012a).

The major television channels offered a common conspiratorial interpretation of the Pussy Riot event, portraying them as puppets of the West who were striving to split the nation apart (Baranov, 2012). Journalists and public intellectuals used a variety of names to stress the otherness of the members of the band: they were described as witches, blasphemers and provocateurs. Their supporters, who shared their liberal values, were said to be alien to the Russian nation (Pust' govoriat: Besy, 2012; Poedinok s Vladimirom Solov'evym', 2012). On 6 April, in the introduction to the documentary *Hystera Ænigma*, broadcast by the major television channel NTV, the commentator posed the question: 'Why are gays demanding that the Cathedral of Christ the Saviour be demolished?' A representative of Moscow's gay community, Nikolai Alekseev, supposedly responded with 'Yes, that is true'. However, Alekseev's words had been subject to a massive editorial cut, in order to give the impression that the LGBT community was in cahoots with Pussy Riot and that they did indeed want the cathedral to be destroyed. The rest of the documentary continued in this same conspiratorial vein and portrayed the members of the band as immoral sexual perverts who wanted to trigger a revolution in Russia (CHP. Rassledovanie: Hystera Ænigma, 2012a).

The distinction between the 'Orthodox majority' (*pravoslavnoe bol'shinstvo*) of 'the people', and the 'minority of perverts and liberals' who were, again, depicted as 'the Other', played an important role in developing the notion of Russian identity by means of conspiratorial discourse. In an aggressive media campaign, spokespersons of the Church, pro-Kremlin intellectuals and journalists sought to into establish the notion of a threat to the nation through internal subversion by a conspiring 'fifth column', supposedly with the West's support of the West. A trilogy of talk-shows *Provocateurs* (*Provokatory*) was introduced by Arkadii Mamontov, a prominent television presenter known for his coverage of the war conflicts and conservative, statist views. This series of highly opinionated documentaries provided the case with a conspiratorial narrative.

On 29 April, the state television channel Rossiia-1 broadcast the first episode of the weekly talk-show *Spetsial'nyi korrespondent (Special correspondent)*, which articulated the subject: the battle being waged for Orthodoxy and the nation in the face of opposition from the 'blasphemers' (*koshchunitsy*), supported by the 'West'. The documentary opened with scenes from the 22 April collective prayer service and later referred to the supposed conspiratorial origins of the Pussy Riot performance. Mamontov posed the question 'What shall we do, people?' (*Chto delat' budem, liudi?*) to the viewers and the studio audience, hence separating them from the 'Other' represented by Pussy Riot. (Spetsial'nyi korrespondent: Provokatory, 2012) 'The people' he appealed to were represented in the studio by an Orthodox nun; by Vladimir Legoida, press-secretary of the Moscow Patriarchy; and by several actors, journalists, and academics who pledged their allegiance to Orthodox Christianity.

Criminal investigators also participated in the programme. Showing the audience the Canadian residence permit of Nadezhda Tolokonnikova, one of the members of the band, they linked her to the intelligence services of a foreign country. Nikolai Starikov stressed that if the 'blasphemers' could desecrate Russian sacred heritage (*relikvii*), 'we shall cease to be a nation' (Spetsial'nyi korrespondent: Provokatory, 2012). Almost all participants agreed that the Russian Orthodox Church was under attack and that the Pussy Riot performance was a way of testing the ability of the Russian people to defend national values.

The programme's journalists and guests downplayed the links between the Orthodox Church and the authorities. The guests constantly emphasized that the Church, as the keystone of the nation, was the main target of the 'war'. The Church's leaders had previously been criticized by the opposition because of their close relationship with the authorities; it is likely that the Kremlin needed to defuse these tensions and shift public attention to the subversive nature of the church's critics. The conspiratorial interpretation of the Pussy Riot incident made it possible to link the band members to a subversive 'fifth column' of liberals with corrupt values, who were supported by the West. As Mamontov contended:

> They wanted to disrupt society, to divide it and split [it]. That is what the organizers of this horrible provocation wanted to achieve. They hold nothing sacred. They did not manage to triumph in December–

January and so decided to attack the most sacred thing which the people have – the Church. (Spetsial'nyi korrespondent: Provokatory, 2012)

This account of the conspiring and atheist 'Other' was aimed at promoting the cohesion of Russians as a single nation bound together by Orthodoxy. However, the most important link was that drawn between the political protests held in response to vote rigging at the 2011 parliamentary elections, and the Pussy Riot incident in the Cathedral. The atheism of Pussy Riot's supporters could thus be used both as a strong argument against critics of the regime, and as a way of promoting the idea that Russian identity was based on Orthodoxy.

The decision of the Moscow court on 19 August 2012 to sentence three members of the band to two years each in prison took the media campaign against Pussy Riot to a new level. From August onwards it was possible to identify two distinct currents in the conspiratorial narrative around the case. The state-aligned media channels continued to follow the initial approach of the campaign against Pussy Riot and to defend the Church. Kirill's statements in August and September 2012 followed the line of emphasizing the fundamental role of the Church in the preservation of Russian identity. On 9 September, during a service commemorating the bicentenary of the Battle of Borodino, Kirill drew a parallel between the Napoleonic invasion of Russia in 1812 and the current anti-church scandals. He stated that Western invaders had desecrated churches and sawn up crosses to destroy the Russian spirit (Patriarkh Kirill, 2012b). This mention of sawn up crosses connected the alleged barbarism of the French with an incident that had taken place in Kyiv in August 2012: *Femen*, a Ukrainian feminist group, publicly sawed a cross in half in the centre of Kyiv in support of Pussy Riot (Radio Free Europe/Radio Liberty, 2012). This was followed by several similar events in Russia, serving to promote the idea of a fully-fledged 'war' against the Church.

On the same day as the Borodino address, Rossiia's weekly newscast *Vesti nedeli* (*News of the Week*) broadcast an interview with the Patriarch in which he claimed that the Pussy Riot case was a well-planned act of reconnaissance (*razvedka boem*) (Kiselev, 2012). This was intended to evoke fears of foreign subversion. The members of the band and their supporters were represented as part of a bigger plan to overthrow the Russian government by attacking the foundations of Russian nationhood. The repeated emphasis on the alleged link between foreign intelligence and Pussy Riot served to highlight how dangerous the band members were, both for the Russian nation and for the Church, which was its main pillar. Furthermore, at this stage of the trial, Pussy Riot began to be portrayed not only as a threat to the Church but also to the legitimacy of the authorities' actions. This shift in interpretation significantly changed the media coverage of the story and brought a new theme into the conspiratorial narrative concerning the case.

As the trial of Pussy Riot provoked increasing domestic and international debate, the pro-Kremlin media conceptualization of the performance also underwent considerable change. Numerous world celebrities and foreign political leaders expressed support for the members of the band and criticized the Russian authorities. This international reaction enabled the pro-Kremlin intellectuals and journalists to portray it as part of the West's plan to discredit the Russian authorities and undermine their legitimacy. The Kremlin's concern about the Pussy Riot trial thus became a top-priority issue. Several influential participants in the Church campaign gave statements linking the Pussy Riot case to Putin's defence of Syria in the face of the United States' plans for military intervention. They also connected the campaign of criticism against the Kremlin with the opposition within the country, which began during the 2011 parliamentary elections. For example, Mamontov argued that Pussy Riot's performance had been planned to make Putin vulnerable to criticism because of his position on Syria (Kots and Iakovlev, 2012). Dugin claimed that people who were hostile to Pussy Riot were actually resisting the imperialist aspirations of the USA, and in particular its plan to establish a pro-American regime in Russia (Dergachev, 2012). This shift in perspective, from religion to politics, demonstrates that the main challenge for the Kremlin was now the impact of the Pussy Riot scandal on the image of Russian elites both in the country and abroad. This change in perspective in the official discourse was also reflected in Mamontov's show.

We have already outlined the content of the first episode. The second, broadcast on 11 September 2012, was concerned primarily with Boris Berezovskii, a fugitive oligarch and political émigré who was resident in the UK. Berezovskii was one of the important actors in Russian politics under Yeltsin who developed a bad reputation (Klebnikov, 2001), and after he left Russia he was often accused by pro-Kremlin politicians of plotting against Russia (BBC, 2013). Several guests of the show claimed he was preparing to stir unrest in Russia by attacking the Church (Spetsial'nyi korrespondent: Provokatory-2, 2012). However, the programme gave almost equal weight to a discussion of the international controversy over Pussy Riot. The studio guests contended that the British public relations agency *BellPottinger* had promoted Pussy Riot and used it to sling mud at the Kremlin's image in the world. The show also included an interview with Paul Craig Roberts, a former official in the Reagan Administration and a controversial writer, who stated that the Pussy Riot debacle had been used 'to demonize the Russian government for standing up to Washington's intention to destroy Syria' (Roberts, 2012). Roberts' remarks were aimed at giving credibility to the conspiratorial notions spread by Russian journalists and public intellectuals. The fact that these experts from the West had similar ideas to those in Russia provided Russian journalists' reports with a pseudo-objective appearance, as though they were presenting how events were seen from abroad. This was a way of countering critical opinions from domestic viewers. This use of foreign experts to provide legitimacy to controversial and, at times, conspiratorial statements appears to be a distinctive characteristic of the official Russian discourse.

In contrast to the first, the report and discussion in the second programme were aimed at explaining the global repercussions of the Pussy Riot case, with the narrative of 'the war against the Church' now relegated to a secondary position. This conceptual difference was even more evident in the third episode of the show, broadcast on 16 October, which was devoted to the 'real' reasons behind the performance. The band's closest supporters were accused of having profited financially from the international campaign around Pussy Riot. Mamontov contended that the organizers of the performance wanted to become rich and famous by undermining Russia's position in the international arena. Pussy Riot's domestic supporters were depicted as greedy, two-faced 'liberals' who worked in close cooperation with Russia's geopolitical enemies in Washington (Spetsial'nyi korrespondent: Provokatory-3, 2012). The scandal was depicted as a new form of 'information warfare' against Russia, which made much use of the Internet and non-government organizations within the country. This conspiratorial narrative was aimed at depicting Pussy Riot as part of a broader Russian opposition. Particular stress was placed on its cooperation with the West.

The perception of the Church now shifted: from being seen as the object of the attack, it was now portrayed as peacemaker able to mediate between social groups in Russia. In turn, these social groups were supposedly set against each other by the Pussy Riot performance. An episode in which two young people tried to set fire to a church but then changed their minds and repented was used to demonstrate that the Orthodox Church can bring about reconciliation

(Spetsial'nyi korrespondent: Provokatory-3, 2012). This significantly altered image of the role of the church served to neutralize criticism of the Church's complicity in the guilty verdict against Pussy Riot.

The Pussy Riot case demonstrates the ways in which conspiracy theories are used to promote national cohesion in Putin's Russia. The debates on the state-aligned television channels about national identity, which were framed by anti-Western conspiracy narratives, have reflected the political challenges faced by the Kremlin. The aim of these debates has been to boost public support for the Kremlin's actions. The vagueness of the nation-building agenda has allowed the authorities to interpret criticism of the regime as a threat to the nation itself, thus connecting two seemingly unrelated issues. The idea of a Western conspiracy and, in particular, of an America's intention to undermine the Putin regime, has further reinforced the Kremlin's argument that Pussy Riot represents a threat to the nation.

The Church played a supporting role by promoting Orthodoxy as the key element in Russia's national identity. Patriarch Kirill and his aides were actively involved in mobilizing people in Putin's support during his 2012 presidential campaign, and used conspiratorial language even before the eruption of the Pussy Riot controversy. This yet again demonstrates the close cooperation between the Kremlin and the leaders of the Russian Orthodox Church (Papkova, 2011). While they were working on the election campaign, representatives of the Church already started to refer to a division within the nation between the anti-religious, anti-state, pro-Western minority and the vast and loyal majority who professed Orthodoxy and supported the authorities.

The need to protect Orthodoxy from criticism at the beginning of the Pussy Riot debacle could be considered to be the core demand of the Church and the political authorities, and was, furthermore, used to downplay the scandals around the Patriarch himself which we referred to earlier. Anti-Western conspiracy theories about the 'information war' against the Church played a pivotal role in the combined efforts of the Church and the authorities to bring together the various groups in Russian society in support of the Church and to undermine the legitimacy of its critics. However, during the final stages of the court proceedings, the Orthodox aspect of the campaign faded away, with emphasis placed instead on the story's political significance and the supposed foreign conspiracy which lay behind the Pussy Riot performance. The narrative of Orthodoxy under threat was replaced by attempts on the part of public intellectuals and politicians to justify the Kremlin's policy in relation to the opposition, with the latter depicted as dangerous and alien. Hence the artificially-created majority of the 'Orthodox people', now represented as the core of the Russian nation, became a crude tool to be used by the Russian political establishment. It was just a tactical political move to draw attention away from the contentious issue of electoral fraud which was wrapped in nation-building rhetoric. Yet, these actions did not include any practical measures for facilitating national cohesion.

Conclusion

Attempts to construct a new Russian national identity based on the political interests of the elites in the 2000s had much in common with similar efforts made by the Yeltsin government in the 1990s. At that time the issue of national identity was used as an instrument for the promotion of political and economic interests and to ensure that self-serving political actors were seen as legitimate (Tolz, 1998). With some success, Putin's government adopted the same strategy to mobilize Russian citizens and ensure their support for its actions. As Hutchings and Tolz (2015, p. 250) demonstrate, the Kremlin's nation-building approach in the mid 2010s reinvented and applied both Imperial and Soviet ideas of national cohesion, even though in some respects they contradicted each other.

Analysing Surkov's concept of Russia as a sovereign democracy provides us with an insight into how the political elites in Putin's Russia use the nation-building agenda to solve specific political problems. Against the background of the Kremlin's ambiguous nation-building policies, Surkov formulated the idea of a single community of 'sovereign Russians'; incorporating elements of both imperial and civic models of national identity, it was hoped that his idea would appeal to the diverse groups within Russian society. Surkov's engagement in the debates on Russian identity was triggered by a fear that Putin's government could lose control over the country; the vagueness of the term 'sovereignty' provided Surkov and other politicians and pro-Kremlin intellectuals with considerable leeway in their definitions, and re-definitions, of the nation-building agenda and of the nation's potential 'Others', in accordance with prevailing political goals.

Surkov's reassessment of Russia's relations with the West had a major impact on the conceptualization of Russian identity and the further dissemination of anti-Western conspiracy allegations. The depiction of the West as a competitor, rather than as an enemy, made criticism of the West – when framed within the conspiratorial narrative – a legitimate part of official political and media discourse. In the language of economic competition, Russia was a wealthy world supplier of natural resources, and this helped present the idea of Russian greatness in economic terms. This argument provided a new framework for fostering patriotic attitudes among Russians and, at the same time, helped to incorporate anti-Western conspiratorial notions into a debate about the economic interests of foreign companies and the West's rapacious desire to help itself to Russian resources.

Anti-Western conspiracy theories became a key instrument for boosting Russia's national cohesion. The notion of the 'conspiring West', competing with Russia for economic wealth and political power, helped to establish the contours of national identity. In the 2000s, Kremlin officials, as well as pro-government intellectuals, spent a great deal of time shaping the image of the USA as Russia's major conspiring rival. Moreover, leading politicians themselves took part in the dissemination of conspiratorial ideas through the government-controlled media. A focus on the USA, as Russia's ultimate rival in the competition for dominance in global politics, has become a central feature in the construction of the image of 'the Other' which was crucial in defining who we, Russians, are and why we are different from Them, people in the West.

Surkov's efforts were not in vain. By the mid 2010s, the notion of the USA as Russia's main enemy had become an essential part of the political and even educational discourse. As Golunov (2015) suggests, the idea that the USA was the main anti-Russian protagonist in conspiracy theories became extremely popular in Russian textbooks on geopolitics. These adopted Western European and American conspiracy theories about the New World Order to emphasize that Russia was encircled by enemies in cahoots with one another to achieve one simple aim: to destroy the regime and divide the country into puppet states. At the same time, the long-term project on the part of the Kremlin's leaders to engage young people in nation-building project failed and was replaced by a more efficient and instrumental plan – to suppress opposition by force. In 2016, the Kremlin established the National Guard, headed by Putin's closest aide and former head bodyguard, Viktor Zolotov (Rozhdestvenskii et al., 2016). After the series of street protests in spring 2017, Zolotov reiterated Surkov's concern about foreign invasion: there could be no genuine domestic protests against the regime. Whenever people took to the streets, patriots needed to watch out for foreign subversion and for attempts at brainwashing by the foreign media (Interfax, 2017).

A campaign to bring together a highly diverse and fragmented population in a bid to achieve national unity was actually used to prevent the possibility of a colour revolution taking place in Russia during the election campaigns of 2007–8. Hence the Kremlin was actually trying to use the aim of national unity to boost political mobilization in support of the political establishment. A sense of belonging to a national community of Russians has been fostered by the constant reiteration of who Russia's enemies are, both inside and outside the country.

During the following electoral cycle, in 2011–12, nation-building strategies were deployed in pursuit of the same goals, and repeated the main narratives of anti-Western conspiratorial discourse, which featured in the earlier period. However, the unexpected wave of civic activism significantly radicalized the Kremlin-sponsored debates on Russian national identity. In other words, these debates became directly linked to the goal of legitimizing Putin's victory. The Pussy Riot performance became a key issue in debates about Russian identity, which highlights with particular clarity how instrumental the shifts in defining this identity actually were. Conspiracy theories about Pussy Riot's threat to Russian identity were used to link the band's supporters with people protesting against election fraud, both of whom were portrayed as a minority. At the same time, the state-aligned media portrayed the various people attending rallies in support of the Church as an undifferentiated Orthodox mass who supposedly constituted the majority of 'the people'; these were said to be ready to protect their faith and their statehood (Kashin, 2012a).

The Pussy Riot trial seems to have had a significant impact on the model of national identity which the Kremlin started to promote during Putin's third term. The campaign against the members of the band included several defining features with which the authorities could define the supposed majority of 'genuine' Russians and the minority of conspiring enemies. The representation of Pussy Riot as sexual perverts working in collaboration with homosexuals, as militant atheists and as opponents to Putin, contributed to the launch of a homophobic campaign in 2013. This was actively supported by the state media and reached its peak in the introduction of a law prohibiting the promotion of 'non-traditional forms' of family among young people (Spetsial'nyi correspondent: Litsedei, 2013). This campaign, along with other political measures, highlighted a turn to a Kremlin-sponsored celebration of so-called 'traditional values' (*traditsionnye tsennosti*), which were, allegedly, inherited by the Russian people from their ancestors (Putin, 2012a). Moreover, an increase in the punishment for insulting religious feelings, which was a direct consequence of the Pussy Riot affair, became one of many ways in which the state could prevent expression of dissent.

Newly introduced federal laws, as well as opinions expressed on numerous television programmes, are examples of this drift towards radical conservatism, and help create the impression that Russia is under siege by its enemies. An opinion poll carried out in November 2013, on the eve of the Ukraine crisis, showed that 78 per cent of Russians believed that Russia had enemies (Levada-tsentr, 2013c). This view, actively encouraged by the state-aligned media, is generated above all through conspiracy theories. Hence despite their long-term destabilizing potential, during Putin's third presidential term, the ruling elites turned conspiracy theories into an important instrument for achieving social and national cohesion. This became even more mainstream during the Ukraine crisis two years later.

5

Battling against 'Foreign Agents'

By the mid 2010s, all of the main spheres of social and political life were influenced by the idea of a conspiring group of people eager for power and wealth. Yeltsin's attempted impeachment, which was based on conspiratorial notions, was a remarkable episode in domestic political life, with conspiracy theories being used to demonize political opponents. In the 2000s the significance of conspiratorial discourses in the public sphere increased still further and became a pivotal element in several political campaigns which changed the course of Russia's political development. The conspiratorial notions served as pretexts for initiating lawsuits and justifying criminal cases against political opponents, at times culminating in legislative changes which have affected the democratic processes in the country.

The campaign against the oil company Yukos and its management, and three campaigns against non-governmental organizations (NGOs) in 2005, 2006 and 2012–13, are the focus of this chapter. They were important milestones in the history of post-Soviet Russia. The Yukos affair sent an important message to the business community and to various law enforcement services; it demonstrated how the state should deal with rebellious businessmen, and what should happen to overambitious entrepreneurs. In turn, the cases against NGOs resulted in changes in Russian legislation regarding third sector organizations and had a harmful impact on the development of civil society. The origins of the campaign against the NGOs can be traced to the shock experienced by the ruling political elites in relation to the 'Orange Revolution' in Ukraine in 2004, and again, later, in response to the massive rallies for fair elections in the aftermath of the parliamentary elections in 2011. The Russian leadership acknowledged the crucial role which NGOs had played during regime changes in the CIS countries. Consequently, through the work of loyal public intellectuals and the media, the activities of NGOs were interpreted through the prism of conspiracy ideas about the West's interests and this prepared the ground for the implementation of a highly repressive set of laws against NGOs. These newly introduced restrictions were sufficient to impede the work of NGOs in the country, and in the Kremlin's view, this would help it to ensure control over society.

The wave of political protests against Putin in 2011–12 (discussed in Chapter 6), which occurred despite the government's preventative measures, resulted in still more negative attitudes towards NGOs on the part of pro-Kremlin intellectuals and politicians, who described them as key facilitators of unrest. In 2012, a law was passed which required all NGOs with any foreign funding to register voluntarily as 'foreign agents'. This had been preceded by a long-running campaign which attempted to establish a link between NGOs and the idea of a 'fifth column' operating within the country, which conspired to destroy the sovereignty of the country and its people.

This chapter looks at how conspiracy notions have been used by the regime as a tool in domestic politics to delegitimize third sector organizations and other political rivals. It will start by looking at the role the notion of conspiracy played in the Yukos affair, because this was the first public campaign against Putin's political rivals which rested on conspiracy theories. It will then consider how regime changes in the CIS countries affected the conspiratorial perception of NGOs among the political elites inside Russia. It will turn next to the ways in which fear of the 'colour revolution', which was disseminated through the media, was used to justify amendments to the legislation regarding NGOs. Finally, the chapter will discuss how post-electoral public activism in 2011–12 triggered another wave of state repressions against NGOs, and what role conspiracy theories played in this.

From Conspiracy Theories to Conspiracy Practices

On 25 October 2003, Mikhail Khodorkovsky, who was then the richest man in Russia, was arrested in Novosibirsk and spent the next ten years in prison, charged with tax evasion. He had been one of the most longstanding leaders of the opposition to Putin and his aides, and so his incarceration illustrates the sort of treatment the Kremlin is capable of meting out to its major opponents. Moreover, this was the first time in the post-Soviet era when anti-Western conspiracy theories were used domestically as a political instrument against one of

Putin's main rivals. Accordingly, in many respects the Khodorkovsky case was a watershed in the use of these concepts as a political tool.

Khodorkovsky's company, *Yukos,* was one of the most advanced and successful companies in Russia. It had influential connections around the world, including political and business elites in the USA and Europe such as the Rockefeller family, Henry Kissinger and George Soros (Khodorkovskii and Gevorkian, 2012). Khodorkovsky himself was an icon of post-Soviet entrepreneurship, whose company was a serious power broker and wielded influence both in Moscow and the regions. In the 1990s Khodorkovsky was one of the oligarchs who played an active part in politics and participated in the 1996 campaign to elect Yeltsin. After the 1998 economic crisis, Yukos was restructured and rapidly became one of the foremost companies in Russia, having grown exponentially to a market capitalization of $30 billion in 2003. As Thane Gustafson (2012, p. 284) writes, Khodorkovsky sought to gain a reputation as 'the indispensable man, the capitalist hero fighting against the bureaucratic enemy, fighting against value-destroying state ownership'. This eventually backfired.

Khodorkovsky was not only interested in money and power, but also made generous investments in the development of civil society. In 2001 he set up a charity organization, *Open Russia,* which funded various civic activities through its branches in the regions and was one of the main drivers in the development of regional intellectual, economic and political elites in Russia. Khodorkovsky's ambitions were not only limited to business and influence, then. There was a good chance that he would begin to challenge Putin for leadership of the country. As a result, he paid a high price for his activities. The clashes between the political and economic elites, compounded by the approaching parliamentary elections in autumn 2003 which the Kremlin saw as crucial if it were to secure its hold on the country, made Yukos and its owner the target of a very real plot.

The case against Khodorkovsky was placed by conservative groups of pro-Kremlin elites in the context of a 'creeping conspiracy of oligarchs' who saw Putin as a weak leader who should be replaced. A powerful example of the conspiratorial framing of this affair can be found in reports by the Council for National Strategy, which was headed by two political consultants, Stanislav Belkovskii and Iosif Diskin. Richard Sakwa (2014, pp. 37–8) argues that this organization has been crucial in forming the ideological views of *siloviki* – a cohort of Russian elites, directly related to law enforcement and intelligence agencies, whose power has steadily grown since Putin's arrival in the Kremlin (Treisman, 2007). Many influential members of Putin's elite are also members of this group; most notably, the prominent Igor' Sechin, one of Putin's most powerful aides, who was head of the oil company Rosneft in the 2010s (Dawisha, 2015). As Khodorkovsky himself acknowledged (Franchetti, 2008), Sechin was instrumental in the conspiracy against him. Reports of the Yukos plot were presented to Putin by Sechin and other members of the *siloviki* to push the president into initiating the case against Khodorkovsky. It turned out that Putin took the threat of conspiracy very seriously, and made his move.

In the autumn of 2002, the Council released its first report under the title *The Great Game of Russia (Bol'shaia igra v Rosiiu)*. It claimed that the government was a 'cabinet of oligarchs' affairs' which the Kremlin was not able to control (Kamyshev, 2002). Thereafter the oligarchs were demonized as the driving force in Russia's politics. In January 2003, the Council released a second report, *The Risks and The Threats to Russia in 2003 (Riski i ugrozy Rossii v 2003 godu)*, which aimed to alarm the Kremlin still further. It argued that the oligarchs had no intention of developing the country in the interests of the nation, let alone of preserving its global power. Still worse, these oligarchs apparently had no compunction in selling Russia to the US in exchange for the legitimization of their personal financial assets. Its principal message was populist and anti-elitist, since it called for the fair distribution of wealth in the country:

> ... [The] ruling class does not consider itself responsible for the preservation of the nation-state and moral foundations of Russia ... At the same time, the ruling class does not consider itself responsible for social peace in the country, or for opportunities to develop in the interests of the majority of Russians, which would require the gap between the richest and the poorest groups in the population to be narrowed ... That is what the majority of people consider important. (Russkii zhurnal, 2003)

The populist call for social equality, and accusations that the oligarchs were the main power brokers in the country but had no interest in serving the people, were an important concept which was actively used in the electoral cycle 2003–4. With the Kremlin's support, the newly formed party *Rodina* (Motherland) had two leaders who shared nationalist and conservative/isolationist views. Sergei Glaz'ev and Dmitrii Rogozin called for a 'natural resources rent' tax in their manifesto, demanding reconsideration of how state property was shared out in the 1990s and heavily criticizing the West as Russia's rival. Their harsh anti-oligarch rhetoric brought them third place in the elections and demonstrated the potential of these ideas for use in domestic political strategies (Sakwa, 2005). Moreover, the denigration of Russia's role in global affairs, the dramatic reading of the Soviet collapse, and the decrying of Yeltsin's policies relating to the selling of state assets, were echoed in the rhetoric used by Putin and Surkov in 2005.

The epitome of the anti-oligarch conspiracy panic came in a third report, entitled *The State and the Oligarchy* (*Gosudarstvo i oligarkhiia*). It unabashedly claimed that the oligarchs – first and foremost Khodorkovsky – were preparing to overthrow the regime. Khodorkovsky indeed had vested interests in changing the government, and did provide financial support to various political parties, in order to wield more influence in the government himself (Sakwa, 2014). The report claimed, in very conspiratorial terms, that this desire for power was concentrated in a small cabal of financial tycoons who profited from extracting fossil fuels, and who would promote their power by appealing to the West for protection. They had neglected the interests of the majority in their attempts to realize their power, and were essentially 'robber barons' who had squeezed out every drop of juice they could from the fruits that the weak Russian state had put on offer. The authors of the report went on to claim that the oligarchs were preparing a coup to depose the president and turn the regime into a parliamentary republic that would allow Khodorkovsky to become prime-minister and, later on, the head of state. The oligarchs allegedly planned to carry out these reforms after the parliamentary elections in autumn 2003, helped by loyal deputies in Parliament. According to this plan, the new government, which had the remit to appoint the prime minister, would have chosen Khodorkovsky (Belkovskii, 2003).

It was rumoured that documents appearing on Putin's desk provided evidence that Khodorkovsky had struck a deal with Condoleezza Rice which gave an assurance that when he was president of Russia, he would abandon nuclear weapons (Zygar, 2016, p. 60). This alleged deal with the US was an important element in the sealing of Khodorkovsky's fate. His openness to the world, political ambitions and willingness to become part of the global financial elite, were taken as indications as to just how alien he was to Russia. During the second trial against Khodorkovsky in 2009–10, Dugin suggested that Khodorkovsky was an agent of the New World Order which aimed to destroy Russia's national sovereignty and place it in the hands of the USA (Onlooker1001, 2009).

This third report triggered off the first arrests of Yukos employees and eventually Khodorkovsky himself. A plan to merge Yukos with Sibneft (another major Russian oil company), and then sell some of its shares to the American oil companies Chevron or ExxonMobil, posed a major threat to the Kremlin (Sakwa, 2014). This would have meant that ownership of Russia's precious natural resources would partially be in the hands of foreigners, and that was completely unacceptable to some groups in the Kremlin. In such a scenario, Yukos, under the protection of a US company, would be untouchable by the Russian authorities. As Vadim Volkov (2008) notes, Khodorkovsky's growing power put him into direct conflict with the state political apparatus: the tycoon was emerging as, potentially, the most powerful person in business circles, with threateningly clear political ambitions.

The attack on Yukos was justified by references to the oligarchic, Western-led plot and represented top businessmen as the powerful and dangerous Other. Russia's natural resources and nuclear weapons, both of which were supposedly under threat, were seen as essential for sustaining the nation's profits, political stability and world power status, and their threatened loss was seen as a justifiable reason for sullying Russia's international reputation and dramatically reshaping internal affairs. For the *siloviki* group of Russian political elites, this was the starting point of their burgeoning power in the country. For the political elite in general, the approaching transfer of power from Putin to Medvedev, as well as challenges from outside the country, led to their empowerment and enabled them to turn the populist anti-Western conspiracy theories from an instrument of intra-elite squabbles into a semi-official political tool.

Defining the Domestic Threat

The 'colour revolutions' in Ukraine and Georgia had a tremendous impact on Russia's domestic politics in the 2000s. Putin's administration feared that the examples of other CIS countries could encourage Russian citizens to protest against the results of the elections in 2007–8. Being concerned about the outcome of the Ukrainian presidential elections in 2004, Pavlovskii argued that Russia was not ready for a new type of revolution and should focus on restraining the influence of the opposition (Samarina, 2004). As Robert Horvath (2013) has demonstrated, the political elites loyal to the Kremlin then began to develop a plan of 'preventative counter-revolution'.

Legislative pressure on NGOs was among the first measures

introduced as a part of this 'counter-revolution'. Scholars have pointed to the important role played by international and non-governmental organizations in fostering civic activism on the eve of and during the events in Serbia in 2000, Georgia in 2003 and Ukraine in 2004 (Chaulia, 2006; O Beacháin and Polese, 2010). The existence of a wide and active network of civic organizations throughout Russia was perceived by the Kremlin as a serious threat to the successful outcome of the parliamentary and presidential elections in 2007–8. NGOs could question the results of the elections, thus creating an atmosphere of uncertainty which, in turn, could delegitimize Putin's successor (Galbreath, 2009). As a result, the regime's need to promote Putin as the nation's leader and delegitimize his opponents made non-governmental organizations, some of which were very critical of the Kremlin, an obvious target for attack, justified, as we shall see, at least in part by conspiracy theories.

The foreign funding of Russian NGOs came in for attack after the events in Georgia in 2003. In his annual address to the Federal Council on 26 May 2004, Putin spoke about those NGOs which received funds from foreign sources and defended the commercial interests of their funders (Putin, 2004). This remark signalled two things: first, the Kremlin's concern about the lack of transparency in funding of NGOs, that can start working against the regime, as had happened in Georgia. Second, Khodorkovsky's active support of civic initiatives throughout the country and beyond (Sakwa, 2009, pp. 123–8) that Kremlin perceived as a serious domestic menace. The actual campaign against NGOs took some time to develop and was only launched a year later, in May 2005. It was preceded by a report from Nikolai Patrushev, then head of the Federal Security Service (FSB), which claimed that foreign intelligence was using new methods of surveillance and operated in the CIS countries under the guise of non-governmental organizations (Saradzhyan and Schreck, 2005). One month later, Putin replied to Patrushev's report by expressing a strong objection to the funding of public activities from abroad and promising to curb it (Human Rights Watch, 2005).

This conspiratorial narrative thus linked NGOs with foreign intelligence, emphasizing their 'otherness' and the threat they posed to the people of Russia. In this new twist in Kremlin-sponsored discourse, it was the activities of NGOs, which were funded by foreign sources, which threatened Russian sovereignty. The term 'sovereignty' became pivotal to the anti-Western conspiracy discourse, which was widely propagated through the media from 2005 onwards.

Russia's sovereignty, along with the development of civil society, were the focus of Putin's address to the Federal Council that year (Putin, 2005). Following his speech, NGOs became strongly associated with foreign subversion and were depicted in the media as an ideological and financial framework by means of which Putin's regime would be overthrown. After 2005, numerous publications by pro-Kremlin intellectuals and spin doctors developed this idea further. Vitalii Ivanov, one of the pro-Kremlin public intellectuals who participated in the campaign against 'Putin's enemies' in 2007, claimed that 'Western foundations' (*zapadnye fondy*) gave donations to a range of opposition parties, regardless of their political views (2006, p. 112). The claim that they were politically indiscriminate was used to convey the cynicism of NGOs and their 'sponsors' from the West, and reinforced the argument that Western foundations were aimed at depriving Russia of her independence.

Another prominent pro-Kremlin public intellectual and Duma deputy, Sergei Markov, claimed that people at the Ukrainian rallies were fighting for freedom and honour, while the organizers of the rallies had become wealthy 'revolutionaries', generously funded by American and European foundations (Markov, 2005). This argument bolstered Putin's accusation that NGOs were interested primarily in commercial benefits, not the well-being of society. Hence the freedom that NGOs enjoyed before 2005, including their ability to get funding from foreign sources, was a privilege which they were now to lose because they were beginning to be put under the control of the government. Many pro-Kremlin public intellectuals depicted NGOs as centres of the 'Orange Revolution'; they enjoyed excessive freedom within Russia, while remaining under foreign financial and organizational control (Iur'ev, 2004).

The work of intellectuals prepared the way for introducing legislative limitations on the activities of NGOs. This goal was achieved at the end of 2005, when the Duma debated and adopted amendments to the law on NGOs despite domestic and international protests. The first set of amendments was approved by Putin on 10 January 2006, and led to much concern among civic activists and foreign diplomats (Khrestin, 2006).

In a press interview, one of the authors of the new legislation used conspiracy theories to substantiate its adoption by claiming that NGOs with foreign affiliation destroyed Russia 'from within', because Russians were too easily impressed by foreign influence:

> It is clear for the West that Russia is a huge store of natural resources. That is why, for example, big Western business is ready to invest money

in the development of Siberia through these organizations. But there is a question: why do they do that? The pragmatic West will not invest money without a reason. (Farizova, 2005)

The authors of the new legislative initiatives, embracing Putin's idea that Russia's sovereignty was its ultimate virtue, suggested a ban on the registration of NGOs in case their aims and goals created 'a threat to sovereignty, political independence, territorial integrity, national unity and the distinctive customs, cultural character and national interests of the Russian Federation' (Rossiiskaia gazeta, 2006). These vague criteria created obstacles for the registration for NGOs, since many of them them did rely on foreign funds; and pro-Kremlin politicians and intellectuals were then in a position to accuse NGOs of subversion.

The obedient media had to contribute to the creation of a negative image of NGOs, since many Russian citizens knew little, if anything, about their activities (Schmidt, 2006). The lack of attention paid by ordinary Russians to third sector organizations created a fertile ground for conspiratorial mythmaking. At the same time, it limited the Kremlin's ability to construct the image of a powerful, subversive 'Other' threatening the lives of ordinary citizens. The regime was well aware of this problem, and so was keen to use the state-aligned media to persuade people that NGOs were linked to foreign subversion.

The Spy Rock

One significant feature of the campaign against NGOs was a documentary broadcast by the state-owned Rossiia television channel, which aimed to delegitimize NGOs by connecting them with foreign intelligence services. The most famous media effort of this type was to claim that British diplomats were involved in Western intelligence; this was a clear reminder of the Stalinist and Cold War periods when the notion of a British spy was central to the state-sponsored campaigns against the dissent. Arkadii Mamontov, who would later mount an attack on Pussy Riot, produced a documentary entitled *Shpiony (The Spies)*. It was broadcast prime time on Rossiia channel on 22 January 2006 and became a significant media event which was subsequently discussed by most of the Russian press and provoked a diplomatic scandal between Russia and the UK (Spetsial'nyi korrespondent: Shpiony, 2006). An eleven-minute film showed an operation against alleged British spies carried out by the FSB. The spies supposedly used a rock in a Moscow park, which was stuffed with sophisticated electronic devices, to exchange information with their informants. Mamontov contended that Marc Doe, the second secretary of the British embassy in Moscow, was a British intelligence officer whose responsibility was to supply Russian NGOs with funding. On screen, Mamontov displayed documents, typed in English and all bearing Doe's signature, showing the names of organizations (e.g. a prominent human rights watchdog, *The Moscow Helsinki Group*), and the amounts of money which had been transferred.

The linking of the two issues (spies and NGOs) was made explicit at the start of the documentary. An FSB officer, Diana Shemiakina, stated that of the thousands of NGOs operating in Russia, only 92 were officially registered with the Ministry of Justice. 'Most of them [NGOs] were created, financed and existed under the patronage of the governmental and civic organizations of the US and their NATO allies' (Fishman, 2006). This supposed connection between NATO, the USA and Russian NGOs created the impression that the NGOs were betrayers of the country. To demonstrate a degree of impartiality, and, perhaps, to emphasize that NGOs could have played a bigger role in the everyday life of the Russians, Mamontov explained that most Russian NGOs were actually innocent organizations which assisted people in spheres where the government was unable to help. Despite this, however, Mamontov insisted that the people who worked in Russian NGOs needed to be more honest, and, unlike those specifically referred to in the documentary, work for the interests of Russia (Steshin and Baranov, 2006).

All the same, the film's narrative was not objective, favouring the Kremlin's position on NGOs and supporting its aim to curtail their rights. It correlated with the major accounts of NGOs which had appeared in Russia in the aftermath of the 'Orange Revolution' in Ukraine. On the one hand, it supported Patrushev's claim that the foreign intelligence services worked through NGOs. On the other, it developed Putin's argument that some NGOs consisted of corrupt people primarily interested in financial gain. Moreover, Mamontov substantiated the claim about the external threat by referring to Condoleezza Rice's criticism of the new law on NGOs, when she was US Secretary of State (Kessler, 2005). In this context Rice's speech, which also praised the successes of Ukrainian civil society, accorded with the conspiratorial view of NGOs as agents of foreign subversion.

Liberal Russian journalists who investigated the making of Mamontov's film discovered that the Rossiia crew played virtually no role in the production; it was almost entirely in the hands of the

FSB. Furthermore, the urgency with which the film was broadcast (it replaced another earlier scheduled programme) is an indication of the government's involvement in the matter (Meteleva and Raskin, 2006). Representatives of the NGOs which were discussed in the programme stated that the documents that were received from the foreign grant organizations were actually signed by the first secretary of the British Embassy, not by Doe (Fishman, 2006).

Astonishingly, Tony Blair's aide, Jonathan Powell, revealed in 2012 that the 'spy rock' had in fact been real and was used to receive information from the British spies stationed in Moscow (Topping and Elder, 2012). This gave considerable support to the Kremlin's arguments against NGOs and the opposition in the later years of Putin's rule. It is probable that Russian special services found out that Doe was a British intelligence officer and used that fact to sling mud at NGOs by creating a story about Doe's cooperation with Russian civil society activists. These facts indicate that the conspiratorial story about the spy rock was deliberately disseminated with the purpose of delegitimizing NGOs and linking them to foreign spying activities in Russia. The wide dissemination by the state-aligned media of the alleged link between foreign spies and NGOs allowed the authorities to reach a large audience and influence ordinary Russians' perception of non-governmental organizations.

The Spies prompted debates among politicians about the need to control NGOs, supplying the supposed 'factual basis' of the NGOs' activities and bringing the conspiratorial interpretation of these activities into the public sphere. Duma deputies expressed concern about the funding of NGOs by foreign intelligence services, but without naming particular NGOs. This created an atmosphere of suspicion towards all NGOs, regardless of their aims and activities. Sergei Mironov, then head of the Council of the Federation, insisted that the spy scandal clearly demonstrated the need for strict laws regulating NGOs (Regnum, 2006). A few days later, Putin came out in support of this argument, complaining that the use of NGOs by foreign intelligence services destroyed the reputation of human rights activists (Kremlin.ru, 2006). Seeing an opportunity to reiterate what he had previously said about the hypocrisy of civil society organizations in Russia, Putin insisted that the new law was legitimate and served to protect Russian sovereignty.

The story of the 'spy rock', and the way it was interpreted in conspiratorial terms in the federal media and among leading politicians, is the first example of state-aligned Russian television taking on the role of pacesetter in the Russian political agenda. The structure of the film's narrative and the fact that no representatives of the accused organizations were invited to appear on the programme provided space for the articulation of all possible conspiratorial allegations aimed at the delegitimization of NGOs by claiming a connection between them and foreign intelligence services. Despite the demands of civic activists that journalists withdraw their accusations, and a lawsuit against Mamontov himself initiated by the leader of the *Moscow Helsinki Group*, Liudmila Alekseeva, the conspiratorial narrative about NGOs continued to play a major role in political discourse from 2006 onwards. Given that funding from foreign bodies was seriously restricted since the mid 2000s and left the state in the position of the major sponsor of NGOs, the conspiratorial narrative about NGOs in the media had a negative effect on the development of civil society and democracy in Russia which became evident over the course of the next few years (Crotty et al., 2014). When the regime faced the new and unexpected threat from the grassroots movement, the conspiratorial narrative was developed further to curtail the work of NGOs and justify the new wave of repressions.

NGOs as 'Foreign Agents'

The unprecedented wave of civic activism in the post-election period in 2011–12 made NGOs a primary object of governmental surveillance and repression. As Daniel Treisman noted (2013, p. 254), the Kremlin's strategy for dealing with the opposition in the aftermath of the rallies was to co-opt, intimidate and disable. The NGOs were at the top of Kremlin's agenda to receive this treatment.

The initial pretext for the new campaign against them was somewhat accidental. In January 2012, during the peak of the protests, *BBC 2* broadcast a documentary entitled *Putin, Russia and the West*. In the second episode, Tony Blair's Chief of Staff, Jonathan Powell, admitted, as we noted earlier, that the 'spy rock' which triggered the campaign against NGOs in 2006 had been real (*Putin, Russia and the West. Episode 2: Democracy Threatens*, 2012). This revelation was truly shocking to members of the opposition, who had believed the 'spy rock' story to have been invented by the FSB. Powell's admission was the headline of the day and was immediately used by pro-Kremlin journalists and public intellectuals in their attack on the opposition and their rallies (Channel One, 2012a; Vesti.ru, 2012). Mamontov gave several interviews to pro-Kremlin journalists in which he criticized leaders of the opposition for being hypocritical and for lacking loyalty towards their country (Cherkudinova, 2012). The conspiratorial ideas which had been elaborated in the mid 2000s by Putin and his supporters were revived and used once again against political opponents.

This unexpected development provided Mamontov with an opportunity to make another documentary on the topic, entitled *Shpionskii kamen'* (*The Spy Rock*) which was broadcast on 22 January 2012 (Spetsial'nyi korrespondent: Shpionskii kamen', 2012). Based on Powell's interview, Mamontov accused several leaders of Russian NGOs of having dual citizenship and thus linked them with the USA, Russia's political Other. The primary object of his attack was Liudmila Alekseeva, who received a US passport in 1982 after being expelled from the Soviet Union for human rights activities (Rights in Russia, 2012). Although having dual citizenship is not uncommon, the Russian authorities and pro-Kremlin intellectuals see it as a sign of potential disloyalty. It is no surprise, then, that after the annexation of Crimea and the increase in authoritarian tendencies, this conspiratorial metaphor was used by various statesmen to justify their adoption of the new law on dual citizenship (Masis, 2016).

Mamontov, following the same line of reasoning, discursively separated NGO leaders from the rest of the nation in accordance with their alleged disloyalty to Russian citizens. Pointing out that every new US citizen must swear an oath of loyalty to the country, Mamontov claimed having dual citizenship inevitably created a conflict of loyalties. The reference to foreign citizenship alongside the presentation of evidence about British espionage served to further enhance the conspiratorial image of civic organizations. Mamontov's programme became the starting point for another round of conspiracy mythmaking against NGOs. To link Alekseeva's dual citizenship to her activity within Russia, Mamontov introduced the term 'foreign agents' (*inostrannye agenty*) to describe organizations which engaged in political activism and were funded from abroad.

To support this, Mamontov suggested that the *Foreign Agents Registration Act* (FARA) in the USA could be used as a template for Russian policy concerning NGOs (Spetsial'nyi korrespondent: Shpionskii kamen', 2012). This law, which was introduced in the USA in 1938, required organizations which were in any way affiliated with foreign powers to register as foreign agents with the Ministry of Justice (Kara-Murza, 2013). Intended primarily for use against any possible Nazi infiltration, the law was amended in the 1960s so that the term 'foreign agent' was applied to any organization which sought to derive income or gain political advantage by influencing

American governmental policies. For the Russians, the main point about this law was that American counter-intelligence was officially responsible for monitoring such organizations.

This highly selective use of foreign legislation is characteristic of Kremlin policies to implement controversial laws. By referring to so-called 'Western practices', pro-Kremlin politicians and loyal intellectuals could justify their actions as 'conventional' (see Schimpfossl and Yablokov, 2014, p. 305). The US law to monitor foreign lobbying groups and organizations operating within their country served to legitimize the introduction of further amendments into the Russian legislation on NGOs. Reference to the US law could also be used to reinforce the notion of an internal enemy and to claim the existence of subversive groups within Russia. In the USA, however, the law is applied to representatives of foreign governments and political parties who are affiliated with that state and represent its interests in the USA. Moreover, for them to fall foul of the law, it must be proven in court that the aim of the 'foreign agents' is to promote the interests of their own countries to the detriment of the USA (Koalitsiia pravozashchitnikov, 2016).

A group of pro-Kremlin public intellectuals and Duma deputies, with the support of the state-aligned media, now carried out a new campaign promoting anti-Western conspiratorial notions. This alliance had proved in the past to be efficient at disseminating far-reaching conspiratorial notions among the public and using them to justify the adoption of more restrictive laws. Veronika Krasheninnikova, former head of the Council for Trade and Economic Cooperation USA-CIS, justified the amendments by reference to her personal experience. In 2006–10 she was a representative of the city of St Petersburg in the USA and was registered as a foreign agent. This, she explained, was 'common practice' in a democratic country (Azar and Krasheninnikova, 2013).

Despite references to the US legislation, in the Russian context the term 'foreign agent' had a different connotation; it recalled the accusations levelled against numerous Soviet citizens during the Great Purges in the 1930s. The reintroduction of the term and its use against NGOs aimed at 'othering' them and demonstrated the Kremlin's engagement with the politics of historical memory (see Miller, 2012a). However, the official initiators of the new law tried to separate the term from the memory of Stalinist repression and link it instead to so-called 'international standards of work with NGOs' (Kostin, 2013). Yet the introduction of terms which are closely related to the memory of the Great Purge demonstrates the dependence of the official political discourse on the vocabulary of the Soviet era. At the same time, as Oushakine has argued (2000, pp. 998–9), using this language of the past demonstrates the remoteness of the context in which it was initially utilized. At the time of Stalin's repressions, being accused of being a 'foreign agent' would result in immediate arrest. However, during the campaign in 2012 it was emphasized that applying the term to an NGO would not necessarily lead to its repression, and that the law simply required an indication in the title of an organization that it was affiliated with a foreign sponsor (Smirnov, 2012).

Vesti nedeli, the television news programme that was often in the forefront of triggering political campaigns during Putin's third term as President, broadcast a report on 8 July 2012 on the parliamentary debates about the new law. It included interviews with Krasheninnikova and with Aleksandr Sidiakin, a Duma deputy who was an active supporter of the new law. It echoed the main tropes of the narrative which had turned NGOs into a subversive 'Other'. Hence Sidiakin contended that in the past few years, approximately seven billion dollars had been transferred from abroad to certain Russian NGOs, and that the biggest transfers had been made during the electoral period. This statement, presented without any evidence, clearly reflected the Kremlin's main concerns: the possibility of foreign influence on the outcome of Russian elections, and the desire to further isolate the country. It also revealed the real aim of the new law: to ensure a safe transfer of power in future elections by restricting the activities of independent observers.

In his interview, Sidiakin stoked popular fears of foreign subversion which had been spread by pro-Kremlin spokesmen during the presidential elections in 2012. He claimed that the law would only apply to the minority of NGOs which were closely related to foreign organizations. The programme then included a statement by Liudmila Alekseeva, who said she had expressed her concern about the new law to the US President. According to the reporter, this clearly demonstrated where the loyalty of such activists lay (Zarubin, 2012). The report showed how this widely-watched state-aligned television channel could provide coverage of the law from the regime's point of view, which relied heavily on conspiratorial ideas which were further developed specifically for this campaign.

In addition to taking ideas from past Soviet propaganda, active supporters of the new law used different conspiratorial theories from the post-Soviet period. For example, while he was presenting the new law to the Duma, Sidiakin wore the St George ribbon; this provided a visual contrast between his initiative and the aims of the anti-regime protesters, who wore white ribbons as their symbol in 2011–12. The St George ribbon was a symbol of soldiers' bravery in Imperial Russia, and after the Second World War was reintroduced as a military award. It was revived by pro-Kremlin journalists in 2005 partly in response to the orange ribbons which were a symbol of the 'Orange Revolution' in Ukraine (Zygar', 2006). According to Miller (2012c, pp. 94–7), the St George ribbon became one of Russia's most successfully constructed symbols of historical memory, commemorating the patriotism and heroic deeds of Soviet soldiers during the Second World War. Sidiakin's use of this symbol was aimed at stressing the patriotic nature of the new law, which would defend the sovereignty of the nation. This stood in contrast to the unpatriotic actions of the opposition. The performative character of Sidiakin's speech was clear when he trampled the white ribbon under foot, symbolizing the country's resistance, by means of the new legislation, to foreign subversion (Piter.tv, 2012). These two symbols, the George ribbon and the white ribbon, were juxtaposed in a conspiratorial way. The intention was to emphasize the otherness of NGOs, and at the same time, to advocate the social cohesion of the rest of the nation, which was emphasized by evoking the memory of the Second World War.

The campaign against NGOs also made use of conspiracy theories regarding the collapse of the Soviet Union. In July 2012, a prominent Russian radio station with liberal credentials, *Ekho Moskvy* (*Echo of Moscow*), broadcast a talk show about the law on NGOs. Discussing the reasons for its implementation, Krasheninnikova accused Russian NGOs of planning to undermine state sovereignty and argued that they were participating in a long-term campaign orchestrated by the United States with the aim of destroying Russia and promoting anti-Russian ideas among Russia's citizens. 'Yes, we destroyed [the USSR] ourselves. This is Washington's idea, [and] look how deeply [this idea] is embedded in your minds', argued Krasheninnikova (Dziadko, Shevardnadze and Krasheninnikova, 2012). The Soviet collapse is being used here as a justification for the change in legislation. This marks the extent to which, by 2012, the idea it had been brought about by the efforts of foreign intelligence had become an essential feature of the country's political discourse.

The label which was to be imposed on some Russian NGOs after the adoption of the new law was so controversial that none of the organizations agreed to be included in the list of 'foreign agents'. As a result, in March 2013, Russian law enforcement initiated a mass inspection of NGOs throughout the country, checking 233 NGOs in 52 regions (Zheleznova, 2013).

Among the first to be targeted were *Transparency International* and *Amnesty International*, major human rights organizations which had often been critical of the domestic policies of the Kremlin. Another target was an independent sociological foundation, the *Levada-Centre*, which was the only independent opinion polling company in the country at that time. The inspection of the *Levada-Centre* demonstrates with particular clarity the vagueness of the terms of the new law and its close connection to conspiratorial discourse. The pretext for inspection was the centre's alleged political activities, which were forbidden for NGOs with foreign funding. In the absence of any definition of political activities, the *Levada-Centre* was accused of influencing the political situation within Russia by publishing the results of opinion surveys which, in the government's view, were subversive (Balmforth, 2013).

A public debate about the inspection erupted, with pro-Kremlin participants using conspiracy-based arguments to defend the actions of the law-enforcement organs. For instance, Evgenii Fedorov, a Duma deputy, contended that the *Levada-Centre* was part of the 'framework' of 664 NGOs which were created to establish external control and exploitation of Russia by the West (Turkova, 2013). This conspiratorial notion was put forward to delegitimize the results of the centre's polls, which demonstrated public disappointment with some of Putin's politics after 2012. The ideas articulated by Fedorov, which were largely based on anti-Western conspiracy theories, could potentially be applied to various concerns in domestic policy; this meant that they could be used as a significant instrument of social cohesion in the post-electoral period.

The role of conspiratorial narratives increased still further in the media campaign against NGOs in 2013, which signified a change in governmental policies after Putin's re-election in 2012. Mamontov's documentary of 2006 had featured one of a relatively small number of conspiratorial stories broadcast by the federal television channel when the campaign against NGOs first started, but the frequency and diversity of such programmes and public speakers during Putin's third presidential term increased exponentially.

The talk show *Politika*, broadcast by the state-aligned television Channel One in May 2013, demonstrated that despite the participation of discussants with different points of view, the programme gave particular prominence to conspiracy theories by means of editing, giving more voice to loyal intellectuals, and allowing moderators to manipulate the debate. Attempts on the part of speakers opposed to the Kremlin to demonstrate the mistakes made in recent inspections were interrupted by the moderators, who immediately posed another question to the loyal public intellectuals. This moved the discussion in a different direction and enabled the use of conspiratorial rhetoric. For instance, the issue of civic activism, in which some NGOs were involved, was diverted into a discussion about the colour revolutions and the supposed role of the intelligence services in them (see, for example, Viacheslav Nikonov and Mikhail Remizov's remarks: Politika, 2013). These manipulative practices created the impression of a plurality of opinions; but the domination of conspiratorial ideas and the biased approach of the moderators determined the overall contours of the narrative and served to delegitimize political opponents of the Kremlin.

A new campaign against NGOs carried out in 2012–13 eventually impacted on public perception, and established a conspiratorial image of third sector organizations in public discourse. According to a sociological poll conducted in May 2013 by the *Levada-Centre*, which continued functioning despite intimidating inspections and critical media coverage, 43 per cent of respondents considered influence on the domestic policies of Russia as the main aim of NGOs with foreign funding. Furthermore, 19 per cent perceived such NGOs as an internal threat to the country. Even though less than one fifth of respondents saw NGOs as clearly conspiring entities in Russia, almost half of them perceived third sector organizations as a problematic factor in domestic life. Hence attempts to delegitimize the Kremlin's opponents by turning NGOs into the subversive Other could be assessed as moderately, but not fully, successful.

The prevalence of conspiratorial rhetoric in public discourse encouraged people to see a link between the term 'foreign agent' and the conspiratorial notion of the 'fifth column', thus effectively discrediting NGOs as spy agencies. Russian sociologist Denis Volkov noted at the time of the campaign that according to their research, approximately 60 per cent of Russians connected the terms 'foreign agent', 'fifth column' and 'spy'. Fifty-six per cent believed that at least some non-governmental organizations were spying on behalf of foreign governments (Dymarskii, Larina and Volkov, 2013). As a result of the campaign, twenty-two organizations were subsequently declared by the law-enforcement organs to be 'foreign agents', and, as a rule, most of these organizations had a critical stance on the Kremlin's domestic policies (Gorodetskaia, 2013). In sum, it has become evident that by 2013 anti-Western conspiracy theories turned out to be fully embedded in domestic politics.

Conclusion

The conspiratorial conceptualization of Russian NGOs, which was promoted in the public sphere from 2004 onwards, was one of the most significant, long-lasting ideological and political projects initiated by the Kremlin. Russian NGOs as political actors were important in fostering the values of a democratic society after the collapse of the Soviet Union. They provided people with assistance and filled the educational and social-support gaps left by the disappearance of the old system of state-sponsored social provision. Despite their relative weakness and inability to attract large numbers of activists, they were one of the main sources of civil education, and this is what enabled them to advance democratic values (Ljubownikow, Crotty and Rodgers, 2013). Moreover, despite the relative atomization of Russian society the population's inclination towards cooperation and activism remain fairly high, especially in circumstances which are challenging for individuals (Greene, 2014). Therefore, the threat the Kremlin perceived in the colour revolutions made civil society institutions the first target for attack. As the case of Yukos demonstrated, the application of anti-Western conspiracy theories, together with the actions of law-enforcement agencies, could bring fruitful results. Accordingly, the campaign against NGOs was harsh and conspiratorial.

With the help of the state-aligned media and public intellectuals, conspiracy mythmaking became a key tool in the discursive construction of the negative image of Russian NGOs. As exemplified by the Yukos affair, conspiracy theories proved to be very useful in ruining the reputation of political enemies. The campaign that unfolded a few years later makes it clear that conspiratorial notions were used to help the Kremlin deprive independent civil society institutions of legitimacy and thus of the possibility of becoming important political actors which could challenge the Kremlin.

The campaigns against NGOs, promoted by the media and shaped by conspiracy theories, served to justify legislative changes and, at the same time, to explain these changes to the public. These measures caused a two-fold decrease in the number of NGOs, from approximately 400,000 in 2005 to less than 227,000 in 2016 (TASS, 2016). Given the absence of effective government support for social and humanitarian initiatives, this drop in the number of NGOs had an adverse influence on the development of civil society in Russia. The allegation against NGOs that they lacked loyalty to the Russian nation paved the way for the government to create from above supposedly civil society actors who were in fact fully loyal to the Kremlin (Biriukova and Zheleznova, 2013).

The process of othering NGOs, carried out by public intellectuals and politicians through anti-Western conspiracy discourse, was primarily aimed at ensuring that civic organizations were perceived negatively by the majority of Russians. In fact, political elites were concerned that they themselves could lose legitimacy because of the activities of NGOs, and this further encouraged the use of anti-Western conspiracy theories as an important instrument of political practice. The significant increase in conspiracy fears about NGOs during Putin's second and third presidential terms allows us to trace both the evolution of the anti-Western conspiracy discourse and the continuity of methods which were used in solving domestic political issues.

The campaign against NGOs in 2005–6 was carried out by a few highly influential media outlets, and it began to shape public opinion regarding the work of NGOs. It was not difficult for the Kremlin to create a conspiratorial image among ordinary Russians of NGOs as a 'fifth column' because both knowledge about and interest in their activities were relatively low. However, the unstable political situation in the aftermath of the presidential elections in March 2012 significantly radicalized the official political discourse. The dramatic decrease in public support for the government forced pro-Kremlin politicians and intellectuals to use all available discursive tools to ensure social cohesion and public support of the regime. An image of NGOs as the dangerous conspiring Other had already been established; the subsequent escalation of the Kremlin-led campaign against NGOs can be seen as a straightforward way to suppress one of the few noticeable opponents of the regime. The crisis in Ukraine, discussed in Chapter 7, would bring another wave of repressions.

6
Shadows of the Revolution

The shadow of 1917 hangs over Putin and his elites. In 2017, a hundred years after the revolution, there is no indication that any official ceremonies will be held to commemorate the event that shook the world and changed the country forever. Instead, after eighteen years of the Putin presidency, the establishment has become accustomed to looking for signs of an insurgency which could end his regime, in the same way that the regime of Emperor Nicholas II collapsed in 1917. The state-aligned media keep on airing programmes about the Western spies who destroyed the great Imperial state from within, making pointed references to the current global state of affairs (Zygar, 2017).

The gradual insulation of the country from foreign influence, and its development into a 'fortress' (at least on the level of political rhetoric), began under the pretext of preventing revolution from being 'imported' into Russia from the West. The first regime changes in the CIS countries in the mid 2000s met with great concern in Moscow. They disrupted existing relations between the political elites of the former Soviet republics and, in the eyes of the Kremlin leaders, posed a serious challenge to the smooth transfer of power during the 2007–8 Russian elections. Russia's power brokers did not want to violate the constitution, which would raise questions about their right to rule; instead they used all the tools available to them to redesign the political system in such a way that Vladimir Putin could legitimately remain in power. Elections have been key to this process.

The importance of regular and fair elections cannot be overestimated. They guarantee political stability, and the peaceful renewal of the positions of the elites; they enable the interests of various social and political groups to be expressed; and they help to solve political crises. Furthermore, they provide citizens with the means of changing the ways in which political, economic and social policies are carried out (Przeworski, 2015). Gorbachev's reforms and the first free elections in the USSR, in 1989, had a significant impact on the country's political development. All the same, free elections posed new challenges to the citizens of these countries, and, even more so, to the political elites. As McFaul and Petrov note (2004), during the 1990s, the Russian political elites managed to reduce the uncertainties associated with competitive elections and learned how to use particular political tools to preserve their leading positions, while at the same time sustaining the public image of the country as a democratic state. Attempts by the authorities to weaken the electoral system, both on the federal and regional levels, were successful both in the 1990s and the 2000s (Ross, 2009). As a result, by the 2010s, the Russian electoral system had become a loyal instrument in the hands of the ruling elites (White, 2011).

The electoral period of 2007–8 was particularly crucial for the Kremlin. The parliamentary and presidential elections, which were to take place in December 2007 and March 2008 respectively, were intended to ensure Putin's political future after the expiry of his second term in the office. Consequently, they were of enormous importance to the country's political establishment. The pre-election period coincided with turbulent changes in the CIS countries, where former political elites lost their positions, in some cases because of electoral defeat, in others of post-electoral opposition campaigns. Claiming that these changes were orchestrated by Washington, Russian political elites articulated the idea of a 'Western plot' to undermine Russian stability and sovereignty, specifically using elections. This concept became central both in the 2007 parliamentary election campaign, and in the 2011–12 parliamentary and presidential campaigns. By the next electoral period, in 2016, the Kremlin had no need for a massive popular mobilization around conspiracy theories, since the Ukraine crisis and the Crimean annexation were doing that job.

The electoral periods in post-Soviet Russia have provided the opportunity for the revitalization of mythmaking. Wilson (2005) has demonstrated the pivotal role played by political technologies in gaining a desired election result, and outlined the various methods by which public opinion is manipulated. Other experts have focused on the Russian elections and have explored the ways in which other candidates fall victim to character assassination, locating and analysing this phenomenon within the Russian electoral context (Sigelman and Shiraev, 2002; Samoilenko and Erzikova, 2017). Surprisingly, the role played by conspiracy mythmaking in Russian elections has been neglected by scholars. This chapter aims to fill this gap, focusing precisely on this aspect of the two electoral campaigns. The conspiracy narratives can be found at the heart of the popular mobilization campaign, and were used to justify repression against any potential rivals.

Putin as National Leader

The transition of power to a carefully chosen successor, and maintaining a central position for Putin in the political system, became the main goals of the pre-electoral period (Furman, 2007). As Henry Hale suggests, in the post-Soviet world political regimes are very dependent on patrons who create networks which function as the backbone of these regimes (Hale, 2015). Preserving the patrons means sustaining the power of these networks; accordingly, in crisis situations there are determined attempts to ensure that these networks survive. After people in Ukraine refused to elect a pro-Russian candidate in their presidential elections, pro-Kremlin spin doctors and politicians spent a great deal of time and resources establishing an image of Putin as the only viable national leader. Through the publication of books and aggressive media campaigns they depicted Putin as the keystone of Russia's national independence and economic stability.

Since the realization in the late 1990s that anti-Western conspiracy theories were a useful tool for public mobilization, their development became a priority for pro-Kremlin intellectuals. The two years in which 'sovereign democracy' had been used as an ideological framework were enough to prepare the arguments which would ensure that Putin remained in power after 2008. By the beginning of the electoral season in 2007, the Kremlin had at its disposal a set of conspiratorial ideas with which to undermine the positions of its opponents, and instruments with which to promote these ideas among Russian citizens. The parliamentary elections which were held on 2 December 2007 served as a form of referendum in support of Putin's policies and of the United Russia Party, in which Putin took the position of chairman. The pro-Kremlin pre-election campaign paid particular attention to the supposed subversive actions of the opposition, which consisted of United Russia's political opponents and international observers, whose statements could undermine the legitimacy of the regime in the eyes of foreign observers. A ferocious media campaign, as well as changes to the state legislation, marginalized the opposition and helped the pro-Putin party to secure a key political position.

After completing two consecutive presidential terms, Putin continued to hold a leading position on the political scene and became more than just a politician (Cassiday and Johnson, 2010). By the crucial electoral period of 2007–8, the Kremlin had devoted much effort to turning the president into a popular icon (Goscillo, 2011). Pictures of a bare-chested Putin riding a horse, videos of young women declaring their love for the president, which went viral on the Internet, and the specific targeting of women as a potential support group, was a deliberate Kremlin policy which was aimed at creating the nucleus of Putin's electorate (Pavlovskii, 2012). This focus on gender and masculinity, as Valerie Sperling notes (2015), has been one of the Kremlin's strategies of legitimization both of Putin and his regime. A poll conducted by the *Levada-Centre* in July 2007 revealed that 52 per cent of respondents would support Putin in 2012 if he ran for another presidential term (Levada-tsentr, 2007). This extensive level of support, in part achieved through manipulative media coverage, was highlighted during the 2007–8 electoral campaign, in which Putin was represented as the main defender of the Russian state (Baraulina, 2006, pp. 24–7; Hutchings and Rulyova, 2009, pp. 29–56).

As Dugin (2007) claimed, among Putin's biggest achievements in the 2000s were the restoration of the country's territorial integrity, the prevention of Russia's collapse, and her newly regained reputation as a world power 'which everybody else takes into account'. Pro-Kremlin spin-doctors further attempted to attach global significance to Putin by stressing his role in resisting US hegemony. Shortly before the elections, Pavlovskii (2007) contended that the Russian global mission was not the country's 'return to former greatness', but its successful containment of the USA, which only Putin was able to achieve:

> You cannot invent a global mission, but you can choose it out of a short list of real, eagerly sought goals. Putin did it. In the world of the simultaneously destructive and utopian 'Bush doctrine', the demand for resistance to the US is impossible. However, there is a global demand for this resistance. . . . The containment of the US is Russia's function for the next few years. Most of humankind, including its Western part, will tacitly support all Russian actions in this sphere even without openly expressing public support. Putin found a unique niche of unarticulated global demand for particular policies and occupied it. (Pavlovskii, 2007)

Consequently, Putin was gradually developing some exceptional features and becoming a unique political figure in post-Soviet Russia. He was expected, among other things, to help unite the various social and ethnic groups in Russian society into one nation. At its meeting in May 2007, the United Russia Party voted in favour of the so-called *Plan Putina* (*Putin's plan*), a set of vague ideas about socio-economic and political projects scheduled for realization in the years following the 2007–8 elections (Orlov, 2007). This initiative was mainly used to demonstrate the continuity of the regime's policies and to emphasize the stability in Russia's domestic policies, which was perceived as one of Putin's main achievements. Apart from socio-economic projects, the most important part of the plan was 'the strengthening of Russian sovereignty', defined as Russia's right to independently determine the direction of its political development. The leaders of United Russia stressed the uniqueness of 'Russian civilization' and emphasized Russia's independence from the West. One of the party leaders at that time, Andrei Vorob'ev, stated that *Putin's plan* did not signal an end to Russia's commitment to democracy; however, 'democracy in Russia is the power of the *Russian people*' [emphasis added – I. Y.]. Thus, Vorob'ev implicitly referred to the wave of 'colour revolutions', which were now said to be organized by Washington to impose on Russia a peculiarly 'Western' type of democracy which was alien to its own political traditions (Vorob'ev, 2007). In this context, the figure of Putin was used to demonstrate the will of 'the people' to democratically choose the country's leader regardless of the will of the 'Other', the United States.

While high-ranking politicians only vaguely hinted at the possible threat of external invasion, pro-Putin intellectuals had more opportunities to express conspiratorial ideas in public. For instance, Dugin's rather Manichean interpretation of *Putin's plan* reduced it to the traditional opposition of Russia to the West and the latter's purported attempts to destroy Russia in the 1990s with the help of corrupt and treacherous domestic elites:

> Putin's personal achievement was the fact that he did not listen to political elites, who had an anti-national orientation. . . . He did not listen to various foundations that led him to the West, pushed him towards ultra-liberalism, towards Russophobia, towards his own suicide, [as well as the destruction of] his course, the country, the nation. He did not listen to these elites, but listened to the voice of history, the voice of the people, and the voice of geopolitics. (Dugin, 2012, p. 26)

This interpretation of *Putin's plan* reflects the main conspiratorial notion which was widely used in the 2007–8 campaign: a general threat to the political order coming from the West. The threat was embodied in the 'treacherous' activities of NGOs and the irresponsible actions of political elites in the 1990s. These elites bore the main responsibility for the collapse of the Soviet Union and the subsequent economic disorder. *Putin's plan* did not contain any real political measures, but, through actions which were largely performative, it served to divide society into two groups, the loyal majority and a subversive minority. The original descriptions of the threat were vague, but they were later elaborated on by high-ranking politicians.

For instance, Boris Gryzlov, *United Russia*'s chairman, claimed (2007) that without Putin, Russia would be open to plunder: 'Contemporary Russia is Putin. "Russia without Putin" is a Russia without governance, a Russia without will. It is a Russia which could be dismembered and which could be used in whatever way. Russia up for grabs (*Rossiia kak dobycha*)'. Gryzlov's text represented a mixture of alarmist ideas about a permanent threat from internal and external enemies, and assurances that the political establishment was able to resist any sort of intrusion into domestic politics. It appealed to negative public attitudes about NATO, which at the time was seen as Russia's rival and potential menace (Levada-tsentr, 2009). Gryzlov also mentioned the threat of the 'colour revolutions' and linked this to the activities of Russian NGOs. Russia was presented as a large, 'sovereign' community of Russian citizens led by Putin, whose actions were aimed at ensuring the prosperity and greatness of the state and its people. 'It is time to remind ourselves: we are Russia. The scenario in which "public" organizations operating in the country are pumped with money to destabilize the situation will not take place here. The right of Russian citizens to shape their country's destiny is not for sale' (Gryzlov, 2007).

On 2 October 2007, at the United Russia party congress, Putin became the official leader of the party, which allowed pro-Kremlin speakers to claim that the parliamentary elections were in effect a referendum on Putin's policies (Mashkarin, 2007). The positioning of Putin at the head of the party served to create the impression that Russia, as a whole, supported both him and his party. Those who did not support them, or held different political views, were either non-patriots or outright enemies. In this discourse, Putin, as leader of the party, not only represented 'Russia', but his policies and actions reflected the aspirations of ordinary citizens. Thus, he was now depicted as the spokesperson of the 'people', set against a minority of political opponents who represented the West. This image was further promoted by means of a media campaign which involved ordinary people. The Kremlin-aligned media claimed that these people were concerned about Putin's political future, and were calling on the president to remain in a leadership position (Vasil'ev, 2007).

Another initiative was to attract voters with no specific political sympathies by means of a campaign entitled *V podderzhku Putina* (*In Putin's support*). Its initiators claimed that 70 per cent of the Russian population could be mobilized to support Putin and that most Russians would join forces with the purpose of 'helping Putin to work for the benefit of the Russian people' (Bagdasarian, 2007). In the speeches of the campaign's activists, Putin was placed in opposition to disloyal politicians, who had betrayed the country after the demise of the Soviet Union. This viewpoint was endorsed by the concept of the *tumultuous '90s* (*likhie devianostye*), the time of economic and political chaos, which could only have happened with the connivance of irresponsible politicians who cooperated with the West and ultimately took the Russian people to the brink of starvation. In the words of spin doctors, intellectuals and journalists, Putin's policies were aimed solely at ensuring stable lives for ordinary people after the chaos of the 1990s. This propaganda transformed Putin into the country's saviour and 'the people's leader'.

During the first rally of the *V Podderzhku Putina* campaign, Vladimir Voronin, the representative of a Cossack movement, who made it clear that he did not endorse any of the political parties, expressed concern about the possible return of the instability of the 1990s:

> Our logic – the logic of non-partisans and people detached from power – is simple: on 2 December 2007 we do not want to wake up in a different country, where governments change like in a film. . . . We do not want a power vacuum like in the 1990s. We want the preservation of stability and continuity of government, and we can only see Putin as its guarantor. (Emel'ianenko, 2007)

Reference to the recent traumatic experience of the 1990s became a pivotal element in the electoral rhetoric of the 2007–8 campaign. Every spokesperson stressed that a stable future was not yet guaranteed, meaning that the return of instability was still possible. Hence, the division was made still sharper between 'the people', who wanted the continutation of the stability and relative prosperity which Putin had provided in the last eight years, and the internal 'Other', a troublesome minority who were trying to return to power and would bring chaos in their wake.

When accepting the leadership of the party, Putin emphasized that in the previous century, 'our Motherland passed through many convulsions', such as economic 'shock therapy', territorial collapse and moral decay. By contrast, in the 2000s his government had provided ordinary Russians with economic stability, agricultural successes and improved social support (Putin, 2007b). This demonization of the 1990s – first featured in Putin's landmark speech in 2005 – not only reminded Russian citizens about recent traumatic experiences, but it also served to define more clearly the main opponents of Putin and United Russia, now commonly called 'Putin's enemies' (*vragi Putina*). In the words of pro-Putin politicians and intellectuals during the campaign, the ultimate goal of these people and organizations, backed by the West, was to restore a regime interested solely in national plunder and disintegration.

'Putin's Enemies'

In 2006–7, pro-Putin intellectuals and spin doctors further elaborated narratives about how to define the enemies of Russia and Putin. By the time of the elections, the *Evropa* publishing house, which was closely affiliated with Pavlovskii, published two books which dealt with the 'subversive Other' in Putin's Russia. One was focused on individuals, the other on organizations.

The first of these publications could not have been more explicit; its title was *Vragi Putina* (*Putin's enemies*). Written by a group of pro-Kremlin journalists and published in November 2007, at the peak of the electoral campaign, it included stories about opposition politicians and oligarchs who had either left Russia to avoid arrest or, like Khodorkovsky, had been convicted. The second book, by a PR-specialist Maksim Grigor'ev, was titled *Fake-struktury. Prizraki rossiiskoi politiki* (*Fake-Structures: The Shadows of Russian Politics*). This focused on NGOs and various organizations which were opposed to the Kremlin. The author claimed that the declared goals and principles of these organizations were deceitful; in reality their sole aim was to undermine Russia by means of cooperation with American and European funding bodies (Grigor'ev, 2007). The publication of these books was widely advertised by the pro-Kremlin media as a newsworthy event. The authors were invited to give several interviews, which allowed them further to elaborate their arguments (Malysheva, 2007).

The overarching narrative of these publications was to make out that Putin and Russia were virtually the same thing. Therefore, any criticism of Putin and the existing political system could be interpreted as a hostile stance towards the nation. Pavlovskii noted in an interview given at this time at the Echo of Moscow radio station that the term 'enemy' helped to stress the difference in the political views of Putin and his opponents (Al'bats and Pavlovskii, 2007). Thus, the use of that term was justified because it made it clear, on the eve of the elections, who were the Kremlin's allies and who were its opponents.

Vitalii Ivanov, deputy head of the pro-Kremlin Centre for Political Conjuncture (*Tsentr Politicheskoi Kon'iunktury*) and one of the pro-Kremlin spin doctors, wrote in the preface to *Vragi Putina*:

> Putin's regime carries out policies which respond to the aspirations of the nation, the policies which restore Russian power, consolidate the state, support domestic order, which correspond to our political traditions and strengthen patriotism. ... It is not important why a person rejects Putin's regime and becomes its enemy. It is important that, in the current situation, this person automatically becomes an enemy of the state and the nation, an enemy of our Motherland. (Danilin, Kryshtal' and Poliakov, 2007, p. 6)

The central idea of *Vragi Putina* was to compare Putin to his 'political enemies' and demonstrate how 'immoral' these people were in comparison to the president. To do that, the authors assigned a cardinal sin to each of the 'Putin enemies'. Boris Berezovskii was guilty of wrath, which pushed him into battle with Putin over returning control over the country to the people. Mikhail Kas'ianov, Russian prime minister from 2000 to 2004, and subsequently a staunch opposition leader, was accused of greed, since he preferred a luxurious lifestyle and foreign trips to dealing with ordinary Russians. The Yukos oil company's owner Mikhail Khodorkovsky's sin was the envy of Putin, which resulted, in the words of the authors, in him planning to dismantle Russia, destroy most of the population and give the country's nuclear weapons to the Americans (pp. 53–4, 125, 183–4).

Fake-structures had a different angle: it developed the idea that Russian NGOs were a tool of foreign-government subversion, which contributed to the destruction of Russia's unique political culture and society. Khodorkovsky's *Open Russia*, like other NGOs, tried to monopolize the very notion of 'Russian civil society', and criticized Putin from the position of civil rights activists. Grigor'ev criticized the coalition *Drugaia Rossiia* (*the Other Russia*), formed by various Russian opposition activists critical of the Kremlin. The author emphasized the title of the coalition – the *Other* Russia – and pointed out how alien Putin's opponents were in relation to Russian society, which Putin represented (Grigor'ev, 2007).

The creation of an 'Other' by insisting on a connection between former oligarchs and NGOs was yet another tactic to separate the main critics of Putin's policies from 'the people'. This conceptualization was reinforced by stressing the critics' affiliation with the West. At a time when most people were struggling financially, rich business people who had made their fortunes by use of the highly unpopular reforms in the 1990s, were a particularly easy target. Grigor'ev's critique argued that these people were alienated from their country and had links with financial interests abroad. The parliamentary elections of 2007 were presented as a way for Russian people to decide the future of the country, in contrast to the 1990s, when decision-making was controlled by the West (Dobrov et al., 2007).

International Observers as 'Fake Structures'

The concept of 'fake structures' was also applied to international observers of the parliamentary and presidential elections. The Russian political establishment supported the international monitoring of the elections because it reinforced the regime's legitimacy. However, international observers who acted outside the Kremlin's control were cause for concern. In late October 2007, conflict between the Central Election Commission of the Russian Federation (CEC) and the Organization for Security and Cooperation in Europe (OSCE) reached its peak when the OSCE criticized the Russian government for not ensuring that election observers received their visas on time. OSCE subsequently received a letter of invitation from the CEC proposing a reduction in the number of international observers; this prompted OSCE to refuse to participate in the monitoring of the 2007–8 elections (OSCE, 2007).

In response, pro-Kremlin reporters and intellectuals claimed that OSCE was acting on the orders of the US government and was preparing reports about the elections well before they had actually begun. The observers were alleged to have been tasked with delegitimizing Putin, whose position would be even stronger after the elections. Portraying international observers in this way helped create a sense of danger in relation to international monitoring organizations, which supposedly wanted to delegitimize Russia's parliamentary elections and thereby 'undermine' Russian statehood. At a press conference about the issue of international observers, Grigor'ev claimed that Washington had set OSCE the goal of undermining the Putin regime and making it dependent on foreign institutions. Accordingly, he called for a complete ban on international observers at the elections (Malysheva, 2007). Conspiracy ideas in this particular case were used to justify the current policies of the Russian government concerning the elections. At the same time, conspiracy theories which pointed to USA control of the international observers justified their exclusion.

These accusations coincided with intensified US activity in post-Soviet countries. President Bush actively supported the political changes in the CIS countries, stating that we live 'in historic times when freedom is advancing, from the Black Sea to the Caspian, and to the Persian Gulf and beyond' (BBC, 2005). References to US involvement in the politics of the post-Soviet space, to the detriment of Russia's interests, as well as a massive propaganda campaign promoting the notion of 'sovereign democracy', contributed to the image of Russia as a 'besieged fortress'. In this context, the regime did not expect the absence of international observers to have an impact on the public perception of the elections' legitimacy. At the same time, claims made by alternative international observers from Serbia and CIS states that the elections were carried out in accordance with democratic standards, were widely reported in the pro-Kremlin media (Izvestiia, 2007).

In this context, anti-Western conspiracy theories worked as a tool to delegitimize foreign observers. The possibility of challenging the validity of the elections in December 2007 was pre-empted by anti-Western conspiracy theories which were disseminated on the eve of elections. Claims that the OSCE observers were biased provided an argument as to why the Russian public should ignore external criticism of the election results. At the same time, any criticism of the Kremlin's policies in the 2000s was counterbalanced by references to the chaos of the 1990s, and the possibility of a revival of those terrible times if *United Russia* were to lose the elections. This prospect, framed by conspiracy narratives, was at the heart of Putin's speeches on the eve of the elections.

The Leader Defines the Enemy

A mass rally of Putin's supporters was held at the *Luzhniki* stadium on 21 November 2007; this was a key feature of the campaign to establish Putin as the irreplaceable Russian leader and strengthen the position of *United Russia*. Putin's active engagement in the campaign during its final stage was of crucial importance. The conspiracy narratives, which were developed by various pro-Kremlin speakers and disseminated by the state-aligned media in the previous months, were reflected in Putin's speeches. Having received formal approval from the leader, their inclusion in public discourse was seen as wholly legitimate. The main goal of Putin's speeches was to destroy popular support for any opposition leaders or parties which could challenge *United Russia*'s predominance. Putin explained that his presence at the rally was motivated by concern about Russia's future, which could be secured only by *United Russia*'s policies.

The successful collaboration between Putin and *United Russia* in the interests of Russia was juxtaposed to attempts by their rivals to undermine the country. At least half of the speech Putin delivered on 21 November at *United Russia*'s congress was concerned with evocative descriptions of the political elites who had robbed the country's citizens in the 1990s. He also made reference to those irresponsible politicians who had contributed to the collapse of the Soviet Union in 1991, and to foreign embassies and NGOs of the present day which were attempting to cause divisions in Russian society. Putin's speech, then, reflected the conspiratorial themes that had been developed by pro-Kremlin spin doctors in the previous years. Referring to the unreliable elites who had ruled the country in the past, Putin maintained:

> Those who confront us do not want our plan to be realized, because they have completely different aims and designs for Russia. They need a weak and sick state. To engage in underhand dealings behind society's back (za ego spinoi obdelyvat' svoi delishki), to get dividends (poluchat' kovrizhki) at our expense, they need a disorganized and disoriented society, a divided society. (Putin, 2007c)

This part of the speech came close to repeating, – at times, almost word for word – *Vragi Putina*. Its authors, Danilin, Kryshtal' and Poliakov, had claimed: 'These particular persons are Vladimir Putin's real enemies. They are all united by hatred of the president [because he] did not let them engage in their underhand dealings behind the scenes (obdelyvat' svoi delishki) at the expense of the entire society, the entire state' (Danilin et al., p. 10). Since the book had been published before the rally, these parallels demonstrate a close relationship between Putin's speechwriters and the ideas elaborated by the pro-Kremlin spin doctors. Using the conspiratorial notion of underhand, behind-the-scenes activities on the part of elites who opposed Putin promoted, by contrast, an image of Putin himself as a genuine 'people's leader' who acted for the good of the nation.

Putin's speech included sections that were designed specifically to cast certain social groups as a threat to the Russian people and to

Russian greatness. One of its crucial points was the labelling of political opponents as 'jackals who beg for scraps at foreign embassies, foreign diplomatic missions, who count on foreign funds and governments, rather than the support of their own nation' (Putin, 2007c). This description served to differentiate the Russian people, led by Putin, from 'unpatriotic' politicians of the Yeltsin era who sought a return to power through parliamentary elections. This accusation was primarily directed at the Union of Right Forces (*SPS, Soiuz Pravykh Sil*), the liberal party led by a young and newly elected leader Nikita Belykh. The party could potentially have challenged the domination of *United Russia* in the new parliament. The list of SPS candidates included a few well-known politicians who had served in Yeltsin's government. Danilin also accused the party of lying to voters and having to rely on spin doctors to create the impression of a truly 'national' party (Danilin, 2007). Two months later, his arguments were reflected in Putin's speech:

> None of these people have stepped back from the political stage. You can find their names among the candidates and funders of certain parties. They wish to have revenge; they want to return to power, to their spheres of influence. . . . [They want] gradually to restore an oligarchic regime based on corruption and lies. They lie even today. They will not do anything for anyone. . . . They will also take to the streets now (*Vot seichas echshe na ulitsy vyidut*). They took a bit [of knowledge] from Western specialists; [they] were trained in neighbouring republics, so, now [they] will arrange provocations here. (Putin, 2007c)

Without actually naming his party, Putin identified the one political opponent who could put up a plausible challenge to *United Russia*. Had SPS managed to achieve any credible success at the elections, it would have thrown into question the country's absolute support of *United Russia* and complicated the process of transferring power to Putin's chosen successor. To suppress this opponent, the Kremlin put financial pressure on wealthy members of SPS threatening their businesses; they had either to leave the party or stop funding it. At the same time, when members of the party took part in street protests, this gave pro-Kremlin spin doctors the opportunity to promote conspiracy theories about SPS participation in a colour revolution (Guseva and Fishman, 2007).

On 29 November Putin warned Russian television viewers about a group of politicians who planned, in defiance of the wishes of the Russian people, to return to the 'years of indignity, dependency and collapse' (Stott, 2007). Broadcast in a prime-time news bulletin on

Channel One a few days before the elections, this address to the nation was intended to bring about a high turnout of Putin supporters, which would demonstrate the legitimacy of both the parliament and the future president. Although a conspiratorial narrative was not at the centre of this address to the nation, it did make an appearance; and yet again it was used to divide the country into the 'patriotic' majority, led by Putin, and a minority of 'pro-American liberals' and fugitive oligarchs who wanted to enrich themselves at Russia's expense.

The parliamentary elections of 2007 can be seen as a central episode in the political development of post-Soviet Russia, as they were harnessed to the task of achieving a smooth transfer of power from Putin to his chosen successor and legitimizing the political system over which he presided. As Duncan (2013) noted, uncertainty about the future created a sense of fear in the elites in Russia; and this fear was in part reflected in the proliferation of anti-Western conspiracy theories, which claimed that there was a subversive minority in the country which aimed to destroy the political and economic achievements of the 2000s.

After United Russia's success in the December 2007 elections, the political establishment altered its overarching political narrative; instead of the threat of a 'colour revolution', the principal danger was the slow modernization of the economy. This became the central trope of Medvedev's presidential term. According to *Russian Newsweek*, Medvedev personally removed all references to the Western threat of 'colour revolution' from his speech to a meeting of civil activists in January 2008, and focused instead on how to increase the socio-economic prosperity of the Russian people (Fishman et al., 2007, p. 17). This conceptual shift in Medvedev's rhetoric suggested that anti-Western conspiracy notions were regarded by the political establishment as an efficient tool of popular mobilization, particularly during sensitive periods for the regime. The next electoral period, in 2011–12, again demonstrated that anti-Western conspiracy ideas could protect the regime at a critical time.

The White Ribbon Divides the Country

The major protest activity in the 2011–12 electoral period can be attributed largely to misjudgements on the part of the Kremlin. Lack of information and understanding about popular attitudes, and the conflicting signals sent by the Kremlin to local authorities about who will run again for the president's office, allowed the opposition to seize their opportunity and organize what turned out to be the biggest rallies since the time of *perestroika* (Petrov, Lipman and Hale, 2014, pp. 17–18). At the beginning of the electoral campaign, the main goal of the pro-Kremlin narrative was to justify Putin's return to presidential office for a third term. The official announcement that he was running for president again was made at the *United Russia* Party congress on 24 September 2011, when Medvedev announced that he would not be seeking a second term himself. Referred to by the Russian media as a reshuffle (*rokirovka*), this swap resulted in disillusionment among many Russians and provoked criticism in the independent media about Medvedev as a politician. In the run-up to the elections, liberal journalists argued that Putin would have a hard time explaining to ordinary Russians why he was returning to the Kremlin, and justifying Medvedev's decision not to seek re-election. Putin failed to resolve these issues during the campaign (Kamyshev, 2011).

On 20 November 2011, at the Mixed Martial Arts Tournament, Putin was booed by the crowd. High-ranking supporters, including his press secretary, Dmitrii Peskov, tried to account for the crowd's reaction, making out that it was the defeated foreign fighter who was booed (Kates, 2011). Nevertheless, the incident demonstrated the fact that Putin was having difficulties in achieving wide public support. This caused a dramatic shift in the campaign strategy (Kukolevskii, 2011), which revived the conspiratorial concepts which had been used in the previous electoral campaign.

'The Voice from Nowhere'

As early as 27 November, at the United Russia Party conference, Putin stated: 'We know . . . that representatives of some foreign countries are gathering those they are paying money to, so-called grant recipients, to instruct them and assign work to influence the election campaign themselves' (Bryanski and Grove, 2011). In this way, Putin and other members of the Russian political establishment attempted to delegitimize the activities of NGOs on the eve of the elections and make the results of alternative polls and monitoring vulnerable to criticism. Yet genuine non-biased monitoring would have demonstrated massive fraud and violations of the law.

These pronouncements were backed by a clear increase in the dissemination of anti-Western conspiracy ideas by the Russian media. The

NTV television channel made a documentary about the Association in Defence of Voters' Rights, 'Golos', which would later be nicknamed *Golos niotkuda* (*The Voice from Nowhere*). The programme was broadcast on prime-time television on the eve of the elections (CHP. Rassledovanie: Golos niotkuda, 2011). The filmmakers, from a special NTV department which had been created specifically to produce this kind of mudslinging (Afisha, 2012), claimed that Golos was affiliated with foreign sponsors, and that it received funding precisely to bring about Russia's collapse by claiming that the 2011 parliamentary elections had been rigged. This story was followed by the closing down of the *Karta narushenii* (*The Map of Violations*) project, produced by Golos in collaboration with the news website *Gazeta.ru* to monitor the quantity and specific details of violations during the parliamentary elections (Sidorenko, 2011).

At the same time, Anton Beliakov, a Duma deputy from the pro-Kremlin *A Just Russia* Party, stated that the USA, as Russia's geopolitical opponent, had financed Golos for the purpose of demonizing and undermining the country's reputation, and so damaging her investment climate (Makeeva, 2011). Beliakov and his Duma colleagues filed an inquiry at the General Prosecutor's Office to check if Golos' intervention in the electoral process had been carried out in the interests of foreign countries (Bashlykova, 2011). Nikolai Levichev, the head of *A Just Russia,* also accused Golos of being a 'puppet master' (*kuklovod*) with 'messianic' aspirations to influence the results of the elections (Gazeta.ru, 2011).

This joint attempt by television channels and politicians to link Golos with 'foreign masters' served to throw both its reputation, and the results of the monitoring of the elections, into doubt. Although the organization disclosed all the necessary information about its funding, the conspiratorial narrative, disseminated through the mainstream media during the parliamentary election campaign, described Golos as an important tool of foreign influence on domestic politics. In the first decade of December, during the street rallies protesting the rigging of the election results, the following appeared on the pro-Kremlin website Vzgliad:

> 'Golos' became 'the entry point' for 'Western partners' into Russian domestic politics; precisely through this association pressure was applied which eventually brought about a situation whereby today the non-systemic opposition claims the illegitimacy of the Russian elections and ineffectively tries to protest in the streets against their results. (Afanas'eva, 2011)

The political establishment feared a loss of legitimacy during the process of the transition of power, and tried to pre-empt this by means of conspiratorial narratives about Golos. This was the same method that had been used against OSCE observers in 2007. Before the parliamentary elections, some experts decided that there would be more evidence of political manipulation in these elections than had been the case in the previous ones, and that this would pose a threat to the political legitimacy of the United Russia Party and Putin himself (Belanovsky and Dmitriev, 2011). With public support for Putin lower than it had been in the 2000s, and the Kremlin unable to offer the public a sufficiently good reason to return Putin to the presidency, pro-Kremlin politicians and spin doctors were very keen to utilize the old tactics. Through active use of the media they attempted to mobilize 'the people' against the pro-Western 'Other', which made independent observers of the elections the first, and most vulnerable, target, just as they had been in the 2007 parliamentary elections.

'The White Ribbon Aims to Shed Blood'

Street protests and activism after the parliamentary elections in December 2011 triggered a wave of conspiracy speculations about a possible colour revolution supported from abroad. This notion had been fostered by pro-Kremlin intellectuals since 2005 and they could now proclaim that it had become a very real danger. Nikolai Starikov described the events in Moscow as a well-tested plan for revolution which had been designed in Washington to establish friendly political regimes in the post-Soviet nations and plunge them into chaos:

> The [foreign] partners and their Fifth Column are now trying to promote in Russia the same scenario which they have repeatedly tested in the post-Soviet space of Kyrgyzstan, Georgia, Ukraine – it has been the same everywhere. Elections and cries about their falsification by the authorities, [then] people in the streets, [then] an orange revolution (insurrection), [then] total control of the political life in this country by Washington. (Starikov, 2011f)

One of the protesters' symbols was a white ribbon; it was used to emphasize the unity of those discontented with the election results (El Mariachi, 2011). Shortly after the protests, Starikov and another pro-Kremlin blogger, Dmitrii Beliaev, contended that the white ribbon was proof of a 'colour revolution', and that this was a plan invented in the USA to provoke clashes with the authorities and bring about the deaths of Russian protesters. According to Beliaev, the website *Belaia lenta* (*The White Ribbon*) had been registered in the USA two months before the Russian parliamentary elections; this was proof, he argued, of a foreign plan to provoke post-electoral unrest in Russia. He also alleged that just before the website was registered, Aleksei Navalny, a prominent Russian opposition leader, travelled to London where he purportedly received instructions from Boris Berezovskii, while another leader of the opposition, Boris Nemtsov, travelled to the USA supposedly to get approval for the plan. After the December elections, Navalny and Nemtsov urged people to join street protests; Beliaev claimed that 'the ideological backup' for these actions was provided by individuals with dual citizenship. He pointed out that several popular media personalities – the inventor of the white ribbon, writer Arsen Revazov; Dem'ian Kudriavtsev, the then general director of the *Kommersant* publishing house; and another well-known blogger, Anton Nossik – held Israeli passports. Another person mentioned in Beliaev's post, Konstantin von Eggert, was a former BBC journalist and member of the Royal Institute for International Affairs in London, and had previously had close connections to Great Britain; Beliaev took this as an indication of his involvement in anti-Russian subversive activity (Beliaev, 2011).

When the Moscow authorities refused permission for an official opposition rally, and opposition leaders called on people to hold unauthorized protests, Starikov and Beliaev warned their readers that the real aim of the white ribbon movement was to shed blood on the streets of Moscow and try to blame the government for the violence:

> On 10 December, people gather not to express [their] protest, but solely to shed blood and infuriate the mob, to cause disorder. This has happened in many countries in the Middle East, and the same happened one hundred years ago in Russia. 'The White Ribbon', according to the intentions of organizers, should become red. Then this symbol has a completely different meaning. (Starikov, 2011a)

The peaceful atmosphere of the first rally against the election results, held on Moscow's Bolotnaia Square, belied the warning of bloodshed. However, the state leadership chose another tactic to undermine the opposition: refocusing the criticism from rigged elections to Putin himself. Putin's own comments on the white ribbons were extremely pejorative, but they initially backfired. At a press conference held on 15 December he compared the ribbons to condoms, which was meant to defame the protesters' symbol (Elder, 2011b). These comments triggered a wave of anti-Putin criticism that was expressed on protesters' banners during the next demonstration, held on 24 December. Yet Putin's comments did have an important influence on the course of the electoral campaign, and inadvertently supplied the pro-Putin intellectuals with further arguments to link the supposed internal enemy with the West.

Putin's deprecating comment on the white ribbons became, in fact, the key moment of the Kremlin campaign to win the elections. It helped transform the protesters' message, enshrined on numerous banners, into personal criticism of Putin, rather than a demand for fair elections. This shift crucially shaped the subsequent campaigns. Putin became the focal point of both anti-government protests and the pro-government campaign; and this helped to bring about a highly performative official discourse. Pro-Kremlin intellectuals and journalists depicted Russian society as divided between 'the real people of Russia', also called 'Putin's majority', who for the most part represented provincial Russia, and the so-called 'creative class', a dissatisfied minority consisting of hipsters (fashionable young people), internet users and so-called 'liberals' (Ross, 2016). The elections in March 2012 were, then, transformed again into a referendum in support of Putin and his policies. The pro-Putin campaign, carried out by the state-aligned media, also attempted to turn the image of Putin into a symbol which could unify disparate social groups to broaden his electoral base. At the same time, it served to demarcate the boundaries between 'Us' and the subversive 'Other', a broad category which included almost every citizen critical of Putin and his policies.

The 'Spoiled Muscovites' vs. 'The Real Russia'

The division of Russian society into the majority of people and the minority of protesters was effected through the creation of media personalities who, it was claimed, shared the values of Putin's electorate. For instance, during the same press conference on 15 December which was referred to above, Putin received a question from Igor' Kholmanskikh, a worker from Nizhnii Tagil, who expressed concern about the opposition rallies:

> We don't want to go back. I want to say about these rallies, if our militia, or, as is it called now, the police, do not know how to work, cannot cope, I, together with my men, are ready to go out and assert our stability . . . (Zygar, 2016, p. 218)

This episode signalled the start of Kholmanskikh's media career that ended soon after the elections; in the winter of 2011–12 he was transformed into an iconic personality and a recurring character in the campaign, representing the 'real, working Russia' in contrast to the 'cubicle rats' (*ofisnyi plankton,* a derogative term for office workers) of Moscow. In an article published on 18 January 2012, Kholmanskikh wrote:

> It is our country. It is not for them to be the best people in the country and the salt of the earth, but for us all. The country should be developed in the way that all people think is right. . . . I think that if I am ready to vote for Putin in the presidential elections and am ready to encourage others to do the same, it does not mean I am on 'the side of the authorities'. I am on the side of the people. (Nakanune.ru, 2012)

These words echoed Putin's statement, made in a pre-election article he wrote for the newspaper *Izvestiia,* about a certain section of the Russian elites, who always tried to initiate revolution instead of promoting stability (Putin, 2012b). The focus of the pro-Putin rhetoric was the juxtaposition of the stability and prosperity of the ordinary Russian people, versus a corrupt, pro-Western minority, which was attempting to get rid of Putin and hand control of the country to the West. The subsequent course of the presidential campaign was based on this juxtaposition: the 'real people of Russia' against a 'fat, ambitious, absolutely addle-brained, forgetful minority', in the words of Mikhail Leont'ev, a famous pro-Kremlin journalist who became one of the frontmen of Putin's campaign (Polianskaia, 2012).

Although the conspiratorial narratives of the elections in 2007 and in 2012 had certain similarities, the 2012 presidential campaign was distinguished by a vagueness in the pro-Kremlin speakers' definition of the subversive 'Other'. Between 2008 and 2011, as Vladimir Gel'man (2013, p. 5) notes, the number of groups unsatisfied with the regime was growing. People who were affected by the world economic crisis, and motivated by Medvedev's calls for modernization, hit the streets to express their discontent with the status quo. The diversity of social and political groups disappointed with the prospect of Putin returning to the presidency made it difficult for the Kremlin to clearly and quickly identify the object of conspiratorial mythmaking. Consequently, diverse groups of people who protested about the rigged elections in December 2011 and questioned the stability of the regime were discursively united into a single group, 'the people from Bolotnaia'. All of the members of this vaguely defined social group supposedly shared a hatred of Putin and had links to the West.

Sergei Kurginian, another prominent participant in the campaign, posited a division between 'the pro-Western, conspiring minority' and Russian patriots in a manifesto called, revealingly, *Oni i My* (*Them and Us*). The central argument of the manifesto defined the attendees of the first Bolotnaia rally and its leaders as agents of a 'foreign evil will' (*ispolniteli inozemnoi zloi voli*) which had been preparing for *perestroika-2*. Kurginian drew a parallel with the last years of the USSR and Gorbachev's failure to reform the country, which had resulted in economic collapse; and he accused Yeltsin of plundering the country in the 1990s. He directed his populist call to the economically worst-affected group of the population in the 1990s, the intelligentsia, many of whose representatives did not have high incomes, in contrast to the attendees of the opposition rallies, most of whom were said to have relatively high income (Volkov, 2012, p. 74):

> So, THEY want the final breakdown of the country. If you wish it, go to THEIR rally. Support their fat bodies with your skinny hands. But THEY, after partitioning the country, will leave for foreign castles and villas. While you will not leave. So, is it worth going to THEIR rallies, supporting THEM? (Sut' vremeni, 2011)

Kurginian's acknowledgement of the justified 'dissatisfaction of professors and doctors, workers and engineers, soldiers, teachers, agrarians' with current governmental policies was clearly aimed at distinguishing the discontent of representatives of 'real Russia' from the dissatisfaction of leaders of the opposition movement. Avoiding references to post-election grassroots civic activity in the country, Kurginian associated the rallies for the most part with politicians from Yeltsin's government, such as Nemtsov, and former tabloid celebrities, like Kseniia Sobchak. Their aim, according to Kurginian, was to destroy the country by manipulating 'justified discontent' with the political situation, as was also done in 1991 (Sut' vremeni, 2011).

At the same time, pro-Kremlin spin doctors and journalists continued to portray the leaders of the opposition rallies as a 'fifth column' working for the US State Department. A substantial part of the conspiratorial narrative during this campaign was disseminated through television documentaries. The most notable example is NTV's series of documentaries, *Zagranitsa im pomozhet* (*Abroad Will Help Them*) and *Anatomiia protesta* (*The Anatomy of Protest*). Each episode in these series summarized the various myths, forgeries and clichés of Russian conspiracy discourse of the 2000s, such as Russia being infiltrated by foreign agents, NGOs and oppositionists, and being financed by foreign governments hoping to destroy Russia and obtain control over its natural resources (CHP. Rassledovanie. Anatomiia protesta, 2012b).

However, the key aim of these documentaries was to lay the blame for electoral fraud on the anti-Putin opposition. Numerous videos were screened about vote-rigging engineered by foreign intelligence services. On the other hand, as early as 4 February 2012, the Investigative Committee of the Russian Prosecutor General's Office declared that most videos about the Kremlin's falsification of results during the 2011 parliamentary elections 'contained elements of video editing' and were later placed on US Internet servers (Channel One, 2012c). The fact that anyone in the world who had *YouTube* access could upload these videos was of no interest to those making these comments; their emphasis was on the fact that these particular *YouTube* servers were in the USA, and this suggested that anti-government criticism had been staged by the USA. Moreover, at the peak of the campaign, Stanislav Govorukhin, the chief of Putin's campaign office, declared that the Internet was a scrapheap (*pomoika*) which belonged to the US State Department (NTV, 2012). Thus, the videos about electoral fraud, which were widely recorded and disseminated via the Internet by ordinary Russians, were interpreted as a part of a subversive American plan, rather than a grassroots initiative by Russian citizens calling for fair elections.

Although conspiratorial notions were placed in the public space, the policy of delegitimizing those opposed to Putin had a limited impact on public opinion. According to a poll conducted by the *Levada-Centre* in January 2012, only 13 per cent of respondents adhered to the idea of 'Western sponsorship' of the rallies (Levada-tsentr, 2012). Given this result, it might be concluded that although anti-Western conspiracy theories were a useful item in the Kremlin's political toolbox, they only possessed a limited capacity. Their ability to polarize society was evident only when they were placed alongside other populist rhetoric which referred to current socio-economic and political problems. During the electoral campaign, the authorities aggressively used anti-Western conspiracy notions to achieve a short-term mobilization of all potential supporters. However, the division of Russian society into the 'people', represented by Putin, and a mixed community of protesters supposedly linked to the West, was used to channel away from the Putin regime the dissatisfaction of large numbers of Russian citizens with the economic and social inequality in the country. Alarmist conspiracy theories about a 'fifth column' supported the populist claim about the preservation of existing stability, and were used to bring about the swift mobilization of those voters who were financially dependent on the government.

Michael McFaul: 'Ambassador for Colour Revolutions'

A comment addressed to Putin by US Senator John McCain that the Arab Spring 'is coming to a neighbourhood near you', and Secretary of State Hillary Clinton's 'concerns about the conduct of the election', helped to substantiate conspiracy fears (Spillius, 2011; Labott, 2011). In response to international criticism, Putin stated that Clinton's words had no factual basis, but they set the tone for some 'figures within the country and provided a signal. They [the members of opposition] heard this signal and, under the auspices of the US State Department (*gosdep*), started active work' (Elder, 2011a). Hence, the notion of *gosdep* (an acronym of *gosudarstvennyi departament*) – another conspiratorial metaphor – became a central feature in the body of conspiratorial mythmaking related to the 2011–12 electoral period.

In Russia's official discourse, the new US ambassador to Russia, Michael McFaul, who arrived in January 2012, came to symbolize American conspiracy against the country. His meetings with leaders of the opposition allowed pro-Kremlin journalists and writers to claim that he had arrived in Russia to supervise a colour revolution; indeed, he was soon given the nickname 'Ambassador for colour revolutions' (Bohm, 2014). The image of the new Ambassador which appeared in the Russian media provided an important conceptual connection between the opposition rallies, the notion of the colour revolution, and the collapse of the USSR.

These three things were crudely lumped together by Mikhail Leont'ev in his programme *Odnako*, which was broadcast on Channel One on 17 January. Leont'ev's pronouncements followed a report which had just been broadcast on the previous programme, *Vremia*, about Ambassador McFaul's first Moscow meeting with opposition leaders (Channel One, 2012b). Leont'ev described McFaul as an expert on 'colour revolutions', referring to an article published on the popular Russian website *Slon* entitled *Poslom v Rossiiu priezzhaet spetsialist po revolutsiiam* (*The arriving ambassador to Russia is a specialist on revolutions*) (Baunov, 2012).

According to Leont'ev, McFaul's main specialization was the 'promotion of democracy'. He backed up this claim with a quote from McFaul's interview with *Slon* about his positive impressions of the last years of *perestroika* and his friendship with 'Russian democrats'. Leont'ev suggested that McFaul financed and trained so-called 'democratic leaders' who then took leading positions in Russia in the 1990s, and that in 2010 McFaul had played a central role in the training of the opposition leader Aleksei Navalny at Yale University. Hence Leont'ev tied together the collapse of the USSR, the harsh economic reforms supported by pro-American economists, and the current activities of the opposition movement, implying that these processes were all part of one plan coordinated by one person, Michael McFaul. Later, Leont'ev referred to the US periodical *Foreign Policy*, which noted that McFaul was the second non-career diplomat appointed to Moscow; the first was Bob Strauss, who, according to Leont'ev, had 'serviced the collapse of the USSR'. In addition, he held that McFaul was the author of hundreds of 'anti-Putin' articles and a book, *Russia's Unfinished Revolution: Political Change from Gorbachev to Putin*. This title gave Leont'ev the opportunity to hypothesize that the new ambassador had arrived in Moscow in order to complete the revolution (Analiticheskaia programma 'Odnako' s Mikhailom Leont'evym, 2012). The previous academic interests of Ambassador McFaul and, in particular, his research on the origins of the political changes in Ukraine in the mid 2000s (Aslund and McFaul), enabled Leont'ev to speculate about McFaul's comprehensive knowledge both of the funding schemes of the 'colour revolutions', and the financial support provided by the USA to encourage similar events in Russia.

Leont'ev's short report on Ambassador McFaul's appointment, broadcast on prime-time television, became another element in the conspiratorial allegations about the presidential electoral campaign. Igor' Panarin described McFaul as the archetypal conspiratorial mastermind:

> Time has shown that he knows how to withstand pressure, quickly adjusts to a changing situation, and obviously has some secret plans about how to implement Aleksei Navalny's project. So, it is too early for the Kremlin to relax – the fight to prevent chaos and to preserve Russian statehood is yet to come. (Panarin, 2012)

Meeting with opposition leaders on his first day in office made McFaul stand out from traditional diplomats. In addition, he had connections with the Russian political elites of the 1990s, many of whom were considered by pro-Kremlin propagandists to be representatives of the West, and he was very open to dialogue with members of the opposition (Makfol and Pozner, 2012). For these reasons he became an obvious target for anti-American conspiracy theorists. In the ensuing campaign against McFaul they were able to exploit negative Russian attitudes towards the USA: throughout the 2000s, between 25 and 30 per cent of Russians held such attitudes (Levada-tsentr, 2015). McFaul was portrayed as the conspiratorial personification of the USA, supposedly the key coordinator of subversion of the Russian state.

Poklonnaia Hill vs. Bolotnaia Square

The apex of this conspiracy hysteria was the 'Anti-Orange' rally on Moscow's Poklonnaia Hill which was held on 4 February 2012, where leading anti-Western public intellectuals gathered to denounce 'the orange threat' (Analbaeva, 2012). This rally was the first in a series of street events that were used to demonstrate the numerical predominance of pro-Putin forces over oppositionists. Among the slogans were: 'Yes – to fair elections, no – to orange ones'; 'We won't let the country collapse'; and 'Stop begging for scraps at foreign embassies'. These slogans provided a link between the electoral campaigns of 2007 and 2011–12 that also accused 'foreign embassies' and the opposition of working to undermine Putin's regime. The Poklonnaia Hill rally became the 'patriotic answer' to the opposition's third demonstration for fair elections which took place in Moscow on the same day. The 'patriotic' rally was supposed to symbolize the attitude of 'real Russia' to Putin, as opposed to the anti-Putin rhetoric of the opposition. This same approach would be used later in the Pussy Riot affair.

The Poklonnaia Hill rally had two main aims: to resist the 'orange threat', and to express support for Putin. The large number of protesters served to demonstrate that Putin represented the majority of the Russian people, who opposed the minority of 'dissatisfied Muscovites'. The coverage by state-aligned media channels also stressed the numerical superiority of the pro-Putin demonstrators, giving the figure of 'more than 100 thousand participants', in contrast to the anti-Putin rally which was said to have drawn only a quarter of that number (Gazeta.ru, 2012). In the words of the leaders of the Poklonnaia Hill initiative, the participants of their rally stood up against the political 'nobody' (*nichtozhestvo*) which was determined to destroy the country (Ivanov, 2012).

Pro-Putin speakers regularly juxtaposed the two rallies. They were said to symbolize the two parts of Russian society and were evidence of the binary division of the world, which is a typical trope of conspiracy discourse. Most Russians, who were represented by Putin, were said to be concerned with securing stability and peace, while the minority had only one goal – to gain power by any means. Putin and his political allies insisted that the opposition was prepared to falsify the election results to delegitimize the authorities.

A few days before the presidential elections, Putin stated that his opponents were ready 'to use certain mechanisms' which would prove that the elections were rigged. 'They [the members of opposition] will themselves be filling in ballots, they will be controlling it [the course of elections], and then they will assert [that there was fraud at the elections] themselves. We can already see it, we already know it' (Polunin, 2012). This statement was a pre-emptive step to deal with the possible appearance of videos about electoral procedure violations, as happened with the parliamentary elections of December 2011. If such videos did appear, Putin's remarks would have prepared the ground for delegitimizing them. If they did not, the legitimacy both of the elections, and of Putin's return to the presidency, would be self-evident. The majority would be entitled to impose its will on the minority in this supposedly democratic state. By claiming subversive actions on the part of the opposition, Putin aimed to undermine any criticism of the elections.

This portrayal of Putin as spokesperson for the patriotic 'majority' was strengthened even more during his pre-election appearance in the Luzhniki stadium, which was timed to coincide with the Defender of the Fatherland Day on 23 February 2012. The rally was preceded by a rally entitled '*Zashchitim stranu!*' ('*[We will] defend the country!*'). In his opening speech Leont'ev stressed that Putin was the real saviour of the country, which would otherwise fall victim to a 'national suicide' every bit as cataclysmic as the collapse of the Soviet Union in 1991 (Radio Ėkho Moskvy, 2012). Reflecting the symbolic meaning of the day on which the rally was taking place, Putin's speech was framed by a call for national unity, and pursued a twofold goal. Above all, Putin pointed to the community of 'the people' which he led, which was open to everyone who shared its patriotic values and was ready to defend them. He then criticized the unreliable minority, which was striving to act against the interests of its own country:

> The main thing is that we are together. We are a multi-ethnic, but single and powerful nation. I want to tell you that we do not reject anyone, do not attach labels (*shel'muem*) or push anyone away. On the contrary, we urge everyone to unite for our country, certainly all those who consider our Russia their own country, who are ready to take care of it, value it, and believe in it. And we ask everyone not to look out at the

distant horizon (ne zagliadyvat' za bugor) ... [not to] go abroad and not to cheat at the expense of our Motherland, but to be together with us, work for it and its people and love the way we love it – with all our heart. (Sholomon84, 2012)

In this crucial remark, Putin reiterated some of the key points of the speech he had delivered in November 2007 at the high point of the parliamentary campaign, when he introduced the notorious idea of 'jackals who beg for scraps at foreign embassies'. The use of similar notions in 2012 demonstrated Putin's consistent use of anti-Western conspiracy theories in electoral strategies that sought to mobilize Russian society by dividing it into 'the people' and the subversive pro-Western minority.

Yet there were differences between the campaigns in 2007 and 2012. In 2007, anti-Western conspiracy theories were part of an elaborate and well-prepared campaign which delegitimized specific organizations and parties to ensure the smooth transfer of power from Putin to his chosen successor. The situation in 2012 was different. The campaign centred on Putin's return; this was the overarching narrative of Kremlin propaganda. At the same time, the protest movement, which erupted in December 2011, significantly radicalized the campaign, turning it into a crusade against the vague and undifferentiated 'orange threat' of the opposition 'from Bolotnaia'. This was heavily based on anti-Western conspiratorial rhetoric.

A corpus of anti-Western conspiratorial perceptions, which became the intellectual base of the 2012 campaign, was developed by public intellectuals in the 2000s. They depicted Russia as a besieged country perceived by the West as a mere repository of natural resources. At the same time, Putin's rhetoric combined conspiratorial allegations, which were based on the discourse produced by his 'support group', and appeals for national unity. The conspiratorial aspect of this rhetoric was mainly focused on the supposed threat represented by treacherous opposition politicians and irresponsible intellectuals (Malinova, 2012, p. 83). Every conspiratorial allegation used by Putin was aimed at delegitimizing the arguments of his political opponents and was disseminated by means of newspaper articles, blog posts and documentaries shown on state-aligned television channels. The campaign vividly juxtaposed the images of 'the real people' and the 'Other' by organizing an 'Anti-Orange' rally that mirrored the street activities of the opposition, as well as marches in support of Putin, both of which were widely covered in the media.

Conclusion

In autumn 2014, amid the Ukraine crisis, Viacheslav Volodin, Surkov's successor as first deputy of the Presidential administration, stated: 'If there's Putin, there's Russia; if there were no Putin, there would be no Russia' (Sivkova, 2014). Thus, the Kremlin's new ideologist revealed the extent to which the cult of Putin is pivotal for post-Soviet nation-building. The propaganda campaign that pervaded Russian society in 2014 helped create the illusion of an encircled nation that was led and protected solely by Putin. As this chapter has demonstrated, the first steps leading to this situation were taken back in the 2000s to secure the transfer of the presidency to Medvedev. Both electoral campaigns, in 2007–8 and 2011–12, were tests to see if the regime was able to preserve its leadership and patronal networks and prepared a set of ideas and policies to sustain the Kremlin's grip on power.

Constructed by spin doctors and intellectuals in Luzhniki and on Poklonnaia Hill, 'Putin's majority' of 2012 in fact consisted of diverse social groups that could not be convincingly brought together under a single descriptive term, nor even considered to exist in real life. Through biased television programming and sociological polls (Morar', 2007) produced by Kremlin-funded polling agencies, the architects of electoral campaigns created the image of an overwhelming majority of 'the people' who supported Putin's candidacy.

The image of Putin which appeared in the Kremlin-controlled media during the electoral campaigns consistently made him out to be a genuine 'people's politician'. His public appearances and the staged support from ordinary working people combined to establish his connection with 'real Russia' and sustain his leadership position. The campaign thus followed well-established populist tactics. Panizza describes the populist leader thus: (2005, p. 21): 'a political figure who seeks to be at the same time one of the people and their leader, the populist leader appears as an ordinary person with extraordinary attributes'. Attempts on the part of intellectuals loyal to the Kremlin to create an image of Putin which stressed his global importance, and to create a public cult around him, emphasized this 'extraordinary aspect' of a populist leader (Sedakov, Vernidub and Guseva, 2007). Moreover, Putin was presented as the embodiment of 'the people', who were expected to unite over the populist demands for sovereignty and independence from the West. This Manichean division of the population into in-groups and out-groups is another marker of the populist approach taken by Putin's team, an approach which was also practised by other populists across Europe (Mudde, 2007).

Research suggests (Colton and Hale, 2014) that the public response to this division has been fairly positive. Despite the drop in the country's economic performance and hence in personal incomes after 2008, many Russians continued to support Putin. This populist division of society, which was used once again during the presidential campaign of 2012 to ensure Putin's victory in what was a critical period for the regime, seems to have proved an efficient means of mobilizing citizens in support of Putin.

The 2007 parliamentary elections were grounded in Putin's personal popularity. The uncertainty of his political future after 2008 created the opportunity for alarmist appeals to protect the country from a 'plunder' which would be as catastrophic as the dramatic changes of the 1990s which, as we have discussed, were alleged to be connected to a 'Western conspiracy'. Seeing the 2007–8 electoral period as a crucial event in the fate of the regime, the ruling political elites prepared the necessary ideological background to justify Putin's continuation in power. Anti-Western conspiracy theories, which had been actively developed by Kremlin-aligned intellectuals with the aim of delegitimizing potential opposition, were an integral part of this project.

In contrast, the application of anti-Western conspiracy theories during the 2012 presidential campaign was an attempt to deal with the decrease in public support for Putin and his regime. The authorities had failed to note important shifts in society, and had to face the consequences of this failure when the protest demonstrations began after the 2011 parliamentary elections. Because it was so vague and fragmented, the idea of the 'Putin majority' had to be actively promoted again, and this was accomplished by means of an aggressive media campaign which took place in January–March 2012 and which demonized political opponents and civil activists. In short, anti-Western conspiratorial mythmaking became an essential part of electoral practices. It was used to provide a simple explanation of current events, shift responsibility for social and economic problems onto other social actors, and delegitimize political opponents. Numerous spin doctors and public intellectuals contributed to the anti-Western agenda. In charge of think tanks and publishing houses, they were able to initiate media campaigns and create conspiratorial schemes with the aim of helping the Kremlin achieve its political goals and, above all, securing Putin's victory in the presidential elections. Their power to divide the country will become even more obvious during the conflict in eastern Ukraine.

7
The War has Begun

The conflict in Ukraine and the annexation of Crimea in 2014 marked a watershed in post-Soviet Russian history. The Sochi Olympic Games, which were to celebrate the greatness of Putin's Russia, closed at the same time that blood was being shed in the centre of Kyiv. A day later, the Ukrainian president Yanukovich fled to Russia, and to fill the resulting power vacuum, Ukraine installed a 'revolutionary' interim government. The backlash in Russia came very quickly. Within a few months, the country had been divided into 'Us', those who allegedly supported the Kremlin's handling of the Ukraine crisis, and 'Them', those who were critical of Russia's involvement in the conflict, and of its annexation of Crimea a couple of weeks later. Indifference was not an acceptable position; in the view of the Kremlin, either you supported the authorities and their interpretation of events, according to which they were part of a Western plan to attack Russia, or you were considered to be an enemy. The Russian authorities, along with those intellectuals who sided with them, saw the new Ukrainian leaders as 'illegitimate Western puppets', and insisted they had no right to try to take control of Eastern Ukraine's rebel territories (TASS, 2014). Pro-Kremlin intellectuals regarded the Ukraine crisis as an act of war against Russia, aimed at getting rid of Putin and partitioning Russia into several puppet states under the control of the USA.

These narratives had a clear influence on public opinion; Putin's popularity rating reached its highest in the 16 years of his rule (Cullinane, 2015). At the same time, negative attitudes towards the West (i.e. the USA and the EU) also increased enormously (Mukhametshina, 2015). Popular support for the government and public hatred of the West helped the Russian authorities to demonize the opposition and downplay its importance on the domestic political stage. Putin's press secretary, Dmitry Peskov, called those who opposed the annexation of Crimea a 'nano-fifth column' supported by the West (Bershidsky, 2014), and this became a popular phrase used by many pro-Kremlin speakers to convey the idea that Western conspirators had yet again penetrated the country.

The use of a highly charged conspiratorial term by such a top-ranking politician to describe dissenting voices within the country reveals a major shift in the post-Soviet Russian conspiratorial discourse. As previous chapters demonstrated, anti-Western conspiracy theories had been gradually creeping from the margins into mainstream political discourse from 1991; but politicians of the rank of Peskov and Putin very rarely voiced conspiratorial ideas directly, leaving this job to public intellectuals and journalists. Moreover, conspiracy panics were spread tactically by the authorities, over short periods of time, in order to ensure that particular political goals were achieved. After 2014, this dramatically changed.

At the peak of the Ukraine crisis the Russian political elites, as well as the state-aligned media, started using conspiracy theories and making shameless accusations that their opponents, together with the West, were waging war against Russia. From the inception of the conflict up to late 2016, when the Russian authorities felt that the situation inside Russia had been brought under control, there was an overwhelming sense that the country was encircled by enemies (Jablokov, 2015). The events which unfolded between 2014 and 2016 revealed the entire set of ideas and methods applied by the Kremlin as part of its anti-Western conspiracy theories. After ten years of active investment in the creation of an anti-Western conspiratorial culture in Russia, the fruits of this work proved to be very useful. They reveal the huge potential that conspiracy theories have for the mobilization of Putin's supporters and the suppression of the opposition.

The Ukraine crisis has also become a supposedly legitimate reason for 'tightening the screws' in domestic policies. As scholars note, this was largely carried out because of the growing economic instability and the decrease in incomes within the country; this made 'co-opting' the opposition (Gel'man, 2016, p. 32) and taking control of society extremely difficult. The popular revolt against the corrupt authorities in Ukraine was interpreted by the Kremlin, with good reason, as a direct threat to its own domestic security. Therefore, the wave of repressive laws against non-state political actors, which began in 2012, continued throughout the 2014–16 period. The state has carried out several reforms of the law enforcement services aimed at suppressing revolt and has imposed harsher criminal punishments for dissenters.

Such actions were, nevertheless, just part of the arsenal of tools employed by the Kremlin to keep the country under control. The most important source of power and legitimacy for authoritarian leaders nowadays is the ability to manipulate information in such a way that it allows the authoritarian ruler to survive. This is particularly clear during economic downturns, when, as Guriev and Treisman (2015) discovered, the authoritarian leader sets out to increase the flow of state propaganda. The state-aligned television channels, which are the primary source of information for most Russians, played the most significant role in the discursive division of the nation in 2014–16 (Volkov and Goncharov, 2014). During the Ukraine crisis, the state-controlled media switched to a 24 hour 'propaganda mode', in which they portrayed both internal and external criticism of the authorities as part of the Western plan to destroy Russia. Hutchings and Szostek (2016) have concluded that anti-American narratives have been major plotlines in the coverage of the Ukrainian conflict on Russian television. The 'fifth column', 'national traitors' and 'Ukrainian fascists' became the main conspiratorial protagonists in news reports. As Borodina (2014) notes, the prolonged and aggressive anti-Ukraine campaign which has been aired continually on Russian television has pushed aside all other news stories, leaving Ukraine and the Crimea at the forefront of both domestic and international news. Less loyal media outlets were either disbanded or put under the strict control of staunch pro-Kremlin owners who had a direct impact on their news coverage (Fredheim, 2016). In spring 2014 the news broadcasts televised by the two state-aligned channels contained ten reports on Ukraine, each of which was seven to ten minutes long; the length of the news broadcasts also doubled. In other words, everything that the Russians watched on television was about Ukraine and it was presented in a way which was most favourable to the Kremlin's political goals.

This media campaign had a particular goal: to attract people who had previously been less interested in the consumption of news produced by state-aligned channels. The steady decline in viewer numbers for these channels was dangerous for the ruling elite as it was slowly eroding support for the Kremlin, while the opposition was getting more prominent. As Rogov argues (2016), the outbreak of the war and the fact that a clear enemy was appearing on screen attracted the audiences less engaged in politics and less informed about their specifics, which in turn increased Putin's support base among the electorate and helped mobilize the majority in his favour. As we shall see, the anti-Western conspiracy theories which were developed and disseminated over the latest fifteen years of Putin's rule were not in vain; on the contrary, they quickly morphed into the central element of this mobilization campaign.

This chapter will be looking primarily at news reports from the weekly programme *Vesti Nedeli*, which from autumn 2012 was hosted by Dmitrii Kiselev. There are several reasons for this. Firstly, anti-Western conspiratorial discourse in the Russian media space became so widespread between 2014 and 2016 that it needs to be narrowed down for analysis. Secondly, in the period of the Ukraine crisis, *Vesti Nedeli* has been one of the most popular news shows on Russian television (Meduza, 2016b). As a consequence, and given the popularity of television in the country, the conspiratorial ideas which were produced and reproduced in the programme rapidly spread across the country. Thirdly, Dmitrii Kiselev is the central figure in Russia's media elite (Schimpfossl and Yablokov, 2014) and has strong connections to the Kremlin. During the crisis in Ukraine he was promoted and became head of the state media holding Russia Today, which has under its umbrella the news channel of the same name; this is another prominent source of anti-Western conspiracy theories (Yablokov, 2015). The EU and the USA placed Kiselev on their sanctions list – one of the few Russian media personalities to be included – because of his active engagement in the production of anti-Western and anti-Ukrainian propaganda. All in all, this makes Kiselev and *Vesti Nedeli* particularly interesting cases through which to explore the conspiracy culture at the time of the Ukraine crisis.

Ukraine, 'The Puppet State'

Euromaidan, the protest of Ukrainians against president Yanukovich and his crony regime, was not only a matter of concern for the Ukrainian ex-President, but also for the Russian authorities. From the Russian perspective, signing the EU agreement would open the door to an influx of untaxed goods from the EU and bring Ukraine closer to the sphere of EU influence. This was seen by both the Ukrainian authorities and the protesters as the first step on the road to becoming part of the EU. It was meant to send a strong signal to the Europeanized element in Ukrainian society, which regarded the ever-present Russian influence as an undesirable hangover from the past (Snyder, 2015). Yanukovich's refusal to sign the EU agreement, and his decision to opt instead for an economic deal with Russia, reinforced by the repressive legislation of 16 January 2014, triggered clashes with the police and became one of the milestones in the process of overthrowing the regime (Wilson, 2014).

The rapid escalation of the conflict in Kyiv resulted in the defection of Yanukovich to Russia and the victory of the pro-US and pro-European forces. This was interpreted by the Russian authorities as evidence of a Western plan to interfere in the post-Soviet space and a potential threat to Russian security. In the aftermath of the February revolution in Kyiv, an image of the Ukrainian government as 'Other' was achieved by portraying Ukraine as Russia's main enemy and insisting that Ukraine's new revolutionary leadership was controlled by the US government. This, it seems, had the required result: in the polls, the USA and Ukraine currently occupy the top positions in Russia's list of adversaries (Levada-tsentr, 2017). Russian journalists and political elites created a connection between the new post-revolutionary Ukraine, whose leadership opposed the Russian establishment's support of Yanukovich, and Russia's geopolitical archenemy, the USA. A leaked tape of a conversation between the US ambassador to Ukraine, Geoffrey Pyatt, and Assistant Secretary of State, Victoria Nuland, in which they discussed possible members of the new Ukrainian government, became key evidence that the USA was in full control of Ukraine (BBC, 2014). The former Ukrainian political leadership – ex-prime minister Azarov and Yanukovich himself – reinforced this notion by describing the new leaders as 'American puppets' (BBC, 2015; RIA Novosti, 2016).

Russian state-aligned media continuously repeated and developed the idea of Ukraine as a 'puppet state' in their reports. Anonymous sources suggested that after the presidential elections the newly elected president, Petro Poroshenko, spent the night at the US embassy and that the ambassador convinced him to start the invasion of the Donbass and promised that its negative consequences would be downplayed in the Western press (Kiselev and Rozhkov, 2014b). Another set of reports suggested that the CIA and the White House stood behind the rise of the Ukrainian revolutionaries as well as the invasion of Eastern Ukraine, and had sent troops and money to support the Ukrainian forces (Kiselev, 2015a; Kiselev, 2016a). Kiselev's *Vesti Nedeli* suggested that the CIA had masterminded the attacks against rebellious Eastern Ukrainian regions and that the operation in Eastern Ukraine began after the CIA director visited Kyiv under a false name (RIA Novosti, 2014).

When the US Vice-President, Joe Biden, visited Kyiv, the *Vesti Nedeli* reporter mentioned the American flag waving over the Ukrainian parliament building, and the US Ambassador chairing a meeting with

Ukrainian deputies. Against the background of a shot of Biden with the words 'The Verkhovna Rada of Ukraine' (The Ukrainian Parliament) on show behind him, the reporter explained that the US Ambassador settled the US vice-president into the Ukrainian Speaker's chair, 'as if [he wanted] to demonstrate who really ruled the country' (Kiselev and Balitskii, 2014).

From 2014, an exceptional number of high profile Russian politicians gave statements asserting that there was an intimate relationship between the USA and the new Ukrainian government. For example, Nikolai Patrushev, head of the FSB from 1999 to 2008 and now Secretary of the Security Council, openly claimed that the USA was the main instigator of the Ukrainian conflict. For Patrushev, it was clear that the motive behind the Ukraine crisis was not a desire on the part of Ukrainians for the country to be more democratic; rather, it was about the USA's desire to create a new generation of Ukrainians who despised Russia and who would ensure that Ukraine was removed from Russia's sphere of influence. It was trying to bring this about by financing anti-Russian NGOs in Ukraine (Rostovskii, 2016).

During the Ukraine crisis, Patrushev has been the main conspiratorial spokesman of the Russian elites. His regular interviews provide a portal into the mind-set of the Kremlin bureaucrats. Patrushev interpreted the conflict as another step in the US plan to dismantle Russia, divide it up and acquire its natural resources (Egorov, 2014). In a twist, Ratnikov's 2006 story about 'Madeleine Albright's mind',[1] which posited that the US hated Russia for its abundance of natural resources, resurfaced in Patrushev's interviews. On several occasions, Patrushev referred to this story as if it were undisputed fact; the Kremlin's policies in Ukraine were hence justified, as they provided some protection from the American-led war against the Russian state (see Egorov, 2014; Chernenko, 2015). Propaganda videos released at that time reiterated Patrushev's point of view: Russia's actions were a defensive operation to prevent further escalation of the war against Russia itself. The makers of the videos suggested that the Ukraine crisis was a pretext for the USA to start World War 3, occupy Russia and confiscate its natural resources, which would allow the USA to prosper economically (Okeiamnet, 2014). Hence, the conspiratorial story which began as rhetoric, a means of criticizing the USA during the challenging period of the presidential succession from Putin to Medvedev in 2006–7, later developed into a mainstream tool used by

---

[1] See Chapter 4 for more details.

top-ranking Russian politicians to explain global politics (Etkind and Yablokov, 2017).

Kiselev's *Vesti Nedeli* also featured the US conspiracy against Ukraine and Russia to take over natural resources. In one of the programmes the presenter contended that the 'real' purpose of the Ukrainian military invasion of Eastern Ukraine in May 2014 was for the USA to gain control of the rich natural resources located in the Donbass region. A report broadcast on 18 May 2014 showed two maps: the first was of the territories in Ukraine with the allegedly richest natural resources, and the second was of the battleground in Eastern Ukraine. The two maps overlapped, showing that the centres of conflict between Ukrainian and separatist forces were located precisely in the areas most rich in resources. According to Kiselev, the appointment of Joe Biden's son, Hunter, to the board of the private Ukrainian oil and gas company *Burisma* (Risen, 2015) was a clear indication of the reasons behind the White House's interest in Ukrainian domestic affairs:

> The Americans act with Ukrainian nationalists like [Europeans] with aboriginals, as if [the Ukrainians] were a wild tribe. [The Americans] tell them about democracy, while thinking of [the Ukrainian] fossil fuels. It is a usual thing to wage wars for fossil fuels. However, it's not fashionable for Americans to do that. Let the aboriginals do that instead. (Kiselev and Bogdanov, 2014)

This quotation exemplifies the attitude of the pro-Kremlin Russian elite who, through conspiratorial discourse, seek to denigrate the importance and political/intellectual capability of the Ukrainian elite, as compared to those of Putin's Russia. In the narratives of Russian pro-state speakers, Ukrainians are not citizens of an independent nation, but rather as a mob controlled from abroad. This negative image of Ukrainians reflects some of the ideas enshrined in Surkov's theory of sovereign democracy which were implanted in the public consciousness in the 2000s. The close connection between the idea of Russia's greatness and the Russian elites' fear of losing control of Ukraine generated a wave of conspiracy panics which demonstrated the Kremlin's concern about losing part of its sphere of influence, and were aimed at demonizing Ukraine in the eyes of television audiences for Russia's political ends.

These powerful descriptions – of Ukraine as Russia's enemy, alien to the Russian nation, and of the new Ukrainian leadership, as under the control of the USA – were aimed at supporting the mainstream conspiracy theories. Ukraine's inability to protect its own independence, along with its new leadership's readiness to cooperate with Russia's rival, alienated Ukraine from the 'Russian people' and ensured that any cooperation with Ukraine would be regarded as national betrayal. Although Ukraine might seem to be a rather weak enemy in comparison with the economic and military might of Russia, various rhetorical tools were deployed to frame Ukraine as an external and dangerous 'Other'. In addition, the accusation on the part of the Russian leadership that the new Ukrainian authorities were allies of the USA served as justification for Russia's annexation of Crimea (Krym. Put' na rodinu, 2015). The state-aligned media and Russian politicians carried out a metaphorical division of the world, into nations which were allied to Russia, and those which were not; this was based on their relations with the USA.

The 'Selfish' Minority vs. The 'Patriots'

The dramatic division of Russian society into those who opposed both the annexation of the Crimea in March 2014 and Russia's military involvement in the Ukraine crisis, and those who supported them, became key to the increased popularity of Putin's policies during his third presidential term. Claiming the existence of a potentially disloyal minority whose political views radically differed from those of the majority of Russians who supported the regime, was a useful and clever move on the part of the Kremlin to justify its aggressive foreign policy and new authoritarian legislation by generating fear of domestic subversion. Putin himself contributed to this several times by making conspiratorial allusions about the opposition, which eventually developed into the supposed division between the loyal and supportive majority and the 'dangerous minority' supported by the West. He first spoke about the opposition in a key speech when the Crimea was accepted as a new Russian region in March 2014:

> Some Western politicians are already threatening us with not just sanctions but also the prospect of increasingly serious problems on the domestic front. I would like to know what it is they have in mind exactly: action by a fifth column, this disparate bunch of 'national traitors', or are they hoping to put us in a worsening social and economic situation so as to provoke public discontent? We consider such statements irresponsible and clearly aggressive in tone, and we will respond to them accordingly. (Putin, 2014)

The response on the part of the Russian authorities' state-aligned media and pro-state activists to dissenting views regarding Crimea and rebellious regions in Eastern Ukraine was swift and harsh. Many reports, websites and editorials about the opposition – disparate, corrupt, self-interested, loyal to the West – skyrocketed. Given the spike in Putin's popularity and the overwhelming support for his policies, it was not hard for various pro-state speakers to emphasize how small and alien the opposition was. Russian media and various pro-Kremlin speakers applied derogatory labels to those who were against the annexation of Crimea in March 2014: 'intelligentura' (a fusion of the Russian words intelligentsia and agency), the 'fifth column', 'traitors', 'aliens' (Kiselev and Rozhkov, 2014a). In addition, unknown Putin activists created a website under the title 'National traitors. The 5th column' that collected the names of all opposition activists and politicians critical of Russia's Ukraine policies (*Natsional-predateli Rossii. 5-ia kolonna*). The reaction to those who did not support the authorities has been harsh and aggressive, at least on the rhetorical level. Russian writer and politician Eduard Limonov called the opposition protesters 'lost people' whose 'miserable' loneliness, affection for the West and hatred of Putin made them 'aliens' in the country, and they should be expelled by the authorities (Limonov, 2014). Reference to the 'alien' nature of the Russian opposition later appeared in a campaign to publicly criticize those individuals who opposed the confrontation with Ukraine. The poster juxtaposed an image of an alien, taken from the popular Hollywood film of that name, with pictures of Russian opposition leaders, to serve as visual evidence of the 'otherness' of the Kremlin's critics (Glavplakat, 2014).

The Russian political leadership also contributed to the establishment of a conspiratorial notion of a 'fifth column' in official discourse. During a press conference on 18 December 2014, Putin emphasized that the 'fifth column' was a social force 'totally dependent on foreign authorities and acts in their interests'; yet again, he was legitimizing the use of a conspiratorial and negatively charged term in public discourse (Izvestiia, 2014). Although the Kremlin has a very peculiar understanding of the term 'democracy' which tends to suit its own ad hoc needs, Putin insisted that Russia is a democratic country with an official opposition and that it would be a mistake to merge all opposition activists into a single subversive group of internal enemies. This idea was expressed by Putin in, for example, a speech to the FSB in March 2015 which was reported by *Vesti Nedeli*. However, the line between the 'loyal opposition' and the subversive 'fifth column' tends to be drawn according to how close a particular opposition group is to the Western Special Services (i.e. CIA) (Kiselev, 2015c).

Another major defining marker of a person's loyalty to the nation is his or her attitude towards the economic sanctions against the Russian elites and companies. A report on 23 March 2014 about the reaction of the Russian political establishment to the first round of EU and US sanctions contrasted the unity of prominent Russian politicians with the 'cunning' actions of the opposition leaders, who allegedly supplied the US and EU with a list of people who would be subject to sanction. In the report's introduction, Kiselev spoke about the limited effect of the sanctions, which, he claimed, damaged only a small circle of businessmen who were personally loyal to Putin. However, he continued, the list of people under sanction was created 'in Moscow by our "fifth column", which seeks the support of the West and receives it. [Publisher and journalist] Parkhomenko, [opposition leader] Navalny – these are the heroes of that circle. Let's classify it as a result of complexes, and the absence of real popular support' (Kiselev and Popov, 2014a). In this way the threat from outside, initiated by the USA, was projected onto the domestic political scene and used against the opposition leaders.

The report itself featured interviews with several prominent Russian politicians who praised the annexation of Crimea. Much of the report consisted of interviews with the loyal political elite which demonstrated that the majority were on the side of the Kremlin. However, the journalist also noted that US President Obama released a new list of people under sanction soon after an article by Aleksei Navalny about the sanctions was published in *The New York Times*. The journalist insisted that this 'outrageous disloyalty' on the part of the Russian opposition surprised even the Americans: 'It is ill-mannered to criticize your own country abroad. There is a special term for the authors of the sanctions lists – "inside man". One way to translate this is a pointed gun, another – our man (A dlia sostaviteli spiskov est' spetsial'nyi termin – inside man. Odin perevod – navodchik, drugoi – svoi chelovek)' (Kiselev and Popov, 2014b).

Alliance with the West, and in particular with US foundations and intelligence, is used as a marker of the involvement of the opposition in the conspiracy against the Russian people. This is especially evident in the media representation of the leaders of the political opposition as a dangerous and conspiring minority. Television reports about the activities of the opposition, and about the anti-war marches, have sought to create the same negative image and compare Russian protesters with the activists who had overthrown Yanukovich's regime. Kiselev's report about the 'March for Peace' in September 2014 in Moscow opened with the reporter questioning the national loyalty of the protesters who came on the peace march. He then questioned why the protesters did not show support for the victims of the shelling of the cities in Donbass and did not protest against the murdered Russian journalists who died trying to tell the truth about the conflict. This served to detach the protesters from the supposed majority of Russians who supported the rebellious Donbass region. Kiselev's introductory remarks served to create a split in the unity of the opposition forces as well as to query the sincerity of their intentions. The march was described as an alliance of random forces, from LGBT activists to radical Russian nationalists, who did not have any specific demands apart from opposing the Kremlin's policies. One example of the way the protesters were cast as aliens can be seen in a quote from the march's manifesto calling for the withdrawal of the Russian government's counter sanctions against the EU, which had triggered high inflation in the country. Kiselev pointed out that the cancellation of the sanctions against Russia was not what the protesters wanted:

> They are not asking for them to be revoked. The sanctions against Russia are good and right. They are more concerned about Russia's response. They could have expressed it more briefly: return Italian sausages and French cheese to us. It'd be simpler and more honest. (Kiselev and Medvedev, 2014)

Many pro-state media reports on the opposition described it as a small and insignificant minority which was unable to gain the support of the Russian population. This rhetorical strategy was aimed at downplaying the importance of dissenting voices and deflecting attention from their arguments (Kiselev and Zarubin, 2016). At the same time the pro-Kremlin media strategy tried to explain why the opposition was so foreign to the Russian nation and why its opinions had to be countered by means of hostile political campaigns. Support for the Western sanctions and the new Ukrainian authorities turned the opposition into an internal 'Other' whose loyalty lay with the West. As Limonov put it: 'Liberals ... took the position of traitors, supporting the USA and the West in the war with Ukraine; this position is opposed to the opinion shared by the majority of Russian people' (Limonov, 2016).

Vesti Nedeli's attempt to separate the 'conspiring minority' of Russian opposition leaders from both the majority of the Russian people and the 'loyal' opposition was carried out against the background of supposedly very low popular support for the opposition leaders. Indeed, during the Ukraine crisis the popularity of the opposition parties did significantly drop (Levada-tsentr, 2016b). Various pro-state speakers explained that the most prominent leaders of the

Russian opposition were working with Western intelligence because the resources and power that the West could provide compensated for their lack of support from Russian voters. This is a clear example of how a conspiratorial populist discourse manifests itself in today's Russia. Although an extremely low rating indicates the opposition leaders' unpopularity among ordinary Russians, this does not prevent the authorities from seeking to ruin their reputation with conspiratorial allegations of close collaboration with US and EU intelligence.

One *Vesti Nedeli* report, broadcast on 26 April 2015, elaborated on Putin's idea of what constituted a 'healthy' political opposition and why those who sought the support of the West were not part of it. The report discussed the trip made by Mikhail Kas'ianov, the leader of the opposition party RPR PARNAS, to the USA to hand over a list of suggestions for further economic sanctions. Kiselev's opening statement made it seem as though Russia was the freest country in the world, where everyone had the freedom to speak out. According to Kiselev, a 'normal' opposition would seek support among the people and endeavour to convince them that its economic programme and leadership skills would enable it to run the country. Conversely, Russian opposition leaders did not choose to seek support from the Russian people, but instead travelled to Washington with a list of people on whom to impose sanctions (Kiselev, 2015b). This contrast between a 'healthy' and an 'anti-national, subversive opposition' exemplifies how the political opposition in Russia could be turned into a dangerous internal 'Other' and its reputation undermined by conspiratorial allegations.

Showing the opposition leaders' support of Ukrainian independence, and their criticism of the Russian intervention, is another way of portraying them as the internal 'Other' which is related to the dangerous and conspiring external 'Other', the West. A *Vesti Nedeli* report from 8 March 2015, which detailed the US Congress hearings on Ukraine and Russia, included a quotation from Russian chess player and politician Garry Kasparov, who described the Russian authorities as 'a cancerous growth', and asked the American Congress to 'place their bets' on new people. Kasparov's comment was followed by one by the journalist: 'Those people in Kyiv, on whom Americans put bets, started out by capturing governmental buildings and [throwing] Molotov cocktails. Soon they switched to tanks. A year later, according to the UN, there are six thousand people on the list of victims' (Kiselev and Bogdanov, 2015).

The Russian opposition's alliance with the new Ukrainian authorities, as well as with the US administration, was, for *Vesti Nedeli* journalists, evidence that the opposition leaders were prepared to assist in the destruction of Russia and the plunder of its resources, in exchange for being appointed leaders of the new country, just as the Ukrainian opposition became the new leaders of Ukraine after February 2014 (Kiselev and Zarubin, 2016). The *Vesti Nedeli* reports became a powerful political instrument in shaping domestic public opinion about the Kremlin's opponents. Particularly after 2012 they had a major influence on public opinion, improving the image of the Kremlin's authoritarian policies and turning Putin into an unassailable and uncontested national leader.

The 'People's' Leader and the 'Treacherous Elites'

One of the Russian authorities' objectives in relation to the Ukraine crisis was to increase Putin's popularity among different factions in Russian society. Encouraging people to 'rally around the flag' made it possible for the Kremlin to increase public support for the authorities even among groups which used to be critical of their actions (Greene and Robertson, 2017). From the middle of the Ukraine crisis Putin's popularity has been stable and heartfelt (Volkov, 2015; Frye et al., 2017).

The state-aligned media has found various ways of supporting the notion that there is overwhelming support for Putin, and that he is a man of 'the people'. Firstly, it has quoted pollsters who have supposedly demonstrated overwhelming public backing for the president. Secondly, it has shown images of happy crowds gathered at events attended by Putin. For example, the *Vesti Nedeli* report about a concert on the Day of Russia in June 2015 stated that every centimetre of Red Square was filled with people celebrating Russia's independence and glory. The total turnout was an unexpected forty thousand. The report depicted Crimea as an inseparable part of Russia, and resistance to attacks by the West – the sanctions imposed on Russia, for example, and the West's criticism of the war in Ukraine – served as the basis for solidarity among Russians who pledged their support for Putin. The author of this report quoted Putin as saying: 'Nobody has ever managed to decode Russia and shift its standards. They can't excommunicate us, turn us away, isolate us from our roots and origins' (Kiselev and Zarubin, 2015). These conspiratorial allusions also helped to boost societal cohesion and serve nation-building practices. In contrast to the divided Ukrainian nation, a 'failed state' (The New Times, 2014; Korovin, 2015) as pro-Kremlin speakers described it, the Russian people stood united behind its leader and were ready to protect the nation's prosperity and security.

The notion that 'the Russian people' were a united community loyal to the leader was also conveyed in reports about the so-called Antimaidan movement. The ideological approach of this recently created movement, led by Nikolai Starikov, was solely based on anti-Western conspiracy theories. The people attending the Day of Russia celebration and the Antimaidan rallies were depicted by the state-aligned media as the 'real' Russian people loyal to Putin. One *Vesti Nedeli* report stated that while ten thousand people had been expected to attend the rally, fifty thousand people turned up, representing seventy-two regions, which was almost all of Russia (Kiselev and Skabeeva, 2015a). A report on Channel One also emphasized the number of people who came both from the Russian regions and from Ukraine (Batukhov, 2015). The unifying mantra at these marches was resistance to Western attempts to undermine Russian statehood and Putin. The visual depictions of the people served to demonstrate the overwhelming support for the authorities in the face of the biggest military clash with the West in the post-Soviet era. Thus, the 'Antimaidan' march created the image of 'truly patriotic Russians', the proactive majority of the 'people' ready to defend the country from any 'colour revolutions' and American conspiracy. Starikov drew attention to the shadow of American intelligence which was cast over the events in Kyiv and insisted that Euromaidan represented the threat to overthrow Russia and instigate revolution. In Starikov's view, the pro-state rallies demonstrated the capability of Russian society to protect itself from foreign invasion and represent real opposition to the government; he contrasted them with the 'fifth column' of Russia haters whose goal was to destroy Russia rather than improve the lives of its people.

In the same conspiratorial fashion, Western criticism of Russia's actions in Ukraine, and of Putin personally, was treated as part of the Western war against Russia. This was particularly clear in the report broadcast on 31 January 2016 by *Vesti Nedeli*. The BBC documentary 'Putin's Secret Reaches', which argued that Putin has substantial financial assets, was taken as yet more proof that the Americans were behind the media attacks on Russia, and was used to justify further criticism of the Western media. Statements made by the US Treasury official Adam Szubin in a film about supposed corruption on the part of the Russian president, were taken as evidence of the White House's plan to cause unrest in Russia before the parliamentary elections in September 2016. The presenter claimed that the US official's accusations were not grounded in any evidence, but were simply a way of tarnishing Putin's reputation, which would make it easier for the opposition to start a revolution. Again, this was likened to the situation in Ukraine in 2014 (Kiselev, 2016b). Resistance to the US-led New World Order has been adopted as the best means of strengthening Putin's popularity across the world. Kiselev said of the media campaign to smear the presidential image:

> Putin is like a bone lodged in their throat. He hampers their plans to start wars based on false allegations, the terms of peace in Iraq; hinders them from destroying countries, just as they did in Libya. Putin prevents the US placing the world under its control, because he doesn't give up. (Kiselev, 2016b)

Traitors are in the Kremlin

In the harshest period of the conflict between Russia and Ukraine, in the autumn of 2014, the elite's support of Russia's Ukrainian policy, as well as its loyalty to Putin, were unexpectedly questioned by the most ardent authors of anti-Western conspiracy theories. The limited and largely covert involvement of Russian forces in eastern Ukraine triggered criticism on the part of those who wanted immediate annexation of the region, which would thereafter be called Novorossiia. The regions of eastern and southern Ukraine, which had been part of the Russian Empire, were seen by anti-Western Russian philosophers as a major battleground with the West (Laruelle, 2016b). The Kremlin used the idea of Novorossiia to justify both the federalization of Ukraine and Russia's resistance to the Ukrainian authorities. Use of this term in mainstream Russian political and media discourse was to a large extent an instrument of propaganda, and it faded away after 2015 (O'Loughlin, Toal and Kolosov, 2017). All the same, for nationalists the idea of Novorossiia remained hugely important; for them it signified liberation from capitalism and the onset of a conservative revolution in Russia (Laruelle, 2016a). Some, such as Dugin, saw it as the start of the long-awaited 'war of the continents'; for others, it represented the start of a new cold war (Akopov, 2014; Balmforth, 2014). Yet none of this was on the Kremlin's agenda.

Active supporters of Novorossiia – most notably, Dugin, and Igor' Strelkov, the notorious commander of pro-Russian rebels in the Donbass and Crimea – suggested that a 'fifth column' of pro-US supporters had been working in Putin's government. Dugin extended this idea, introducing another term – the 'sixth column' – to draw a distinction between street opposition activists like Aleksei Navalny, and high-ranking bureaucrats in Putin's cabinet who were secretly plotting against him and undermining his policies. Dugin claimed that the biggest threat from this cabal of pro-Western actors, which included top managers of state-run corporations, supposedly loyal oligarchs and 'enlightened bureaucrats', was that they would stop Putin from initiating anti-Western policies and revitalizing Russian identity. '[The sixth column] is invisible, cowardly, ignoble, self-confident; it is an integral element in the regime's institutes, is well-organized, and closely follows the plan developed by the West' (Dugin, 2014). Eventually, Dugin accused the 'lunar Putin' – the supposedly pro-Western version of the Russian leader – of exchanging the support for Novorossiia for the deal with the West. After that statement, he lost his chair at Moscow State University (Wilson, 2014, p.186).

A few months after the publication of Dugin's article, Stelkov, who had just returned from the Donbass, accused the political establishment of undermining the rebels in eastern Ukraine. He claimed that the high-ranking bureaucrats responsible for the Kremlin's foreign policy had put forward arguments for a peaceful solution to the Ukraine crisis. The Minsk Agreements aimed at settling the peace in the rebellious territories, and the failure to use the military in southern and eastern Ukraine, had made it possible for the West to deliver military forces and ammunition to Ukraine. In Strelkov's opinion, the role of the 'fifth column' was to seize power and overthrow Putin in accordance with orders from the West, which threatened to confiscate the assets held by its members in Western banks if they did not comply (Strelkov, 2014). In December 2014 Strelkov named Surkov, who had been appointed by the Kremlin in 2014 to negotiate the terms of peace in Ukraine with European and US leaders, as one of the high-ranking bureaucrats working in consort with the West (Rosbalt, 2014).

The application of conspiracy theories by the Russian elite to the domestic situation demonstrates a number of interesting aspects about the country's tangled politics. The criticisms levelled against Surkov and Putin show that the hard-line producers of anti-Western narratives, despite being part of the conservative elite and in some cases recruited by the Kremlin to support its policies, tried to spread, albeit unsuccessfully, negative ideas about the beliefs and activities of other elite members. Attempts on the part of Strelkov and Dugin to accuse Surkov and other liberal-minded members of Putin's close circle of acting in the interests of the West is a sign of clashes within the Russian establishment.

The annexation of Crimea, and the application of international sanctions, did have negative consequences for the Russian political and economic elite, which had been well integrated into the global economy. Accordingly, some members of the elite voiced concern over the escalation of the Russia–West conflict and called for a peaceful solution (Sukhotin, 2014). Yet most members of the Russian establishment showed no sign of dissent and were strong supporters of the regime (Volkov, 2016). The conflict in Ukraine made the Kremlin hard-liners more powerful, and further isolation of Russia from the West would have been to their benefit (Krastev and Leonard, 2014). According to this paradigm, a retreat from the conflict, and the possibility of a peaceful solution, could have been seen by people like Dugin and Strelkov as a failure on the part of the hard-liners and a big climb-down in the conflict with the West.

Despite the blatant conspiratorial rhetoric which appeared throughout the media, genuine supporters of conspiracy theories do not play a major role in decision-making on important matters, unless their views benefit the Kremlin's plans. Throughout this book, I have shown how the Russian elites use conspiratorial discourse as an instrument for securing support and legitimizing their actions. The Ukraine crisis is no exception: conspiracy theories have been applied by authorities tactically and instrumentally to achieve their goals. Yet while some members of Putin's elite openly admit their belief in these theories, they rarely become the rationale of Kremlin policies. For example, Putin's economic adviser, Sergei Glaz'ev, accuses the 'small group of people in Putin's government' who devise the country's economic policy of being agents of the West 'serv[ing] the interests of banks and financial speculators' (Adrianova, 2016). In retaliation, he proposes to isolate Russia from global financial markets and ensure that it does not use the US dollar in its transactions (Glaz'ev, 2016). Glaz'ev was allegedly involved in instigating public unrest in eastern Ukraine and the Crimea in 2014: at that point, his reputation as the pre-eminent anti-Western hawk was used to ensure public support of Kremlin policies in the rebellious Ukrainian regions of Donetsk and Luhanks and in Crimea (Meduza, 2016a). Yet, his radical economic views, which would arguably destroy Russia's economy if they were actually implemented, seem too detached from reality even for the Kremlin. Accordingly, his advice remains on paper.

Seek and Destroy:
The Conspiratorial Legitimization of the New Laws

The crisis in Ukraine triggered another wave of repressions which furthered the authoritarian trend following the 2012 elections. In December 2013, amidst the growing conflict in Kyiv, Putin signed a law which criminalized calls for Russia's disintegration (Meduza, 2016c). Putin's later proposals for federalization in Ukraine and autonomy for Donbass backfired domestically. Similar movements reemerged in the Russian regions, such as Kuban' and Novosibirsk, demanding more autonomy (Podrobnosti, 2014; TSN, 2014). These were perceived by conspiracy theorists as the subversive acts of Russia's enemies, and Starikov's followers called for the imprisonment of the people behind the movements. Putin's remark that the Internet was a 'CIA project' (MacAskill, 2014) served to kick-start the Kremlin's offensive against the Internet industry (Soldatov and Borogan, 2015). Putin's aides, including Patrushev, regularly suggested that the Internet was used by Russia's rivals to undermine the country's statehood and therefore should be closely controlled (Kommersant, 2017).

The most conspiratorial of the new laws related, once again, to legislation on NGOs, which the Kremlin saw as instrumental in overthrowing the Yanukovich regime. Even though some changes to the law on NGOs took place shortly after Putin's return to the Kremlin in 2012, another more recent cycle of repressive laws was justified by the escalation of the Ukraine crisis and the desire of politicians to protect Russia from 'external threat' by 'undesirable organizations' (Koshkin, 2015). The perception of foreign NGOs as a direct threat to internal security was the starting point for this new round of legislative amendments. Valentina Matveenko, Head of the Council of Federation which was formally behind the introduction of the new legislation, claimed unequivocally that the purpose of these organizations was to undermine the internal stability of the State and had brought coups d'etats in the countries where they had previous been active (i.e. Libya, Ukraine) (TASS, 2015).

Putin signed the law on so-called 'undesirable organizations' in May 2015. It granted the General Prosecutor's office the right to close any foreign organization which the Russian authorities considered dangerous. One of the Duma deputies immediately requested that the Russian security services check out the *Carnegie Foundation*, *Amnesty International*, *Human Rights Watch*, *Transparency International* and *Memorial Foundation* (Makutina, Tagaeva and Khimshishvili, 2015).

In June 2015, a member of the Council of the Federation introduced the so-called 'patriotic stop-list', which included twelve organizations that were mostly from the USA. The grounds on which organizations were to be included in the list were not clear; indeed, the senators pointed out that the information about the 'subversive activities' of these foundations had come 'from undisclosed, but various sources' (Korchenkova and Goriashko, 2015a). During the debates on the new law at the Council of the Federation in July 2015 it was revealed that the senators had consulted the General Prosecutor and the FSB before pushing the initiative forward (Bocharova, 2015).

The new media campaign against foreign foundations replicated the tactics which had been used during the periods when the anti-NGO legislation was first proposed in 2005, and when it was introduced in 2013. As in previous years it relied heavily on anti-Western conspiracy theories broadcast by the major television channels and pro-Kremlin experts. Starting from December 2014, *Vesti Nedeli* depicted these organizations as a major threat to internal security (see, for example, Kiseleva and Liadov, 2015). It paid particular attention to the *National Endowment for Democracy* (NED), a foundation closely related to the US Republican Party. This was the first of the American foundations to be banned in Russia under the new law. Even before the initiative was introduced in parliament, Russian television had started depicting this foundation as a cover for the CIA and a menace to domestic order. The first report provided by *Vesti Nedeli* in October 2014 covered a conference of the Russian opposition in Prague which was attended by representatives of the NED, and described the foundation as a major donor to opposition organizations in Ukraine, Libya and Syria, and as the 'wallet' of the State Department and Congress (Kiselev and Popov, 2014b). According to *Vesti Nedeli*, from 2014 the NED had begun to focus on Russia, and the Russian opposition came to Prague to present their ideas for 'undermining' the country from within. Furthermore, it went on to assert that the NED was behind all of the regime collapses which the Kremlin considered to have been successful over the past decade, such as Georgia, Ukraine, Libya and many others; that the techniques of 'colour revolutions' worked; and that these techniques were regularly implemented by the USA against its enemies.

Again, the similarities between the campaign against foundations in 2015 and the previous campaign against NGOs are striking. In the middle of the campaign against NGOs the Rossiia channel broadcast a two-hour talk-show and documentary entitled 'Revolution on demand', which was concerned with the 'colour revolutions' in

Lithuania in 1991, Ukraine in 2014 and Macedonia in 2015. The presenter, Evgenii Popov, who had also reported on the NED meeting in Prague, focused on three events: the protests at the Vilnius television centre in Lithuania in January 1991, which were broken up by Soviet special forces; the Euromaidan protest in 2014; and the rallies against the Macedonian prime minister in Skopje in the summer of 2015. Popov portrayed them all as part of the same plan to extend US dominance around the world with the help of 'colour revolutions'. The programme's anchor, unequivocally following the conspiracists' approach, pointed out, approvingly, that the documentary created the impression that all three revolts were all 'one big event', and illustrated this point by reference to the similarity of the technologies which were used in the protests in Lithuania, Ukraine and Macedonia (Spetsial'nyi korrespondent: Revolutsiia na zakaz, 2015).

One of the speakers in the documentary, a Lithuanian journalist, admitted that a high-ranking US spy, who was stationed in Vilnius before the 1991 events, acknowledged that US troops were already in the country by the end of *perestroika*, and were involved in preparing the riot and promoting the independence of Lithuania. The inclusion of Vilnius in the documentary is crucial for understanding how the conspiratorial discourse spread during the post-Soviet period, and how its main tenets made it so convincing. As discussed in previous chapters, the notion that the independence movements in the Baltic states were encouraged by US espionage networks is central to the post-Soviet anti-Western conspiratorial discourse. This plot line, which connected Vilnius, Kyiv and Skopje, suggested that the West was behind the bloodshed caused by these protests; this meant that the regime changes in those countries placed them all in the same position, as victims of the USA's lust for power. Popular revolts against corrupt and oppressive regimes, even if they are justified, are presented as the results of brainwashing techniques on the part of 'Western sponsors'; this justifies the removal of political opponents within those regimes. In this way, journalists have been preparing the ground for the Kremlin's approach to future protests in Russia against government corruption, following the same violent methods that were applied during the street rallies in spring 2017 (Kremlin.ru, 2017).

As she had done in 2012, Veronika Krasheninnikova provided an expert opinion on the nature of foreign NGO activities. All organizations on the aforementioned list were funded by the CIA and directly involved in making 'colour revolutions' (Korchenkova and Goriashko, 2015b). As non-governmental organizations, they received funding from Western governments, and fulfilled the latter's aim of undermining Russian statehood and defence (Kuksenkova, 2015). Other pro-Kremlin speakers referred to the American left-wing website *CounterPunch*, which published a scathing article about NED (Lendman, 2015). The article, by an American journalist, was a useful reference point for pro-Kremlin intellectuals. A Russian website called, strikingly, 'Antimaidan', posted two interviews with pro-Kremlin experts who referred to the *CounterPunch* article, both of whom praised the Kremlin's efforts to prevent the regime from being overthrown as Ukraine's had been. One of these experts noted that the head of the Russian department in NED is Nadia Diuk, who came from a family of Ukrainian nationalists who had fought against the Soviet Union. This, it was claimed, indicates the real reasons for NED's active engagement with Russia, and Ukraine's involvement in the conspiracy against Russia (Antimaidan, 2015).

All major television channels covered the news of NED's shutdown, quoting the official statement by the General Prosecutor's Office, which accused the organization of subversion against the electoral outcomes and defamation of the Russian state (Channel One, 2015; Channel Five, 2015). This official, yet conspiratorial, statement has been crucial in framing public perception of the organization. However, the key conspiratorial reading was yet again provided by Kiselev's programme.

One week before Putin signed the new law into being, *Vesti Nedeli* broadcast a report about NED's involvement in Russian domestic affairs. It claimed that its funding was increased after the events in Ukraine, that Russia was now its focus of attention, and that it had chosen to support several opposition leaders and organizations (Kiselev and Skabeeva, 2015b). The report's line of argument was somewhat disjointed. After mentioning NED's financing of LGBT activists in Arkhangelsk, the reporter switched to discussing a photograph from the 'Eternal Regiment' march on 9 May 2015 in which people carried pictures of Soviet soldiers in the Second World War, after which several posters of veterans were dumped in a rubbish bin. A rumour circulated among Russians critical of the Kremlin's actions that the people who had come to the parade had been paid to attend. The journalist tried to provide her explanation of that story. Despite providing no proof for her assertion, the reporter insisted that the NED was behind the event: '... Someone apparently tried to galvanize society (using the terminology of NED). Here it is – the evidence ... The liberals went ballistic: The Eternal Regiment is the Kremlin's show-piece' (Kiselev and Skabeeva, 2015b). The claim that the NED had an interest in undermining Russians' unity over the victory in the Second World War – the basis of social cohesion in post-Soviet Russia – supported and perpetuated the conspiratorial propagandist notion of constant anti-Russian attacks by the West.

Conclusion

Russian politics appear to have changed after Putin's return to the Kremlin in 2012 (Gel'man, 2016), when there was a more authoritarian approach and the authorities started to apply conspiracy theories to domestic politics more regularly. Yet, the Ukrainian conflict was an exceptional stage in this process. The mass production and consumption of anti-Western conspiracy theories have become the norm of everyday Russian life. The events in Kyiv – violent clashes with the police, the ousting of the legitimate president Yanukovich, and the conflicts in the Ukrainian regions – served as perfect visual evidence to support Russian fears of a potential revolution initiated by external forces. The images of the 'colour revolution', which first appeared in 2004, and the possible cost of the events to the Russian nation, became still more powerful when television channels broadcast images of policemen being burned alive and the skeletal, shelled blocks of buildings in Donetsk.

The simplicity of conspiratorial explanations and the clear-cut division of the world into the 'righteous Russians' and the 'cunning Americans' who were working in consort with 'bloody Ukrainian fascists' helped shape the state ideology of Putin's regime at a critical moment, when the president's popularity was steadily declining (Kolesnikov, 2015). The state-aligned media's adoption of a propaganda approach helped the Kremlin to ensure public support for its actions, justify the new round of authoritarian legislation and the attempt to further isolate the country from foreign influence, and encourage acceptance of the hardships endured by the masses as the economy declined. In addition, the call to rally around 'Putin's flag' was strong enough to guarantee the success of the ruling party in the parliamentary elections of 2016 and prepared the public for Putin's next presidential term. Both election campaigns – the parliamentary campaign of 2015 and the presidential campaign of 2016 – are notable for the absence of traditional pre-election fear-mongering: the terrible events in Ukraine rendered any more fear-mongering unnecessary.

The Ukraine crisis produced a peculiar phenomenon: for the first time in seventeen years top-ranking politicians, including Putin himself, started to regularly voice conspiratorial notions in public. The idea that the opposition works closely with foreign intelligence, that the fall of oil prices was consciously brought about by the USA and Saudi Arabia in order to damage Russia (Lenta, 2014), or that 'someone' is harvesting biological materials from the Russians (Moldes, 2017), are no longer merely statements made by public intellectuals, but now feature strongly in Putin's speeches. Perhaps it is this shift in Putin's rhetoric, and his shameless attempts to spread conspiratorial panics, that led Angela Merkel to suggest that he has 'lost touch with reality' (Paterson, 2014).

Seeing Russia's elites as simply paranoid is not sufficient to understand what really goes on in Putin's Russia. The emergency in Ukraine, and the need to defend Russian interests there, has opened many opportunities for the authors of conspiracy theories. They planted the seeds of their approach in 1991; some of these have now turned into fruit which the Kremlin has reaped, most effectively since the conflict began. Yet some conspiratorial ideas are too revolutionary even for the Kremlin, and do not match its agenda and tactical goals. People like Glaz'ev and Dugin, for example, may prove to be instrumental in producing narratives to convince Russians that the West is against them. They might even try to use some misconceptions which are still held by Russian elites about the global economy and foreign affairs (Etkind and Yablokov, 2017) in order to make their messages sound more convincing. However, they are too excessively devoted to conspiracies to be part of the rational and cynical Russian politics. As Fyodor Lukyanov notices (2016), the idea that the West is engaged in an ongoing battle against Russia can be accepted and used by the Kremlin elites as it helps them overcome the identity crisis experienced by Russians after 1991. Yet it has limitations, and these hinder the Kremlin's attempt to find its place in today's world order. The conflicts in Syria and, most importantly, Russia's meddling in the US and French elections in 2016–17, both of which triggered the fears of a global 'Russian' conspiracy against democracies, might be a solution to this problem. Projecting Russia's important standing in the world, via anti-Russian conspiracy theories and modern technologies, is, certainly, an elegant way of trying to restore its status as a great power.

Conclusion

In 2012 Vladimir Yakunin, then president of Russian Railway, professor of political science at Moscow State University and owner of a luxurious mansion which included a separate building for fur coats, gave a talk to students at Moscow State University entitled 'The new global class and challenges to humankind'. This revolved around one idea: the West is building a New World Order and if Russia wants to survive as a great state, it has to acknowledge this, resist it and isolate itself, relying only on its natural resources for survival. Yakunin's belief is that the world is ruled by a group consisting of its eight most powerful individuals, who meet in a secret room in the Empire State Building in New York (RUSRANDru, 2012). While it was somewhat surprising to hear about the existence of this global conspiracy from a member of Putin's inner circle (Dawisha, 2015), it was not totally unexpected.

In the years following the collapse of the Soviet Union, anti-Western conspiracy theories gradually moved from the political margins to the centre of official political discourse. By 2017, the image of the West as the conspiring 'Other' had become a crucial element of this discourse and was regularly used by political elites, including top-level politicians, to gain public support for their actions and to delegitimize the opposition. This process of bringing anti-Western conspiracy theories into the mainstream began in the mid 2000s. Major developments in Russian politics in the 2000s demonstrate that Fenster's understanding of conspiracy theories as a populist approach of power is valid not only in relation to US politics, but can also shed light on political developments in post-Communist societies.

Several scholars have noted that the current Russian political regime lacks any clear ideological underpinnings (Krastev, 2011; Shevtsova,

2015). This makes it more flexible than a totalitarian regime would be; it allows citizens to do business, travel abroad and enjoy a somewhat unlimited self-expression. In addition, a positive economic dynamic and the growth of wealth in the 2000s contributed to the popularity of Putin's policies. However, as the second term of Putin's presidency approached its end in 2008, against the background of a wave of 'colour revolutions' in the CIS countries, the political establishment became concerned about the future, and made the preservation of Putin's power its major task. As part of this process, with the support of loyal public intellectuals, the Kremlin formulated a powerful narrative which juxtaposed the Russian nation with the West, from whose intrigues only Putin could protect Russia. This stance has been turned into the main ideological crux of the regime.

Daniel Treisman (2011, p. 256) has pointed out that the ruling elites in post-Communist Russia have always kept a close eye on the results of opinion polls; under Putin and Medvedev this tendency became even more pronounced as all major political decisions had, somehow, to be reconciled with the public mood. This concern with public opinion has been reflected in the constant populist appeals on the part of political leaders to the majority of Russians. This tendency peaked in the 2007–8 and 2011–12 electoral cycles when the so-called 'Putin majority' became a significant factor in domestic politics. Hence in the 2000s, widespread approval of Putin became a key tool for legitimizing the policies introduced by the Kremlin and securing its control over the country. From 2014 to 2016, when the Ukraine crisis was at its height, the imagined 'majority' turned into a real one as support for the Kremlin skyrocketed. Winning the 'war of the West against Russia' in Ukraine, and 'returning Crimea to Russia', proved to be strong enough incentives to bring together different strata and different generations of Russians.

In official discourse, Putin was represented as the only possible leader and even the embodiment of 'the Russian people', whose interests and demands he allegedly fulfilled. Putin's rhetoric was aimed at gathering together different social elements into the broad category of the 'Putin majority'. At the beginning of the 2000s, public demand was for a strong, stable state, and greater social equality. Putin's administrative reforms and attacks on the oligarchs not only partially fulfilled the demand, but also established Putin's authority. From the mid 2000s, the maintenance of economic and political stability in the country was the key issue for many Russians. Accordingly, pro-Kremlin intellectuals and politicians linked the economic growth of the 2000s with the image of Putin as a successful leader. Hence the popular demand to preserve stability was bound up with the need to keep the current ruling elites in power. This goal was achieved by means of the suppression of democratic institutions and attacks on civil society.

The transition towards greater authoritarianism in the mid 2000s was accompanied by a discourse which contrasted the 'Putin majority' to the minority of dissenters who disagreed with the Kremlin's political agenda. Since 2004, dissenting voices have been seen as the 'subversive', 'conspiring' Other, something alien to the Russian nation and more loyal to the West than to Russia. This division in Russian society, based on a conspiratorial reading of both past and current events, gradually evolved into a lens through which Russian domestic developments were seen. With Putin's return to the Kremlin in 2012 the anti-Western conspiracy theories turned into one of the key tools for explaining the need for new legislative initiatives and the suppression of the opposition.

The Kremlin's reaction to the Ukraine crisis provides a clear illustration of how essential anti-Western conspiracy theories have become for the political establishment in Russia. Putin's appeal to the Council of the Federation on 1 March 2014 for permission to deploy military force in Ukraine was explained by the Council's members as a response to the threat of a US invasion of Ukraine, and was supported unanimously (The Council of Federation, 2014). The media campaign supporting Russia's policies in Ukraine has been framed by pro-Kremlin politicians and media as a retaliation against the collapse of the Soviet Union in 1991, which is now said to have been organized by the West. Through the press and television talk shows, public intellectuals and politicians loyal to the Kremlin have interpreted the Euromaidan movement as the outcome of subversive Western actions aimed at brainwashing Ukrainian citizens and turning them against Russia. The new government of Ukraine, under the leadership of Petro Poroshenko, has been described as a 'fascist government' under the protection of the CIA. The intervention in Crimea has been justified by the need to protect Russian 'compatriots' from extreme Ukrainian nationalists backed by the West and the NATO fleet. Crimea's annexation has been described in the state-aligned press as the end of the New World Order in Russia and a key step towards the construction of the Russian nation (Remizov, 2014). The concepts elaborated by US right-wing conspiracy theorists since the mid 2010s have found a place in the rhetoric of Russia's mainstream intellectuals and politicians.

The impact of events in Ukraine on Russian domestic policies is at least as significant as the shock experienced by Kremlin officials in 2004 during the 'Orange Revolution' in Kyiv. Thirteen years ago, the unrest in Kyiv sparked the 'weaponization' of anti-Western conspiracy theories against political opponents. In 2014, it has become a 'weapon of mass destruction' deployed by the loyal Kremlin media to destroy or suppress opposition in the country.

The political changes in Russia in the decade between the two Ukrainian revolutions, and the Russian political elites' response to them, allows us to evaluate the role played by anti-Western conspiracy theories in post-Soviet political development. As discussed throughout the book, the change of regime in Ukraine in 2004 was an important factor in triggering a dramatic increase in the use of conspiracy theories as an instrument of social cohesion. These ideas did not appear out of the blue: the notion of a Western conspiracy, as explained in Chapter 1, was a key part of Russian intellectual life for more than two centuries. However, after 1991 it became an important element of the country's political ideology, exploiting people's nostalgia for Russia's past greatness, justifying the authoritarian turn and providing a basis for social cohesion and popular mobilization. In the 2000s, growing nostalgia for the Soviet Union and the absence of public consensus about events of the recent past allowed the Kremlin to stimulate national cohesion based on the fears of conspiracy. As Chapter 3 demonstrates, Russia's political and intellectual elites in the 2000s made a conspiratorial understanding of the Soviet collapse a crucial feature of domestic policies, portraying internal opposition to the Kremlin as a 'fifth column' conspiring against the Russian nation. Putin's definition of the Soviet collapse as 'a major geopolitical disaster' transformed the attitude of ordinary Russians towards the event into a key marker of loyalty to the state and the nation. Those citizens who did not see the loss of the Soviet state as a disaster found themselves excluded, at least discursively, from the community of Russian people. They were labelled enemies who were working with the West, which had been instrumental in destroying the Soviet Union.

The idea that a 'subversive agency' among the political elites of the Soviet Union and Russia had contributed to the Soviet collapse was fundamental to populist rhetoric on the part of politicians and intellectuals. These ideas appealed to some sections of Russian society and supplied the authorities with arguments with which to undermine the reputations of political opponents who had reputedly benefitted from the Soviet collapse. The attempt to impeach Yeltsin in 1999 had shown that anti-Western conspiracy theories about the Soviet col-

CONCLUSION

lapse could serve as a political tool, rather than simply remaining an element in fringe ideologies. It demonstrated the potential of creating short-term alliances with diverse political groups to pursue political goals. At the same time, the attempted impeachment became the starting point for the relocation of these theories from the opposition's ideological arsenal to official political discourse.

The active use of the conspiratorial reading of the Soviet collapse by Russian officials demonstrates the tactics of the Russian establishment in the 2000s. They have adapted the ideology of the national-patriotic opposition and used it against the Kremlin's current rivals, the liberal democratic and radical nationalist opposition. At first, Kremlin officials borrowed the conspiratorial interpretation of the Soviet collapse from the intellectual set of ideas developed by national patriots who opposed the government. Later, these same people became great advocates of the current regime. Aleksandr Dugin, who called for a complete standoff with the West, as discussed in Chapter 2, joined the coalition in support of Putin in the presidential elections in 2012 and two years later stood at the forefront of the Russian campaign to support the annexation of Crimea. Another leader of the national-patriotic movement, whose media outlet was the key voice of the anti-Yeltsin coalition in the 1990s, was Aleksandr Prokhanov; in an interview with *The New York Times* in 2014, he noted with satisfaction that he was 'regularly invited to Kremlin events' (Barry, 2014). The transformation of these public intellectuals from leaders of the anti-government camp in the 1990s into the Kremlin's closest allies in the 2000s shows that the Kremlin has taken every advantage to ensure that it has maximum support from diverse communities. In fact, as this book argues, public intellectuals and the authorities both benefit from their collaboration. The active involvement of public intellectuals in the production and dissemination of anti-Western conspiracy theories raises their public profile and gains them support – and funding – from the Kremlin. In turn, the Kremlin encourages the intellectuals' endeavours to disseminate anti-Western conspiracy theories as they help reinforce the power claims of political elites.

In the 2000s, the ruling political elites, with the support of prominent public intellectuals such as Gleb Pavlovskii, invested a great deal of time and money in creating a network of public intellectuals and media personalities who even today continue to produce anti-Western conspiracy theories and disseminate them among the Russian public. Regardless of political preferences or professional background, intellectuals loyal to the Kremlin portray the West both as the main external enemy of Russia, and as controller of domestic opposition to Putin. At the same time, the efforts of these intellectuals transformed the figure of Putin into an icon of resistance to the West and the only guarantor of Russia's sovereignty. Moreover, the image of Putin has evolved internationally and has become the embodiment of resistance to the West and the New World Order in the eyes of various foreign audiences. The Kremlin's engagement with far-right and far-left organizations around the world (Shekhovtsov, 2018) plays an important role in the Kremlin's efforts to spread its vision of global affairs, in which anti-Western and anti-American conspiracy theories have become a tool for undermining the credibility of the US and EU governments.

Populist theories of Western conspiracy produced by public intellectuals became a way of legitimizing authoritarian rule and delegitimizing Putin's opponents. The case of Mikhail Khodorkovsky was a watershed in the conspiratorial practices of the Kremlin. One year after Khodorkovsky was put in prison, Ukraine experienced its first colour revolution; this scared the Kremlin and opened the gates for all possible conspiracy allegations aimed at protecting the current regime. Numerous think tanks and foundations led by prominent public intellectuals became an integral part of policies meant to promote Vladislav Surkov's idea that Russia was a 'sovereign democracy'. Chapter 4 shows how Surkov's definition of the West as a competitor helped shift anti-Western rhetoric from the margins of political discourse into a discussion on economy and finance. This, in turn, imbued debates on Russian greatness with pride in the country's vast natural resources and provided an explanation of the reasons for the West's hostility towards Russia. However, Surkov represented Western societies as complex and pluralistic, with only some specific groups wishing Russia ill. This change in anti-Western rhetoric, which had traditionally represented the West as a single, monolithic entity, contributed to the further legitimization of anti-Western conspiracy mythmaking in the public sphere: it was more nuanced and hence more believable.

As well as meeting clearly political needs, the growing presence of anti-Western conspiracy theories in official discourse can be explained by the ability of conspiracy theories to create national identities and promote national cohesion. Russian political and intellectual elites in the 2000s opted for anti-Western conspiracy theories as a method of nation-building. They created a dualistic worldview in which the Russian nation stood against its ultimate, conspiring 'Other', the United States.

The Pussy Riot affair is a case in point. Conspiracy theories about

CONCLUSION

the band's threat to Russian national cohesion were used to link its supporters to protesters demanding fair elections in the country. The campaign against Pussy Riot was a media-constructed event aimed at polarizing society in the post-electoral period. It served as a bridge between a conspiratorial propaganda campaign against the United States, which was embarked on to ensure Putin's victory, and the anti-opposition campaign in the aftermath of the elections. The corpus of anti-Western conspiracy notions used in the debates around the Pussy Riot affair set the parameters of domestic politics during Putin's third term and provided a counter-balance to the opposition's anti-Kremlin views.

This division of the world enabled the Kremlin to simulate cohesion within the highly heterogeneous Russian society on the basis of shared animosity towards the USA. Active social mobilization against the allegedly destructive US policy towards Russia peaked during the electoral cycles in 2007–8 and 2011–12. However, the wave of rallies against the regime from 2011 onwards, the subject of Chapter 6, came as a surprise to the Kremlin and radicalized the search for a domestic 'conspiring Other' connected to the USA and turned resistance to the USA into the basis for legislative initiatives. The Pussy Riot trial was a timely event for the political authorities as it allowed Russian society to be split between the 'Russian Orthodox people' and the subversive 'Other', in the aftermath of a difficult electoral campaign. However, efforts to construct a sense of nation based on an alleged Western-inspired conspiracy against Orthodoxy was only partly successful, and only in the short term.

The impact of anti-Western conspiracy theories on political developments in Putin's Russia had never been so apparent as it was during the parliamentary and presidential elections of 2007–8 and 2011–12, when the struggle to protect access to power was particularly intense. As Chapter 6 shows, well-orchestrated campaigns throughout both electoral cycles portrayed Putin as the embodiment of 'the Russian people', and the only person who could guarantee the country's sovereignty and independence from the West. The Kremlin wanted to create an 'overwhelming majority' of Putin supporters as a way of consolidating the elites and demonstrating the regime's efficiency (Rogov, 2013). Various anti-Western conspiracy theories, which had been developed by public intellectuals and pro-Kremlin politicians, became an efficient instrument of popular mobilization. The two electoral periods of the new millennium became revealing demonstrations of how various state and private institutions cooperated in an effort to maintain the regime. Public intellectuals and think tanks worked together with the state-aligned media to aggressively promote fears of a colour revolution in Russia, which was reportedly being planned by the West and its allies within Russia. In turn, in their public speeches, top-ranking politicians, including Putin, articulated anti-Western conspiratorial notions. This confirmed the conspiracy narrative as an inherent and legitimate part of official political discourse.

As Chapter 5 demonstrated, the citizen activism which had pre-empted Putin's third presidential term resulted in increased government pressure on NGOs, which became the Kremlin's main target in the aftermath of the 'Orange Revolution' in Ukraine in 2004. From then on, pro-Kremlin public intellectuals and the state-aligned media shaped the image of NGOs as the conspiring 'Other' within Russian society; they were supposedly supported by Western foundations and intelligence services and sought to subvert Russian society. This clearly reflected the political elites' fear of the possibility of a colour revolution taking place in Russia. Just after Putin's return to the Kremlin in 2012, NGOs again found themselves at the centre of an aggressive campaign to delegitimize their activities on the grounds that they were dangerous and subversive. The Ukraine crisis has cost Russian civil society the loss of several influential foreign NGOs, and has saddled it with more pressure from the state. The political campaign against NGOs after 2014 relied heavily on a corpus of anti-Western conspiracy theories developed in the 2000s with the active support of the Kremlin. The campaign demonstrated how joint effort by politicians, public intellectuals and the state-aligned media was able to use conspiracy theories to justify repressive measures taken against political opponents. The relative decline in the number of NGOs during the Putin years indicates the usefulness of conspiracy theories in the struggle for redistributing power between different political actors.

This study has also demonstrated that the Russian authorities themselves appear to be the major protagonists and producers of conspiracy theories. In the United States the federal authorities are also partly responsible for the popularity of conspiracy fears among Americans, as Olmsted (2009) has argued, because in the past they made it easier to suppress dissenting voices and conceal real conspiracies. However, for the most part conspiracy theories in the USA emerge from grassroots movements which perceive the federal government as the ultimate conspiring Other.

The picture is reversed in the Russian case. The Kremlin and its public intellectual allies are major instigators of anti-Western conspiracy theories, which are transmitted to the grassroots level of Russian society through channels under government control. This process takes the place of a coherent state ideology and legitimizes Kremlin policies. In addition, unlike in the USA, political and intellectual elites use conspiratorial rhetoric to boost their popularity and build their careers. Yet attempts on the part of independent individuals on the grassroots level to develop and apply their own populist, anti-elite conspiratorial discourses to strengthen their popularity are punished by the state.

While I was writing these final remarks, the Russian law enforcement services announced that they had uncovered a significant plot against the state led by Viacheslav Mal'tsev. Mal'tsev, a popular Youtube blogger from Saratov, made his name by criticizing Putin for being a dictator who regularly violates the Constitution. He was elected to run for parliamentary elections as one of the leaders of the democratic movement RPR-PARNAS in the parliamentary elections in 2016. Mal'tsev did not support the annexation of Crimea and called for peace with Ukraine. He called on his supporters to start a revolution in November 2017 and overthrow the corrupt regime. In summer 2017 he was arrested for a few days and, soon after, left Russia to avoid political pressure (RFE/RL, 2017). Today, FSB claims that Mal'tsev is the head of a terrorist network which planned to stir up a number of regional administrations and set off street violence (Merzlikin, 2017).

The line between using conspiracy theories against opponents and turning them into the driving force in politics is drawn very carefully. As the Ukraine crisis demonstrated, the Kremlin's rulers are willing to engage overtly in the propagation of anti-Western conspiratorial discourse when it is politically expedient. However, the people who genuinely hold conspiratorial views rarely become serious decision-makers in the Kremlin hierarchy; they are more often foot soldiers and middle ranking officers in rhetorical battles against the regime's rivals.

The prominence of anti-Western conspiracy theories in contemporary Russia and their active use in domestic and foreign policy allows us to draw several conclusions about their future prospects and their relationship to the political regime. The rallies in the winter of 2011–12 symbolized a new period in post-Soviet Russian history and forced the Kremlin to reconsider its ways of governing the country. As this study has demonstrated, in the 2000s anti-Western conspiracy theories were concerned only with particular governmental and non-governmental actors who, in theory, were able to undermine the legitimacy of the ruling elite. The principal aim of these theories was to secure victory in the elections. The Kremlin's failure to accomplish a smooth transfer of power from Medvedev back to Putin in 2011 revealed a serious dissatisfaction with the state of affairs in the country on the part of some sections of the elites and middle-class citizens. This highlighted problems within the political system itself and made it clear that it was in need of in-depth reform. As Gel'man (2015) notes, after the rallies in 2011–12, maintaining the status quo by any possible means became the Kremlin's main goal. The Kremlin equated the status quo with the preservation of the positions of incumbent politicians. However, ordinary Russians, with the help of the state-aligned media, perceived it as social and financial stability. Against this background, anti-Western conspiracy theories evolved from being an instrument for delegitimizing political opponents into a widely used method for promoting domestic and foreign policies.

The conspiratorial language chosen by the authorities after 2012 was a tool for explaining and justifying their policies. The incessant juxtaposition of 'the people' of Russia, whose demand was the maintenance of the status quo, with the 'Other', who undermined the integrity of the nation, was a way of dealing with conflicts emerging in the country. The West was portrayed as a powerful, external foe which supported internal enemies within the nation. Attempts to mobilize the population in support of the Kremlin was carried out by means of aggressive campaigns in the state-aligned media and allowed the Kremlin to meet the social, political and interethnic challenges of the post-2012 period. Almost all of the major legislative initiatives of the Duma which were aimed at protecting the regime were presented as acts of resistance to the treacherous West.

The events in Ukraine marked another phase in the evolution of the Putin regime. The effects of the 'Revolution of Dignity' in Kyiv will continue to be felt by Russian citizens and their authorities for years. The Kremlin seems to have realized that playing a passive role in global events could threaten the regime's survival, and so has made it clear that it is prepared to protect its interests at all costs. This explains its active role in the fight against IS in Syria, and its possible meddling in other countries' elections, most notably those of the USA, both of which have dramatically changed Russia's standing in the world. The US and European reactions to the election scandal, which has been used to portray Russia as Donald Trump's puppet master, plays right into the hands of the Kremlin. It is perceived as another excuse to harass Russia, and is used as more 'evidence' that the Kremlin was right in its conspiracy theories about the West.

The Ukraine conflict and Trump's election have demonstrated that the post-truth world has ample room to accommodate all possible conspiracy theories and to bring them into everyday life. Promoting 'Fortress Russia', which Mikhail Iur'ev saw as an ideal approach to regaining the country's past greatness, is a developing project and it promises to bring more interesting twists and turns in post-Soviet politics in the coming years. It turns out that the 'Fortress' is not as isolated from the world – nor, specifically, the West – as the author of this book imagined. The cunning and skilful manner in which the Russian political and intellectual elites have made use of conspiracy theories in the new millennium shows how they can be imported from, and, later, exported to, other countries. Studying the use of conspiracy theories in Putin's Russia can help us reach a better understanding of one of the most controversial intellectual phenomena of our times – and one which is growing in importance.

References

Primary Sources

Articles

Afanas'eva, I. (2011). 'Golos' Ameriki. [online] Vzgliad. Available at: http://www.vz.ru/politics/2011/12/9/545334.html.

Akopov, P. (2014). 'Eto velikaia voina kontinentov'. [online] Vzgliad. Available at: https://vz.ru/politics/2014/2/20/672632.html.

Al'bats, E. and Pavlovskii, G. (2007). *Polnyi Al'bats*. [online] Radio Ėkho Moskvy. Available at: http://www.echo.msk.ru/programs/albac/56546/.

Amerikanskie politiki o budushchem Rossii. (n.d.). *Rech' prezidenta SShA B. Klintona*. [online] Available at: http://militera.lib.ru/science/kapitanetz/08.html.

Analbaeva, A. (2012). *'Ne dadim razvalit' stranu!'* [online] Vzgliad. Available at: http://vz.ru/politics/2012/2/3/557130.html.

Antimaidan. (2015). *Amerikanskie zhurnalisty nazvali 'Natsional'nyi fond v podderzhku demokratii' global'nym intriganom.* [online] Available at: https://antimaidan.ru/article/2431.

Archimandrite Tikhon (Shevkunov). (2008). *The Text of the Film 'The Fall of An Empire – The Lesson of Byzantium'*. [online] Pravoslavie.ru. Available at: http://www.pravoslavie.ru/english/7389.htm.

Azar, I. (2015). *'SMERSH – krasivaia abbreviatura'. Interv'iu lidera 'Antimaidana' Nikolaia Starikova spetskoru 'Meduzy' Il'e Azaru*. [online] Meduza. Available at: https://meduza.io/feature/2015/02/20/smersh-eto-krasivaya-abbreviatura.

Azar, I. and Krasheninnikova, V. (2013). *'Preziraiu politicheskikh naemnikov'*. [online] Lenta. Available at: https://lenta.ru/articles/2013/05/29/krash/.

Azar, I. and Shevchenko, M. (2013). *Sobianin po proiskhozhdeniiu – korennoi evraziets*. [online] Lenta. Available at: http://lenta.ru/articles/2013/07/30/shevchenko/.

Baranov, A. and Steshin, D. (2006). *Telezhurnalist Arkadii Mamontov: ia rasskazal, kak protiv nas shpionit Zapad. A menia nazvali dushitelem svobody*. [online] Komsomol'skaia pravda. Available at: http://www.kp.ru/daily/23648.4/49247/.

REFERENCES

Beliaev, D. (2011). *Belaia Lenta – zadacha prolit' krov'*. [online] Available at: https://dbelyaev.ru/p/2731/.

Belkovskii, S. (2003). *V Rossii gotovitsia oligarkhicheskii perevorot*. [online] Utro.ru. Available at: https://utro.ru/articles/2003/05/26/201631.shtml.

—— (2016). *Liubov' provokatora*. Moscow: AST.

Bohm, M. (2014). *Farewell, Ambassador McFall*. [online] The Moscow Times. Available at: https://themoscowtimes.com/articles/farewell-ambassador-mcfaul-32080.

Brafman, Ia. (2005). *Kniga Kagala*. Moscow: Izdatel'stvo MAUP.

Brezhnev, A., Tukmakov, D. and Shurygin, V. (1999). *Impichment*. [online] Available at: http://1993.sovnarkom.ru/TEXT/STATYI/zavtra_99_285.htm.

Buntman, S. and Shevchenko, M. (2004). *Ishchem vykhod*. [online] Radio Ėkho Moskvy. Available at: http://echo.msk.ru/programs/exit/33513/#element-text.

Cherkudinova, D. (2012). *'Kamen', kotoryi ia derzhal v rukakh, byl tot samyi, angliiskii'*. [online] Izvestiia. Available at: http://izvestia.ru/news/512379.

Chernenko, E. (2015). *'Za destabilizatsiei Ukrainy skryvaetsia popytka radikal'nogo oslableniia Rossii'*. [online] Kommersant. Available at: https://www.kommersant.ru/doc/2752250.

Chernov, V. (2013). *Za chto zhe nas ne liubiat. Interv'iu zhurnalu 'Story'*. [online]. Narochnitskaia.ru. Available at: http://narochnitskaia.ru/interviews/za-chto-zhe-nas-ne-lyubyat-intervyu-zhurnalu-stori-iyun-2013.html.

Chernykh, E. (2011). *Sergei Kurginian: 'Gorbachev soznatel'no razvalil KPSS i SSSR!'* [online] Komsomol'skaia Pravda. Available at: http://www.kp.ru/daily/25647.4/810668/.

Chudodeev, A. (2012). *Inakomysliashchii*. [online] Itogi. Available at: http://www.itogi.ru/spetzproekt/2012/49/184673.html.

Cooper, M. W. (1991). *Behold a Pale Horse*. Light Technology Publications.

Dalles, A. (n.d.). Plan Dallesa po unichtozheniiu SSSR (Rossii). [online] *Russkoe delo*. Available at: http://www.russkoedelo.org/mysl/miscellaneous/dulles_plan.php.

Danilevskii, N. Ia. (2013). *Russia and Europe. The Slavic World's Political and Cultural Relations with the Germanic Roman West*. Bloomington: Slavica.

Danilin, P. (2007). *Partiia 'politicheskogo gerbalaifa'*. [online] Vzgliad. Available at: http://vz.ru/columns/2007/9/24/111577.html.

Danilin, P., Kryshtal', N. and Poliakov, D. (2007). *Vragi Putina*. Moscow: Evropa.

Dergachev, V. (2012). *Evraziitsy prigrozili zakatat' 'Marsh millionov' v asfal't*. [online] Izvestiia. Available at: http://izvestia.ru/news/535209.

Dobrov, A., Danilin, P., Kryshtal', N. and Poliakov, D. (2007). *107 minut*. [online] Russkaia Sluzhba Novostei. Available at: http://prigovor.ru/info/37809.html.

Dostoevsky, F. M. (1995). *Sobranie sochinenii v piatnadtsati tomakh*. Vol.14. Moscow: Nauka.

Dugin, A. (2000). *Osnovy geopolitiki*. Moscow: Arktogeia.

—— (2004). *Filosofiia politiki*. Moscow: Arktogeia.

—— (2005). *Konspirologiia (nauka o zagovorakh, sekretnykh obshchestvakh i tainoi voine)*. Moscow: ROF Evraziia.

—— (2007). *O monarkhii, Putine i Zubkove*. [online] Available at: http://www.profile.ru/items_24124.

—— (2012). *Putin protiv Putina. Byvshii budushchii president*. Moscow: Iauza.

REFERENCES

—— (2014). *Strashna ne tol'ko piataia kolonna, no i shestaia, ne voiuiuchshaia s Putinym napriamuiu*. [online] Novorossiia. Available at: http://novorus.info/news/analytics/16571-aleksandr-dugin-strashna-ne-tolko-pyataya-kolonna-no-i-shestaya-ne-voyuyuschaya-s-putinym-napryamuyu.html.

Dymarskii V., Fel'gengauėr, T. and Gorbachev, M. (2011). *Ishchem vykhod*. [online], Radio Ėkho Moskvy. Available at: http://echo.msk.ru/programs/exit/841196-echo/#element-text.

Dymarskii, V., Larina, K. and Volkov, D. (2013). *2013*. [online] Radio Ėkho Moskvy. Available at: http://echo.msk.ru/programs/year2013/1070590-echo/.

Dymarskii, V. and Pavlovskii, G. (2006). *Proverka slukha*. [online] Radio Ėkho Moskvy. Available at: http://www.echo.msk.ru/programs/proverka/42667/.

Dziadko, T., Shevardnadze, S. and Krasheninnikova, V. (2012). *Oblozhka-1*. [online] Radio Ėkho Moskvy. Available at: http://echo.msk.ru/programs/oblozhka-1/907357-echo/#element-text.

Egorov, I. (2014). *Vtoraia 'kholodnaia'*. [online] Rossiiskaia gazeta. Available at: https://rg.ru/2014/10/15/patrushev.html.

El Mariachi. (2011). *Snezhnaia revolutsiia ili chistyi kreativ*. [Blog] Livejournal. Available at: http://el-mariachi.livejournal.com/37344.html.

Emel'ianenko, V. (2007). 'U nas est' vybor'. [online] *Profil'*. Available at: http://www.profile.ru/items_24677.

Ėlementy. (1992). *Ideologiia mirovogo pravitel'stva*. [online] Available at: http://arcto.ru/article/409.

El'tsin, B. (1994). *Zapiski prezidenta*. Moscow: Ogonëk.

Farizova, S. (2005). 'Oni razrushaiut grazhdan iznutri'. [online] Kommersant. Available at: http://kommersant.ru/doc/630481.

Fel'gengauėr, T. and Shevchenko, M. (2013). *Osoboe mnenie*. [online] Radio Ėkho Moskvy. Available at: http://echo.msk.ru/programs/personalno/1112516-echo/#element-text.

Fikhte, M. and Bolotova, O. (2010). *Kreml' otpravilsia na miting*. [online] Gazeta. Available at: https://www.gazeta.ru/politics/2010/02/01_a_3318769.shtml.

Filipenok, A. (2014). *MGU okonchatel'no rasstalsia s Aleksandrom Duginym*. [online] RBC. Available at: http://www.rbc.ru/politics/01/07/2014/57041eda9a794760d3d3fb46.

Froianov, I. (2009). *Rossiia. Pogruzhenie v bezdnu*. Moscow: Ėksmo.

Ganapol'skii, M. and Dugin, A. (2008). *Osoboe mnenie*. [online]. Radio Ėkho Moskvy. Available at: http://www.echo.msk.ru/programs/personalno/532383-echo/.

Gavrov, S. (2012). '*Zaderëm podol Matushke Rossii*'. [online] Vzgliad. Available at: http://vz.ru/opinions/2012/6/27/585741.html.

Gazeta.ru. (2011). '*Nam kuklovodov i tak khvataet*': *online-interv'iu s predsedatelem partii 'Spravedlivaia Rossiia'*. [online] Available at: http://www.gazeta.ru/interview/nm/s3847282.shtml.

—— (2012). *Gosudarstvennoe TV pokazyvaet Poklonnuiu: net oranzhevoi chume, ne pozvolim utopit' Rossiiu v krovi*. [online] Available at: https://www.gazeta.ru/news/lenta/2012/02/04/n_2191705.shtml.

Gefter, M. (1991). Stalin umer vchera. Beseda s zhurnalistom G. Pavlovskim. In Gefter, M. *Iz tekh i ètikh let*. Moscow: Progress, pp. 235–64.

—— (2013). *Destalinizatsiia*. [online] *Gefter.ru*. Available at: http://gefter.ru/archive/7321.

REFERENCES

Geopolitika. (2017). *Dugin in Alex Jones Show on Inforwars.* [online] Available at: https://www.geopolitica.ru/en/studio/dugin-alex-jones-show-infowars.
Glaz'ev, S. (2014). *SShA ne raz lomali o nas zuby.* [online] Izborskii klub. Available at: https://izborsk-club.ru/4351.
—— (2016). *'Priznat' SSHA agressorom i otkazat'sia ot ispol'zovaniia dollara'.* [online] Business-gazeta. Available at: https://www.business-gazeta.ru/article/324210.
Glavplakat. (2014). *Chuzhie sredi nas. Dos'e.* [online] Available at: http://xn--80aaagd9bdc9a8a.xn--p1ai/article/193.
Golovachev, V. (2012). *Sdavaite kupiury, grazhdane!* [online] Trud. Available at: http://www.trud.ru/article/20-01-2012/271675_sdavajte_kupjury_grazhdane.html.
Goncharova, N. and Shevchenko, M. (2012). *Interv'iu.* [online] Russkaia sluzhba novostei. Available at: http://www.rusnovosti.ru/guests/interviews/58118/233174/.
Gorbachev, M. (1991). *Avgustovskii putch (prichiny i sledstviia).* Moscow: Novosti.
—— (n.d.). *Tsel'iu moei zhizni bylo unichtozhenie kommunizma.* [online] Newsland. Available at: https://newsland.com/user/4297656659/content/gorbachiov-tseliu-moei-zhizni-bylo-unichtozhenie-kommunizma/4074611.
Gorianin, A. (2009). *Fantomnye boli Ameriki.* [online] *Profil'*. Available at: http://www.profile.ru/items_27877.
Grigor'ev, M. (2007). *Fake-struktury. Prizraki rossiiskoi politiki.* Moscow: Evropa.
Gryzlov, B. (2007). *Putin ostaëtsia liderom Rossii.* [online] Rossiiskaia gazeta. Available at: http://www.rg.ru/2007/10/17/grizlov.html.
Gusev, D. G., Matveichev, O. A., Khazeev, R. R. and Chernakov, S. Iu. (2006). *Ushi mashut oslom: sovremennoe sotsial'noe programmirovanie.* Moscow: Alex J. Bakster group.
Iakovlev, N. (1983). *TsRU protiv SSSR.* Moscow: Pravda.
Iliukhin, V. (1999). *Obviniaetsia El'tsin.* [online] Available at: http://www.viktor-iluhin.ru/node/328.
—— (2011). *Pochemu ia vozbudil ugolovnoe delo v otnoshenii Gorbacheva M.S.* [online] Available at: http://viktor-iluhin.ru/node/354.
Interfax. (2017). *Zolotov sravnil protestnye aktsii v Rossii s tsvetnymi revoliutsiiami.* [online]. Available at: http://www.interfax.ru/russia/566865.
Iur'ev, D. (2005). *Oranzhevye polittekhnologii Ukrainy: upravlenie svobodoi.* [online] Regnum. Available at: https://regnum.ru/news/370748.html.
Iur'ev, M. (2004). *Krepost' Rossiia: Kontseptsiia dlia prezidenta.* [online] Novaia Gazeta. Available at: http://2004.novayagazeta.ru/nomer/2004/17n/n17n-s44.shtml.
Ivangogh. (2011). Gleb Pavlovskii i russkaia filosofii', *Livejournal*, 27 April 2011, http://ivangogh.livejournal.com/1469702.html
Ivanov, V. (2006). *Antirevolutsioner. Pochemu Rossii ne nuzhna 'oranzhevaia revolutsiia'.* Moscow: Evropa.
—— (2012). *Putin nameren mobilizovat' bolshinstvo. Putinskoe bolshinstvo. Nuzhno obraschat'sia tol'ko k nemu.* [online] Izvestiia. Available at: http://izvestia.ru/news/511953.
Izvestiia. (2007). *Nabludateli SNG nazvali vybory v Dumu svobodnymi i prozrachnymi.* [online] Available at: http://iz.ru/news/413793.

REFERENCES

—— (2014). *'Piataia kolonna – eto liudi, ispolniaiushchie interesy drugogo gosudarstva'*. [online] Izvestiia. Available at: http://iz.ru/news/580996#ixzz4DWj3BWkp.

Kaftan, L. (2004). *Zamestitel' glavy administratsii Prezidenta RF Vladislav Surkov: Putin ukrepliaet gosudarstvo, a ne sebia.* [online] Komsomol'skaia pravda. Available at: http://www.kp.ru/daily/23370/32473/.

Kara-Murza, S. (2009). *Antisovetskii proekt.* Moscow: Algoritm.

—— (2011). *Rossiia ne zapad, ili chto nas zhdiot.* Moscow: Eksmo.

—— (2013). *FARA and Putin's NGO Law: Myths and Reality.* [online] Institute of Modern Russia. Available at: https://imrussia.org/en/politics/455-fara-and-putins-ngo-law-myths-and-reality.

—— (n.d.) *Manipuliatsiia soznaniem.* [online] Available at: http://www.kara-murza.ru/books/manipul/manipul.htm#hdr_1.

Kartsev, D. (2012). *Plan Andropova-Putina.* [online] Russkii Reporter. Available at: http://www.rusrep.ru/article/2012/10/31/kgb/.

Katkov, M. (1863). Samoderzhavie tsaria i edinstvo Rusi. *Moskovskie vedomosti,* (79).

—— (1865). Sredstva i sposoby tainykh vragov Rossii. *Moskovskie vedomosti* (2).

—— (1880). Natsional'naia i antinatsional'naia politika partii v Rossii. *Moskovskie vedomosti,* (94).

—— (1881). Otkuda berutsiia den'gi u nashikh revoliutsionerov. *Moskovskie vedomosti,* (81).

Kazintsev, A. (2001). *Tri dnia v avguste.* [online] Nash sovremennik. Available at: http://www.patriotica.ru/history/kazintsev_gkchp.html.

Keith, J. (1995). *Black Helicopters over America: Strikeforce for the New World Order.* Illuminet Press.

Khlobystov, O. (n.d.). *Iavliaetsia li 'Plan Dallesa' Fal'shivkoi?* [online] Chekist.ru, Available at: http://www.chekist.ru/article/886.

Khomiakov, A. S. (1982). 'O vozmozhnosti russkoi khudozhestvennoi shkoly'. In Kantor, V. and Ospovat, A. L. *Russkaia estetika i kritika 40-50-kh godov XIX veka.* Moscow: Iskusstvo.

Klussmann, U. and Mayr, W. (2005). *Interview with Kremlin boss Vladislav Surkov: 'The West Doesn't Have to Love Us'.* [online] Spiegel. Available at: http://www.spiegel.de/international/spiegel/spiegel-interview-with-kremlin-boss-vladislav-surkov-the-west-doesn-t-have-to-love-us-a-361236.html.

Kommersant-Vlast. (1991). *Pavlov s"ezdil v Brussel'. Izvinilsia . . .* [online]. Available at: http://kommersant.ru/doc/265267.

—— (1992). *A vse-taki: chto vy delali 19–21 avgusta 1991 goda?* [online] Available at: http://kommersant.ru/doc/6327.

—— (1999a). *Kak progolosuiut deputaty za impichment.* [online] Available at: http://kommersant.ru/doc/218398.

—— (1999b). *Svedeniia o rezultatakh golosovaniia deputatov Gosudarstvennoi Dumy Federal'nogo sobraniia RF po voprosu o vydvizhenii obvineniia protiv prezidenta Rossiiskoi Federatsii dlia otresheniia ego ot dolzhnosti.* [online] Available at: http://www.kommersant.ru/doc/218468.

—— (1999c). *Vrag naroda.* [online] Available at: http://kommersant.ru/doc/218225.

—— (2017). *Nikolai Patrushev: internet primeniaetsia dlia podryva natsional'nogo suvereniteta.* [online] Available at: https://www.kommersant.ru/doc/3305724.

REFERENCES

Korovin, V. (2015). *Konets proekta 'Ukraina'*. St Petersburg: Piter.
Kostin, K. (2013). *'Ne nado smotret' na "tretii sector" kak na piatuiu kolonnu'*. [online] Izvestiia. Available at: http://izvestia.ru/news/547731.
Kots, A. and Iakovlev, A. (2012). *Arkadii Mamontov: 'Sud i prigovor Pussy Riot spravedlivy'*. [online] Komsomol'skaia pravda. Available at: http://www.kp.ru/daily/25949/2892800/.
Krasheninnikova, V. (2007). *Rossiia-Amerika: kholodnaia voina kul'tur. Kak amerikanskie tsennosti prelomliaiut videnie Rossii*. Moscow: Evropa.
Kremlin.ru. (2006). *Zaiavleniia dlia pressy i otvety na voprosy po itogam zasedaniia Mezhgosudarstvennogo Soveta Evraziiskogo ekonomicheskogo soobshchestva*. [online] Available at: http://kremlin.ru/events/president/transcripts/23409.
—— (2017). *Mezhdunarodnyi forum 'Arktika – territoriia dialoga'*. [online] Available at: http://kremlin.ru/events/president/news/54149.
Kriuchkov, V. (2003). *Lichnoe delo*. Moscow: Eksmo.
Krotkov, B. (2007). *Revolutsiia: do osnovan'ia, a zachem?* [online] Rossiiskaia gazeta. Available at: http://www.rg.ru/2007/11/01/revolucia.html.
Kuksenkova, I. (2015). *Deiatel'nost' 'Natsional'nogo fonda v podderzhku demokratii' predstavliala ugrozu bezopasnosti Rossii*. [online] Rossiia-1. Availbable at: http://www.vesti.ru/doc.html?id=2646903.
Kurginian, S. (n.d.). *Sut' vremeni-1*. [online] Available at: http://www.kurginyan.ru/publ.shtml?cat=4&cmd=add&id=77.
Legostaev, V. (2002). *Tseluloid GKChP*. [online] Zavtra. Available at: http://zavtra.ru/content/view/2002-08-2041/.
Lendman, S. (2015). *Russia Challenges America's Orwellian NED*. [online] Counterpunch. Available at: http://www.counterpunch.org/2015/07/31/russia-challenges-americas-orwellian-ned/.
Leont'ev, M., Lur'ev, M., Khazin, M. and Utkin, A. (2005). *Krepost' Rossiia. Proschanie s liberalizmom*. Moscow: Iauza.
Levkovich, E. (2012). *Sekundnoe delo: RS pogovoril o raspade Rossii s Aleksandrom Nevzorovym*. [online] Nevzorov.tv. Available at: http://www.rollingstone.ru/articles/politics/interview/11817.html.
Limonov, E. (2014). *Chuzhie*. [online] Izvestiia. Available at: http://iz.ru/news/576441#ixzz4DWkhttxe.
—— (2016). *Oppozitsiia otkladyvaetsia*. [online] Izvestiia. Available at: http://iz.ru/news/579565#ixzz4DWk863WN.
Liubimov, M. (1995). *'Operatsiia Golgofa': sekretnyi plan perestroiki*. Moscow: Sovershenno sekretno.
Luk'ianov, A. (2010). *Byl li zagovor?* Moscow: Èksmo.
Luzhkov, Iu. (2007). *My i Zapad*. In L. Poliakov, ed., *PRO suverennuiu demokratiiu*. Moscow: Evropa, pp. 195–209.
Malysheva, Iu. (2007). *Nabliudateli podstaviat vybory*. [online] Vzgliad. Available at: https://vz.ru/politics/2007/11/2/122049.html.
Manifest (n.d.). *Rossiia – megaproekt nashego pokoleniia*. [online] Available at: http://ulnashi.narod.ru/manifest.html.
Margaret Thatcher Foundation. (n.d.). *Speeches, interviews and other statements*. [online] Available at: http://www.margaretthatcher.org/search?t=6&pg=2&dt=4&doctype%5B0%5D=4&doctype%5B1%5D=6&page=1.
Markov, S. (2005). *'Oranzhevaia revolutsiia' – primer revolutsii global'nogo soobshchestva XXI veka*. In M. Pogrebinskii, ed., *Oranzhevaia revolutsiia'*.

REFERENCES

Ukrainskaia versiia: Sbornik. Moscow: Evropa, pp. 71–2.

—— (2013). *Pochemu Sergei Guriev vynuzhden igrat' to li svoiu, to lichuzhuiu rol'?* [online] Komsomol'skaia Pravda. Available at: http://www.kp.ru/daily/26084/2987276/.

Marrs, J. (2000). *Rule by Secrecy: The Hidden History that Connects the Trilateral Commission, the Freemasons, and the Great Pyramids*. New York: Harper Collins.

Marzoeva, E. (2008). *Uchastniki mitinga v Severnoi Osetii v kategoricheskoi forme osudili deistviia Gruzii*. [online] Kavkazskii uzel. Available at: http://www.kavkaz-uzel.ru/articles/140183/.

Mashkarin, A. (2007). *Novaia real'nost'. Vybory 2 dekabria obreli novyi smysl*. [online] Pskovskaia lenta novostei. Available at: http://pln-pskov.ru/vybory/analitika/46128.html.

Maslov, O. (2007). *'Vashingtonskii obkom' – kliuchevoi simvol v Rossii nachala XXI veka*. [online] Nezavisimoe analiticheskoe obozrenie. Available at: http://www.polit.nnov.ru/2007/03/19/symbolwashobkom/.

Mediakratiia. (2007). *Andrei Vorob'ev: Plan kampanii*. [online] Mediakratiia. Available at: http://www.mediacratia.ru/owa/mc/mc_project_news.html?a_id=17709.

Minkin, A. (2012). *Voron vorona kleval v glaza. A emu vse bozh'ia rosa*. [online] Moskovskii Komsomolets. Available at: http://www.mk.ru/politics/2012/02/08/669523-voron-vorona-kleval-v-glaza-a-emu-vsyo-bozhya-rosa.html.

Mints, I. (1979). *Istoriia Velikogo Oktiabria*. Moscow: Nauka. Vol. 3.

Morev, G. (2013). *Pavlovskii: my pervymi ispol'zovali internet v politike SSSR*. [online] RIA-Novosti, Available at: http://ria.ru/media_Russia/20130917/962975894.html#ixzz2hmzK3drI.

Morozov, A. (2012). *Gleb Pavlovski: 'Podtirat' za geroiami – eto obiazatel'naia chast' politraboty'*. [online] *Openspace*. Available at: http://os.colta.ru/media/net/details/36463/page1/.

Moskva-Tretii Rim. (2009). *Sekretnyi plan Andropova po perestroike SSSR pod kodovym nazvaniem 'Golgofa' byl razrabotan v TsRU, slugi satany iznachalno predpolagali ritual'no raspinat' Russkii Bogonosnyi Narod na Golgofe!* [online] Available at: http://www.ic-xc-nika.ru/texts/2009/apr/n450.html.

Nadezhdina, A. (2012). *'Pussy Riot': Uznitsy bez sovesti*. [online] Ėkspress-gazeta. Available at: http://www.eg.ru/daily/**politics**/33512/.

Nakanune.ru (2012). *Nachal'nik tsekha UVZ Igor' Kholmanskikh vystupil s obrasheniem: 'Delo daleko zashlo'*. [online] Available at: http://www.nakanune.ru/news/2012/1/18/22260092/.

Narochnitskaia, N. (2001). *Neuderzhimaia tiaga k mirovomu gospodstvu*. [online] *Narochnitskaia.ru*. Available at: http://www.narochnitskaia.ru/in-archive/неудержимая-тяга-к-мировому-господст.html?view=full.

—— (2002). *Deiatel'nost' Vatikana na territorii Rossii: geopoliticheskii aspect*. [online] *Pravoslavie.ru*. Available at: http://www.pravoslavie.ru/analit/vatican prozel.htm.

—— (2003). *Rossiia i russkie v mirovoi istorii*. Moscow: Mezhdunarodnye otnosheniia.

—— (2008). *Spory vokrug Vizantii*. [online] *Rossiiskaia gazeta*. Available at: http://www.rg.ru/2008/02/07/gibel-spory.html.

Narochnitskaia.ru. (2007a). *Nataliia Narochnitskaia: 'My dolzhny stat' natsiei'*. [online] Available at: http://www.narochnitskaia.ru/in-archive/nataliya-

REFERENCES

narochnitskaya-quot-myi-dolzhnyi-stat-natsiey-quot.html?view=full.
—— (2007b). *Nataliia Narochnitskaia: 'V SSHA mogut byt' dovol'ny Kasparovym'*. [online] Available at: http://www.narochnitskaia.ru/in-archive/nataliya-narochnitskaya-quot-v-ssha-mogut-byit-dovolnyi-kasparovyim-quot.html.
—— (2007c). Vystuplenie N. A. Narochnitskoi na kruglom stole 'Fevral'skaia revolutsiia v Rossii 1917 g.: Istoriia i sovremennost' v RGGU. Stenogramma. [online] Available at: http://narochnitskaia.ru/in-archive/vyistuplenie-n-a-narochnitskoy-na-kruglom-stole-quot-fevralskaya-revolyutsiya-v-rossii-1917-g-istoriya-i-sovremennost-quot-v-rggu-stenogramma.html.
—— (2007d). Natal'ia Narochnitskaia: 'Revolutsiia – dukhovnoe detishche intelligentsii'. [online]. Available at: http://www.narochnitskaia.ru/in-archive/natalya-narochnitskaya-quot-revolyutsiya-duhovnoe-detishhe-intelligentsii-quot.html?view=full.
—— (2008). Intelligentsiia s ogliadkoi na zapad. [online] Available at: http://www.narochnitskaia.ru/in-archive/intelligentsiya-s-oglyadkoy-na-zapad.html?view=full.
—— (2009). *Evropeiskie fal'sifikatory istorii*. [online] Available at: http://www.narochnitskaia.ru/in-archive/evropeyskie-falsifikatoryi-istorii.html?view=full.
Natsional-predateli Rossii. 5-ia kolonna. (n.d.). [online] Available at: http://5kolonna.info/5kolonna-v-rossii-spisok/.
Natsional'nyi interes. Episode: 'Gibel' imperii. Vizantiiskii urok'. Obsuzhdenie fil'ma v programme Natsional'nyi interes (2008). [TV programme] Rossiia.
Nastoiashchee vremia. (2016). Samarskii gubernator obvinil Naval'nogo v icpolnenii 'Plana Dallesa'. [online]. Available at: https://www.currenttime.tv/a/27954334.html.
Nilus, S. ([1903] 2012). *Bliz est', pri dverekh*. Moscow: Èksmo.
Noskov, O. (2007). *Razdel sibirskogo nasledstva*. [online] Ekspert. Available at: http://expert.ru/siberia/2007/06/resursy_sibiri/.
NTV (2012). *Glava predvybornogo shtaba Vladimira Putina raskritikoval uchastnikov mitingov 'Za chestnye vybory'*. [online] http://www.ntv.ru/novosti/271313/.
Okeiamnet. (2014). *Zachem Amerike nuzhna Bol'shaia Voina v Evrope*. [video]. Available at: https://www.youtube.com/watch?v=if0eXbIprnw.
Onlooker1001. (2009). *Podlye plany Khodorkovskogo i YuKOSa v otnoshenii Rossii*. [video]. Available at: https://www.youtube.com/watch?v=jIv-aaiOaHw.
Orlov, D. (2006). Politicheskaia doktrina suverennoi demokratii, in: Orlov, D., Migranian A., Rogozhnikov M., Nikonov, V. and Surkov, V., eds., *Suverennaia demokratiia: ot idei k doctrine*. Moscow: Evropa, 2006, pp. 4–12.
—— (2007). *Plan Putina*. [online] RIA Novosti-Rossiia Segodnia. Available at: http://ria.ru/authors/20070521/65794202.html.
OSCE. (2007). *ODIHR unable to observe Russian Duma Elections*. [online] Available at: http://www.osce.org/odihr/elections/49175.
Panarin, I. (2010). *Pervaia Informatsionnaia Voina. Razval SSSR*. Saint-Petersburg: Piter.
—— (2012). *McFaul and the Moscow opposition rallies*. [online] RT.com. Available at: http://rt.com/politics/mcfaul-opposition-rallies-panarin-667/.
Patriarkh Kirill. (2012a). *Slovo Sviateishego Patriarkha Kirilla pered nachalom molebna v zashchitu very, porugannykh sviatyn', Tserkvi i eë dobrogo imeni*.

REFERENCES

[online] The Moscow Patriarchy official website. Available at: http://www.patriarchia.ru/db/text/2177868.html.
—— (2012b). *Slovo Sviateishego Patriarkha Kirilla posle molebna v pamiat' ob izbavlenii Rossii ot nashestviia Napoleona.* [online] The Moscow Patriarchy official website. Available at: http://www.patriarchia.ru/db/text/2457627.html.
Pavlov, S. Iu. (n.d.). Margaret Tetcher pro razval SSSR. [online] *Internet protiv teleèkrana.* Available at: http://www.contrtv.ru/common/2025/.
Pavlov, V. (1993). *Avgust iznutri: Gorbachevputch.* Moscow: Delovoi mir.
Pavlovskii, G. (1995). *Slepoe piatno (Svedeniia o belovezhskikh liudiakh).* [online] Russkii Zhurnal. Available at: http://old.russ.ru:81/antolog/inoe/pavlov.htm.
—— (2000). *Proshchai, Belovezh'e!* [online] Nezavisimaia gazeta. Available at: http://www.ng.ru/politics/2000-12-09/3_belovejie.html.
—— (2007). *Rol' Putina i dal'she budet igrat' Putin.* [online] Moskovskie novosti. Available at: http://novchronic.ru/860.htm.
—— (2012). *Genial'naia vlast'.* Moscow: Evropa.
—— (2014). *1993. Elementy sovetskogo opyta: Razgovory s Mikhailom Gefterom.* Moscow: Izdatel'stvo Evropa.
Pavlovskii, G. and Filippov, A. (2013). *Tri doprosa po teorii deistviia.* Moscow: Evropa.
Perin, R. (2001). *Gil'otina dlia besov. Etnicheskie i psikhogeneticheskie aspekty kadrovoi politiki, 1934–2000.* [online] Available at: http://ezoteric.polbu.ru/perin_giliotina/ch22_v.html.
Platonov, O. (1996). *Ternovyi venets Rossii. Tainaia istoriia masonstva, 1731–1996.* Moscow: 'Rodnik'.
Pleshakova, A. and Narochnitskaia, N. (2009). *Pochemu do sikh por skryvaiutsia fakty o Pervoi i Vtoroi Mirovykh voinakh.* [online] Komsomol'skaia Pravda. Available at: http://www.kp.ru/daily/press/detail/3186/#.
Podrobnosti. (2014). *Sibir' boretsia za federalizatsiiu: griadushchii marsh pugaet Moskvu'.* [online] Available at: http://podrobnosti.ua/987359-sibir-boretsja-za-federalizatsiju-grjaduschij-marsh-pugaet-moskvu-foto-video.html.
Poliakov, L., ed. (2007). *PRO suverennuiu demokratiiu.* Moscow: Evropa.
Polianskaia, M. (2012). *Mikhail Leont'ev: 'Liudi s Bolotnoi – eto sytoe, ambitsioznoe, absoliutno bezmozgloe men'shinstvo.* [online] Kommersant. Available at: http://kommersant.ru/doc/1866640.
Politkom.ru (2007). *Natal'ia Narochnitskaia: 'Natsional'noe chuvstvo – tvorcheskii instrument v gosudarstvennom stroitel'stve'.* [online] Available at: http://www.politcom.ru/4547.html.
Polunin, A. (2012). *Putin zhdet 'sakral'noi zhertvy'.* [online] Svobodnaia pressa. Available at: http://svpressa.ru/politic/article/53122/.
Popova, S. (2007). *Ne boites', chto my russkie.* [online] Trud. Available at: http://www.trud.ru/article/21-06-2007/117365_ne_bojtes_chto_my_russkie.html.
Pozner, V. and Narochnitskaia, N. (2007). *Pozner.* [online] Available at: http://www.narochnitskaia.ru/in-archive/quot-vremena-quot-quot-pochemu-rossiya-ne-evropa-quot-04-03-07-stenogramma.html?view=full.
Pozner, V. and Shevchenko, M. (2009). *Pozner protiv.* [online]. Radio Èkho Moskvy. Available at: http://echo.msk.ru/programs/pozner-protiv/586393-echo/#element-text.
Prezident Rossii. (2012). *Ukaz Prezidenta Rossiiskoi Federatsii 'O Strategii gosudarstvennoi natsional'noi politiki Rossiiskoi Federatsii do 2025 goda' № 1666.* [online] Available at: http://kremlin.ru/acts/bank/36512.

REFERENCES

Ptichkin, S. (2006). *Chekisty skanirovali mysli Madlen Olbrait.* [online] Rossiiskaia gazeta. Available at: http://www.rg.ru/2006/12/22/gosbezopasnostj-podsoznanie.html.

Pushkov, A. (2009). *Grossmeistery zazerkal'ia. P. S. Rossiia i mirovaia politika.* Moscow: Eksmo.

Putin, V. (2004). *Annual Address to the Federal Assembly of the Russian Federation.* [online] Available at: http://en.kremlin.ru/events/president/transcripts/22494.

—— (2005). *Annual Address to the Federal Assembly of the Russian Federation.* [online] Kremlin. Available at: http://archive.kremlin.ru/eng/speeches/2005/04/25/2031_type70029type82912_87086.shtml.

—— (2007a). *Priamaia liniia s Prezidentom Rossii Vladimirom Putinym.* [online] Available at: http://www.president-line.ru/.

—— (2007b). *Vstupitel'noe slovo na s"ezde partii 'Edinaia Rossiia'.* [online]. Available at: http://kremlin.ru/events/president/transcripts/24562.

—— (2007c). *Vystuplenie na forume storonnikov Prezidenta Rossii.* [online] http://kremlin.ru/events/president/transcripts/24713.

—— (2012a). *Address to the Federal Assembly.* [online] Available at: http://www.kremlin.ru/news/17118.

—— (2012b). *Rossiia sosredotachivaetsia – vyzovy, na kotorye my dolzhny otvetit'.* [online] *Izvestiia.* Available at: http://izvestia.ru/news/511884.

—— (2013). *Zasedanie Soveta po mezhnatsional'nym otnosheniiam.* [online] Available at: http://kremlin.ru/events/president/news/17536.

—— (2014). *Address by the President of the Russian Federation.* [online] Available at: http://en.kremlin.ru/events/president/news/20603.

—— (2015). *Direct line with Vladimir Putin.* [online] Available at: http://en.kremlin.ru/events/president/news/49261.

Radio Ekho Moskvy. (2012). *Vystupleniia na mitinge v podderzhku Vladimira Putina: Mikhail Leont'ev, zhurnalist.* [online] Available at: http://echo.msk.ru/blog/echomsk/861846-echo/.

—— (2013). *Vstrecha Vladimira Putina s uchastnikami uchreditel'nogo s"ezda rossiiskogo voenno-istoricheskogo obshchestva.* [online] Available at: http://echo.msk.ru/blog/echomsk/1035290-echo/.

Radio Free Europe/Radio Liberty. (2012). *Femen Activists Cut Down Cross in Kyiv.* [online] Available at: http://www.rferl.org/content/ukraine-femen-cross-pussy-riot/24679942.html.

Regional'nyi sait Kostanaiskoi oblasti. (2011). *Rogozin: vashingtonskii obkom planiruet miting 10 dekabria.* [online] Available at: http://www.altynsarin.ru/world_news/8423-rogozin-vashingtonskij-obkom-planiruet-miting-10.html.

Regnum. (2003). *Gleb Pavlovskii: 'Putinskoe bol'shinstvo – al'ternativa nyneshnei politike i nyneshnei vlasti'.* [online] Available at: https://regnum.ru/news/cultura/85138.html.

—— (2006). *Gosduma osudila britanskuiu razvedku, no ne nazvala 'opasnye NPO'.* [online] Available at: http://www.regnum.ru/news/578894.html.

Remizov, M. (2014). *Zhertva krymskoi kampanii.* [online] Izvestiia. Available at: http://iz.ru/news/567486.

RIA Novosti. (2014). *Vizit Shefa TsRU v Kyiv i operatsiia na iugo-vostoke: sovpadenie ili net?* [online] Available at: https://ria.ru/world/20140415/1004017907.html.

—— (2016). *Azarov: Ukraina eshche nikogda ne byla pod takim sil'nym vliianiem*

REFERENCES

Zapada. [online] Available at: https://ria.ru/world/20160229/1382187242.html.
Roberts, P. C. (2012). Pussy Riot, The Unfortunate Dupes of Amerikan Hegemony. [online] Available at: http://www.paulcraigroberts.org/2012/08/22/pussy-riot-the-unfortunate-dupes-amerikan-hegemony-paul-craig-roberts/.
Rogozin, D. (2012). *Russkii otvet Vladimiru Putinu*. [online] Izvestiia. Available at: http://izvestia.ru/news/513702.
Rosbalt. (2014). *Strelkov: Surkov vedet Rossiiu k pozornoi kapituliatsii v Novorossii i Krymu*. [online] Available at: http://www.rosbalt.ru/ukraina/2014/12/23/1351475.html.
Rossiiskaia gazeta. (2006). *Federal'ny zakon Rossiiskoi Federatsii ot 10 ianvaria 2006 goda № 18-FZ 'O vnesenii izmenenii v nekotorye zakonodatel'nye akty Rossiiskoi Federatsii*. [online] Available at: http://www.rg.ru/2006/01/17/nko-poryadok-dok.html.
Rostovskii, M. (2016*). Nikolai Patrushev: 'Mirovoe soobshchestvo dolzhno skazat' nam spasibo za Krym'*. [online] Moskovskii Komsomolets. Available at: http://www.mk.ru/politics/2016/01/26/nikolay-patrushev-mirovoe-soobshhestvo-dolzhno-skazat-nam-spasibo-za-krym.html.
Runkevich, D. and Malai, E. (2014). *Deputaty trebuiut zavesti ugolovnoe delo na Mikhaila Gorbacheva*. [online] Izvestiia. Available at: http://izvestia.ru/news/568959.
Rusrandru. (2012). *Novyi mirovoi klass i vyzovy chelovechestva*. [video] Youtube. Available at: https://www.youtube.com/watch?v=3OvqfkCyMMc.
Russkii zhurnal. (2003). *Riski i ugrozy dlia Rossii v 2003 godu*. [online] Available at: http://old.russ.ru/politics/20030307-doklad.html.
Samsonova, T. and Shevchenko, M. (2009). *Osoboe mnenie*. [online] Radio Ėkho Moskvy. Available at: http://echo.msk.ru/programs/personalno/585694-echo/#element-text.
Savel'ev, A. (2007). *Plan Dallesa – bred, stavshii real'nost'iu*. [online] Available at: http://www.savelev.ru/article/show/?id=420&t=1.
Shargunov, S. (2011). Gleb Pavlovskii: 'Tak ne tsarstvuiut!' [online] *Medved'*. Available at: http://www.medved-magazine.ru/articles/article_270.html.
Shepelin, I. (2014). *Dmitrii Kiselev: 'Teper' Ukraina – virtual'naia strana, a nash portal nastoiashchii'*. [online] Slon. Available at: https://republic.ru/russia/dmitriy_Kiselev_teper_ukraina_otnyne_virtualnoe_ponyatie_a_nash_portal_nastoyashchiy_-1097998.xhtml.
Shevchenko, M. (2011a). *20 let belovezhskoi tiranii*. [Blog] Livejournal. Available at: http://shevchenko-ml.livejournal.com/3019.html.
—— (2011b). *Sgin'! Otvet Sergeiu Parkhomenko*. [Blog] Livejournal. Available at: http://shevchenko-ml.livejournal.com/3920.html.
—— (2012a). *Byt' protiv Rima, ili Makfol kak imperskii procurator*. [online] *Kavkazskaia politika*. Available at: http://kavpolit.com/byt-protiv-rima-ili-makfol-kak-imperskij-prokurator/.
—— (2012b). *Kolonial'naia retrospektiva Izrailia*. [online] *Kavkazskaia politika*. Available at: http://kavpolit.com/kolonialnaya-retrospektiva-izrailya/.
—— (2013a). *Kavkaz: dva mira – dve kul'tury*. [online] Kavkazskaia politika. Available at: http://kavpolit.com/kavkaz-dva-mira-dve-kultury/.
—— (2013b). *Kavkazskaia politika kak sut' budushchego Rossii*. [online] *Kavkazskaia politika*. Available at: http://kavpolit.com/kavkazskaya-politika-kak-sut-budushhego-rossii/.

REFERENCES

——— (2013c). *My ne Evropa? I slava bogu!* [online] *Moskovskii Komsomolets.* Available at: http://www.mk.ru/specprojects/free-theme/article/2013/02/10/81 0258-myi-ne-evropa-i-slava-bogu.html.
Shironin, V. (2010). *Agenty perestroiki.* Moscow: Ėksmo.
Shved, V. (2013). SSSR: Vse moglo byt' inache. [online] *Stoletie.* Available at: http://www.stoletie.ru/versia/sssr_vso_moglo_byt_inache_967.htm.
Sid, I. (2004). 'Plan Andropova' desiat let spustia. [online] So-obshchenie. Available at: http://soob.ru/n/2004/5/op/1.
Simonyan, M. and Medvedev, D. (2008). *Interview with TV Channel Russia Today.* [online] Available at: http://en.kremlin.ru/events/president/transcripts/1226.
Sivkova, A. (2014). 'Est' Putin – est' Rossiia, net Putina – net Rossii'. [online] Iz.ru. Available at: https://iz.ru/news/578379.
Sopova, A. (2012). *Patriarkh Kirill: protiv Tserkvi vedëtsia informatsionnaia voina.* [online] Izvestiia. Available at: http://izvestia.ru/news/520710.
Stalin, I. V. (1997). O nedostatkakh partiinoi raboty i merakh likvidatsii trotskistskikh i inykh dvurushnikov: doklad na plenume TSK VKP(b). In Stalin I. V. *Sochineniia.* Moscow: Pisatel', Vol, 14, pp. 151–73.
Stanovaia, T. (2005). 'Sekretnyi doklad' Vladislava Surkova. [online] *Politkom. ru.* Available at: http://politcom.ru/288.html.
Starikov, N. (2009). *Zapad protiv Rossii: Za chto nas nenavidiat?* Moscow: Eksmo.
——— (2010a). *Kto finansiruet razval Rossii? Ot dekabristov do modzhakhedov.* St Petersburg: Piter.
——— (2010b). *Shershe lia neft'. Pochemu nash Stabilizatsionnyi fond nakhoditsia tam?* St Petersburg: Piter.
——— (2011a). Belaia lenta – zadacha prolit' krov'. [Blog] Nikolai Starikov. Available at: https://nstarikov.ru/blog/13919.
——— (2011b). Gorbachev. Izmena. [Blog] Nikolai Starikov. Available at: http://nstarikov.ru/blog/14078.
——— (2011c). *Natsionalizatsiia rublia – put' k svobode Rossii.* St Petersburg: Piter.
——— (2011d). Sviaz' vremën. [Blog] Nikolai Starikov. Available at: https://nstarikov.ru/blog/10548.
——— (2011e). Utrachennoe dostoinstvo. [Blog] Nikolai Starikov. Available ahttps://nstarikov.ru/blog/9787.
——— (2011f). Vybory v Rossii i pamiat'. [Blog] Nikolai Starikov. Available at: https://nstarikov.ru/blog/13827.
Stepankov, V. and Lisov, E. (1992). *Kremlevskii zagovor: versiia sledstviia.* Moscow: Ogonëk.
Štěrba, J. (2006). Denník menom Úsvit. [Blog] SMEblog. Available at: http://sterba.blog.sme.sk/c/32738/Dennik-menom-Usvit.html.
Strelkov, I. (2014). *Strelkov: 'Piataia kolonna' v Kremle slivaet Novorossiiu.* [online] Za otvetstvennuiu vlast'! Available at: http://igpr.ru/strelkov_5kolonna-v-kremle.
Sukhotin, A. (2014). 'Prezidenta ostavliaem na brustvere'. [online] *Novaia gazeta.* Available at: http://www.novayagazeta.ru/politics/64784.html.
Surkov, V. (2005). *Stenogramma vystupleniia na Gensovete 'Delovoi Rossii' 17 maia 2005 g.* [online] Radio Svoboda. Available at: https://www.svoboda.org/a/127679.html.

REFERENCES

—— (2006a). *Natsionalizatsiia budushchego.* [online] Ekspert. Available at: http://expert.ru/expert/2006/43/nacionalizaciya_buduschego/.
—— (2006b). *Suverenitet – èto politicheskii sinonim konkurentnosposobnosti.* [online] Politnauka. Available at: http://www.politnauka.org/library/public/surkov.php.
—— (2010). *Texts: 1997–2010.* Moscow: Publishing House 'Europe'.
Sut' vremeni. (2011). *Oni i My: Vozzvanie kluba 'Sut' Vremeni'.* [online] Available at: http://eot.su/node/10279.
TASS. (2014). *Putin: esli rezhim v Kyive nachal primeniat' armiiu vnutri strany – eto ser'eznoe prestuplenie.* [online] Available at: http://tass.ru/politika/1144185.
—— *Putin podpisal zakon o nezhelatel'nykh organizatsiiakh.* [online] Available at: http://tass.ru/politika/1990676.
—— *Nekommercheskie organizatsii v Rossii.* [online] Available at: http://tass.ru/info/671635.
Telen', L. (2009). *Mikhail Gorbachev: 'Chert poberi, do chego my dozhili!'* [online] Radio Svoboda. Available at: https://www.svoboda.org/a/1858368.html
The Council of the Federation. (2014). *Stenogramma trista sorok sed'mogo (vneocherednogo) zasedaniia Soveta Federatsii.* Moscow. [online] Availbable at: http://council.gov.ru/media/files/41d4c8b9772e9df14056.pdf.
The New Times. (2014). *Sergei Karaganov: 'My vernulis' v XIX vek'.* [online] Available at: http://karaganov.ru/content/images/uploaded/24d52797d5347b-c1e3d1b311e6c38069.pdf.
Tregubova, E. (2000). *Rossiiu legko raskrutit' na revolutsiiu.* [online] Kommersant. Available at: http://kommersant.ru/doc/17149.
Trukhachev, V. (2008). *Madlen Olbrait: mechtaiushchaia o Sibiri 'orlitsa s broshkoi'.* [online] *Pravda.ru.* Available at: https://www.pravda.ru/world/northamerica/usacanada/29-10-2008/289810-albright-0/.
Tsenzor.net (2004). *'Sovetnik Putina Gleb Pavlovskii: "V Rossii nazvat' 'zekom' – eto dazhe dostoinstvo."'* [online]. Available at: http://censor.net.ua/resonance/715/sovetnik_putina_gleb_pavlovskiyi_quotv_rossii_nazvat_quotzekomquot_eto_daje_dostoinstvo_znachit_on.
TSN. (2014). *Na Kubani proidet marsh za federalizatsiiu pod lozungom 'Khvatit kormit' Moskvu!'* [online] Available at: https://ru.tsn.ua/svit/na-kubani-proydet-marsh-za-federalizaciyu-pod-lozungom-hvatit-kormit-moskvu-381244.html.
Utkin, A. (2009). *Izmena genseka. Begstvo iz Evropy.* Moscow: Èksmo.
Zatulin, K. and Shevchenko, M. (2012). *Russkii vopros.* [video] Available at: http://www.materik.ru/institute/tv/detail.php?ID=15632.
Zinov'ev, A. (1995). Gibel' 'Imperii zla' (Ocherk Rossiiskoi tragedii). *Sotsiologicheskie issledovaniia,* (1): 92–103.
Zor'kin, V. (2006). *Apologiia Vestfal'skoi sistemy.* [online] Rossiiskaia gazeta. Available at: http://www.rg.ru/2006/08/22/zorjkin-statjya.html.
Zyuganov, G. (1997). *Geografiia pobedy. Osnovy rossiiskoi geopolitiki.* St Petersburg: Sankt-Peterburgskaia tipografiia no.6.

Videos

Analiticheskaia programma 'Odnako' s Mikhailom Leont'evym (2012). [TV Programme]. Channel One. [online] Available at: https://www.1tv.ru/news/

REFERENCES

2012-01-17/102215-analiticheskaya_programma_odnako_s_mihailom_leontievym.
Baranov, E. (2012). *Sotni tysiach pravoslavnykh po vsei Rossii molilis' vmeste vo imia very i v zashchitu tserkvi*. [online] Channel One. Available at: https://www.1tv.ru/news/2012-04-22/100381-sotni_tysyach_pravoslavnyh_po_vsey_rossii_molilis_vmeste_vo_imya_very_i_v_zaschitu_tserkvi.
Batukhov, A. (2015). *'God Maidanu. Ne zabudem, ne prostim!' – marsh v tsentre Moskvy k godovshchine smeny vlasti v Kyive*. [online] Channel One. Available at: https://www.1tv.ru/news/2015/02/21/27671-god_maydanu_ne_zabudem_ne_prostim_marsh_v_tsentre_moskvy_k_godovschine_smeny_vlasti_v_Kyive.
Bol'shaia igra. (2007). [TV Programme]: Channel One.
Channel Five. (2015). *Chto podderzhivaet amerikanskii 'Fond v podderzhku demokratii?'* [online] Available at: http://www.5-tv.ru/news/98916/.
Channel One. (2012a). *Byvshii glava kantseliarii eks-prem'era Britanii podtverdil dostovernost' istorii so 'shpionskim kamnem'*. [online] Available at: https://www.1tv.ru/news/2012-01-19/102448-byvshiy_glava_kantselyarii_eks_premi era_britanii_podtverdil_dostovernost_istorii_so_shpionskim_kamnem.
—— (2012b). *Novyi posol SSHA v Rossii vstretilsia s predstaviteliami oppozitsii*. [online] Available at: https://www.1tv.ru/news/2012-01-17/102214-novyy_posol_ssha_v_rossii_vstretilsya_s_predstavitelyami_oppozitsii.
—— (2012c). *V SK prokommentirovali rezul'taty proverki videorolikov, razmeschennykh v Internete*. [online] Available at: https://www.1tv.ru/news/2012-02-04/103836-v_sk_prokommentirovali_rezultaty_proverki_videorolik ov_razmeschennyh_v_internete.
—— (2015). *'Natsional'nyi fond v podderzhku demokratii' stal pervoi v RF nezhelatel'noi mezhdunarodnoi organizatsiei*. [online] Available at: http://www.1tv.ru/news/2015/07/28/14508-natsionalnyy_fond_v_podderzhku_dem okratii_stal_pervoy_v_rf_nezhelatelnoy_mezhdunarodnoy_organizatsiey.
CHP. *Rassledovanie: Golos niotkuda* (2011). [TV Programme]: NTV. [online]. Available at http://www.ntv.ru/video/peredacha/267383.
—— *Rassledovanie: Hystera Ænigma* (2012a). [TV Programme]: NTV. [online]. Available at: http://www.ntv.ru/video/305205/.
—— *Rassledovanie. Anatomiia protesta* (2012b). [TV Programme]: NTV. [online]. Available at http://www.ntv.ru/video/peredacha/296996/.
Constantine26rus. (2012). *Rossiia. Polnoe zatmenie. Fil'm №1 2012*. [online] Available at: https://www.youtube.com/watch?v=j9yZXVFukOY.
Dugin, A. (1992). *Ideologiia Mirovogo Pravitel'stva*, Elementy, no. 2, Arktogeia, http://arcto.ru/article/409.
—— (2010). *Konspirologiia stala poshloi*. [video] Available at: http://russia.ru/video/diskurs_10526/.
Kiselev, D. (2012). *Vazhnoe interv'iu Patriarkha*. [online] Rossiia-1. Available at: http://vesti7.ru/article/347008/episode/09-09-2012/.
—— (2015a). *'Aidarovskii' bunt: nikto ne khochet voevat' za oligarkhov*. [online] Rossiia-1. Available at: http://vesti7.ru/article/345596/episode/08-02-2015/.
—— (2015b). *Killer rossiiskogo liberalizma: Kas'ianov pokhoronil RPR-PARNAS*. [online] Available at: http://vesti7.ru/video/1487429/episode/26-04-2015.
—— (2015c). *Putin: 'Dialog s oppozitsiei vozmozhen, esli ona ne rabotaet po zakazu izvne'*. [online] Rossiia-1. Available at: http://vesti7.ru/article/342398/episode/29-03-2015.

REFERENCES

—— (2016a). *Amerikantsy tolkaiut Evropu k bol'shoi voine.* [online] Rossiia-1. Available at: http://vesti7.ru/article/345571/episode/15-02-2015/.
—— (2016b). *'Tainye bogatstva Putina': ni faktov, ni dokumentov, no podgadit' khochetsya.* [online] Rossiia-1. Available at: http://vesti7.ru/article/350379/episode/31-01-2016/.
Kiselev, D. and Balitskii, A. (2014). *Kyivskie gastrolery: ot vitse-prezidenta SSHA do ekzortsista.* [online] Rossiia-1. Avilable at: http://vesti7.ru/article/346117/episode/27-04-2014/.
Kiselev, D. and Bogdanov, V. (2014). *Biznes na krovi: slantsevye zalezhi Ukrainy ne daiut pokoia SShA.* [online] Rossiia-1. Available at: http://vesti7.ru/video/1497953/episode/18-05-2014/.
—— (2015). *Amerikantsy khotiat poborot' Putina virusom demokratii.* [online] Rossiia-1. Available at: http://vesti7.ru/video/1497279/episode/08-03-2015/.
Kiselev, D. and Liadov, A. (2015). *V rossiiskii stop-list popali organizatory gosperevorotov.* [online] Rossiia-1. Available at: http://vesti7.ru/article/342730/episode/12-07-2015/.
Kiselev, D. and Medvedev, A. (2014). *Uchastniki 'Marsha mira,' po suti, trebovali zapreshchennykh kolbas i syrov.* [online] Rossiia-1. Available at: http://vesti7.ru/article/345925/episode/21-09-2014/.
Kiselev, D. and Popov, E. (2014a). *Iavlinskii obkhodit Khodorkovskogo storonoi.* [online] Rossiia-1. Available at: http://vesti7.ru/article/345850/episode/19-10-2014.
—— (2014b). *Sanktsii nasmeshili rossiiskii isteblishment* [online] Rossiia-1. Available at: http://vesti7.ru/article/346201/episode/23-03-2014.
Kiselev, D. and Rozhkov, E. (2014a). *Antirossiiskie mitingi: intelligentsia prevrashchaetsia v intelligenturu'.* [online] Rossiia-1. Available at: http://vesti7.ru/article/345880/episode/05-10-2014.
—— (2014b). *Kyiv skryvaet pravdu o krovavykh 'zachistkakh'.* [online] Rossiia-1. Available at: http://vesti7.ru/article/346069/episode/01-06-2014.
Kiselev, D. and Skabeeva, O. (2015a). *Maidan ob"iavil Chicherinu terroristkoi.* [online] Rossiia-1. Available at: http://vesti7.ru/article/345554/episode/22-02-2015/.
—— (2015b). *NED: Kak Vashington lezet v chuzhie dela.* [online] Rossiia-1. Available at: http://vesti7.ru/article/342562/episode/17-05-2015.
Kiselev, D. and Zarubin, P. (2015). *Den' Rossii: Strana nauchilas' gordit'sia soboi.* [online] Rossiia-1. Available at: http://vesti7.ru/article/342631/episode/14-06-2015/.
—— (2016). *Za 'svobodnuiu' stranu: oppozitsionery gotovy otdat' chast' Rossii.* [online] Rossiia-1. Available at: http://vesti7.ru/article/344381/episode/13-03-2016/.
Krym. Put' na rodinu. (2015). [TV programme]: Rossiia-1.
Makeeva, M. (2011). *Mironov ob"iavil Beliakovu vygovor. Ne malo li?* [online] Dozhd. Available at: http://tvrain.ru/articles/geroy_utra_anton_belyakov_dokument_po_golosu_vyglyadel_po_drugomu-99998/.
Piter.tv. (2012). *Video: 'Edinaia Rosiia' topchet beluiu lentu v Gosdume.* [video] Available at: http://piter.tv/event/Video_Edinaya_Rossiya_t.
Poedinok s Vladimirom Solov'evym (2012). [TV programme]: Rossiia-1. [online] Available at: http://vsoloviev.ru/battle/2012/1154/.
Politika. (2013). [TV Programme]: Channel One [online] Available at: http://www.1tv.ru/shows/politika/vypuski/politika-vypusk-ot-11-04-2013.

REFERENCES

Pust' govoriat: Besy (2012). [TV Programme]: Channel One. [online] Available at: http://www.1tv.ru/shows/pust-govoryat/vypuski-i-dramatichnye-momenty/besy-pust-govoryat-vypusk-ot-15-03-2012.

Putin, Russia and the West. Episode 2: Democracy Threatens (2012). [TV Programme]: BBC Two. [online] Available at: http://www.bbc.co.uk/programmes/products/26007.

Revenko, E. (2012). *Patriarkh Kirill: Poias Bogoroditsy dal velikuiu nadezhdu.* [online] Rossiia-1. Available at: http://www.vesti.ru/videos?vid=389143.

Rossiia 1. (2012). *Za Pussy Riot vstupilis' deiateli kul'tury.* [online] Available at: http://www.vesti7.ru/vh?cid=33601.

Rozhkov, E. (2012). *Avtoprobegom po koshchunstvu.* [online] Rossiia 1. Available at: http://www.vesti7.ru/archive/news?id=34503.

Shevchenko, M. (2010). *Kto takie russkie.* [video] Available at: http://russia.ru/video/diskurs_11273/.

—— (2012c). *Prodiusery siriiskoi voiny.* [video] Available at: http://tv.russia.ru/video/diskurs_13146/.

Shevchenko, M. and Pavlovskii, G. (2012). *Shevchenko vs. Pavlovskii. Razluchennyi s Putinym.* [video] Available at: http://www.russia.ru/news/politics/2012/10/26/3447.html.

Sholomon84. (2012). *Putin vystupil na mitinge v Luzhnikakh. Polnaia versiia.* [video]. Available at: https://www.youtube.com/watch?v=xtopeYRdthg.

Spetsial'nyi korrespondent: Litsedei. (2013). [TV Programme]: Rossiia-1. [online] Available at: https://russia.tv/video/show/brand_id/3957/episode_id/699361/video_id/699361/.

Spetsial'nyi korrespondent: Provokatory. (2012). [TV Programme]: Rossiia-1. [online] Available at: https://www.youtube.com/watch?v=-yk4lLQ_9Hg.

Spetsial'nyi korrespondent: Provokatory-2. (2012). [TV Programme]: Rossiia-1. [online] Available at: https://www.youtube.com/watch?v=T8uRGkoqRJw.

Spetsial'nyi korrespondent: Provokatory-3. (2012). [TV Programme]: Rossiia-1. [online] Available at: https://russia.tv/video/show/brand_id/3957/episode_id/167958/video_id/167958/.

Spetsial'nyi korrespondent: Revolutsiia na zakaz. (2015). [TV Programme]: Rossiia-1. [online] Available at: https://russia.tv/anons/show/episode_id/1213003/brand_id/3957/.

Spetsial'nyi korrespondent: Shpionskii kamen'. (2012). [TV Programme]: Rossiia-1. [online] Available at: https://russia.tv/video/show/brand_id/9361/episode_id/113606/video_id/113606/.

Spetsial'nyi korrespondent: Shpiony. (2006). [TV Programme]: Rossiia. [online] Available at: http://www.youtube.com/watch?v=G5ePL1wDuiQ.

TASS upolnomochen zaiavit'. (1984). [Film] Moscow: Tsentral'naia kinostudiia detskikh i iunosheskikh fil'mov im. Gor'kogo.

V Kontekste: Chto stoit za aktsiei 'Pussy Riot' v Khrame Khrista Spasitelia (2012). [TV Programme]: Channel One [online] Available at: http://www.1tv.ru/prj/vkontekste/vypusk/14392.

Vesti.ru. (2012). *'Èkspert: 'shpionskii kamen' stoit desiatki millionov funtov sterlingov'.* [online] Available at: http://www.vesti.ru/doc.html?id=690724.

Zarubin, P. (2012). *Zakon ob NKO vyzval ostruiu polemiku.* [video] Available at http://vesti7.ru/article/347018/episode/08-07-2012/.

REFERENCES

Secondary Sources

Aaronovitch, D. (2009). *Voodoo Histories: The Role of the Conspiracy Theory in Shaping Modern History*. London: Jonathan Cape.

Adrianova, A. (2016). *Putin's Maverick Adviser Defies Nabiullina With $64 Billion Plan*. [online] Bloomberg. Available at: https://www.bloomberg.com/news/articles/2016-10-30/putin-s-maverick-adviser-defies-nabiullina-with-64-billion-plan.

Afanas'eva, E., Shulinskii, I., Kachkaeva, A., and Loshak, A. (2012). *Telekhranitel'*. [online] Available at: http://echo.msk.ru/programs/tv/924973-echo/.

Afisha. (2012). *NTV Lzhet*. [online] Available at: https://daily.afisha.ru/archive/gorod/archive/ntvlies/.

Aleksandrov, A. (2016). *'Levada-tsentr': rossiiane stali eshche khuzhe otnosit'sia k Khrushchevu, Gorbachevu i El'tsinu*. [online] Tvrain. Available at: https://tvrain.ru/articles/levada-404640/.

Ambrosio, T. (2009). *Authoritarian Backlash: Russian Resistance to Democratization in the Former Soviet Union*. Burlington: Ashgate.

Amirian, T. (2013). *Oni napisali zagovor. Konspirologicheskii detektiv ot Dena Brauna do Iulii Kristevoi*. Moscow: Falanster.

Applebaum, A. (2004). *Gulag: A History*. Anchor Books.

Arkhipov, I. and Kravchenko, S. (2013*). Putin's Men Targeting Migrants as Moscow Mayor Race Heats Up*. [online] Bloomberg. Available at: http://www.bloomberg.com/news/print/2013-08-14/putin-s-men-crack-down-on-migrants-as-moscow-mayor-race-heats-up.html.

Aslund, A. and McFaul, M. (2006). *Revolution in Orange: The Origins of Ukraine's Democratic Breakthrough*. Washington DC: Carnegie Endowment for International Peace.

Astapova, A. (2015). *Negotiating Belarusianness: Political Folklore betwixt and between*. PhD. University of Tartu.

Atwal, M. (2009). Evaluating Nashi's Sustainability: Autonomy, Agency and Activism. *Europe-Asia Studies*, 61(5): 743–58.

Atwal, M. and Bacon, E. (2012). The Youth Movement Nashi: Contentious Politics, Civil Society, and Party Politics. *East European Politics*, 28(3): 256–66.

Azar, I. (2015). *Rasserzhennye patrioty*. [online] Meduza. Available at: https://meduza.io/feature/2015/02/21/rasserzhennye-patrioty.

Bagdasarian, A. (2007). *S tverskoi strast'iu*. [online] The New Times. Available at: https://newtimes.ru/stati/others/archive-7309-s-tverskoi-strastu.html.

Bagdasarian, V. E. (1999). *Teoriia zagovora v otechestvennoi istoriografii vtoroi poloviny 19–20 vv*. Moscow: Signal.

Balmforth, T. (2013). *Levada Center, Russia's Most Respected Pollster, Fears Closure*. [online] Radio Free Europe/Radio Liberty. Available at: https://www.rferl.org/a/russia-levada-center-foreign-agent/24992729.html.

—— (2014). *From the Fringes toward Mainstream: Russian Nationalist Broadsheet Basks in Ukraine Conflict*. [online] Radio Free Europe/Radio Liberty. Available at: https://www.rferl.org/a/26534846.html.

Baraulina, A. (2006). Kul't distantsionnogo upravleniia. *Russkii Newsweek*, (6): 24–7.

Barbashin, A. and Thoburn, H. (2014). *Putin's Brain. Alexander Dugin and*

REFERENCES

the Philosophy behind Putin's Invasion of Crimea. [online] *Foreign Affairs.* Available at: https://www.foreignaffairs.com/articles/russia-fsu/2014-03-31/putins-brain.

Barkun, M. (2003). *The Culture of Conspiracy: Apocalyptic Visions in Contemporary America.* Berkeley: University of California Press.

Barry, E. (2014). *Foes of America in Russia Crave Rupture in Ties.* [online] The New York Times. Available at: http://www.nytimes.com/2014/03/16/world/europe/foes-of-america-in-russia-crave-rupture-in-ties.html?hp&_r=3.

Bartal, I. (2005). *The Jews of Eastern Europe, 1772–1881.* Philadelphia: The University of Pennsylvania Press.

Bashlykova, N. (2011). *Deputatskoe zaiavlenie protiv 'Golosa' initsiirovala LDPR.* [online] Kommersant. Available at: http://kommersant.ru/doc/1827619.

Bassin, M. and Aksenov, K. E. (2006). Mackinder and the Heartland Theory in Post-Soviet Geopolitical Discourse. *Geopolitics,* 11(1): 99–118.

Baunov, A. (2012). *Poslom v Rossiiu priezzhaet spetsialist po revolutsiiam.* [online] Slon. Available at: http://slon.ru/world/spetsialist_po_antidiktatorskim_dvizheniyam-730708.xhtml.

BBC. (2005). Text: Bush's speech in Georgia. [online] Available at: http://news.bbc.co.uk/1/hi/world/europe/4534267.stm.

—— (2011). *Peskov: 'Gorbachev, razvalivshii stranu, Putinu ne sovetchik'.* [online] Available at: http://www.bbc.com/russian/russia/2011/12/111226_peskov_gorbachev_putin.shtml.

—— (2013). Berezovskii: intelligent i manipuliator. [online] Available at: http://www.bbc.com/russian/russia/2013/03/130324_berezovsky_death_reaction.

—— (2014). *Ukraine crisis: Transcript of leaked Nuland-Pyatt call.* [online] Available at: http://www.bbc.co.uk/news/world-europe-26079957.

—— (2015). *Ianukovich pokhvalil Oppozitsionnyi blok i 'svalil' Evromaidan na oligarkhov.* [online] Available at: http://www.bbc.com/ukrainian/ukraine_in_russian/2015/12/151209_ru_s_Yanukovich_new_interview.

—— (2016). *'Putin is corrupt' says US Treasury.* [online] Available at: http://www.bbc.co.uk/news/world-europe-35385445.

Bearak, M. (2017). *Russian Ambassador Mirgayas Shirinskiy is seventh Russian diplomat to die since November.* [online] Washington Post. Available at: https://www.washingtonpost.com/news/worldviews/wp/2017/08/24/the-russian-diplomat-found-dead-in-his-pool-in-sudan-is-the-seventh-to-die-since-november/?tid=sm_fb_wd&utm_term=.f68dc3f8ca8d.

Beauchamp, Z. (2017). Democrats are falling for fake news about Russia. [online] Vox. Available at: https://www.vox.com/platform/amp/world/2017/5/19/15561842/trump-russia-louise-mensch.

Belanovsky, S. and Dmitriev, M. (2011). *Political Crisis in Russia and How it May Develop.* [online] The Center For Strategic Research Foundation. Available at: https://csis-prod.s3.amazonaws.com/s3fs-public/legacy_files/files/attachments/110330_CSR_Political_Crisis_in_Russia.pdf.

Benford, Robert D. and Snow, D. A. (2000). Framing Processes and Social Movements: An Overview and Assessment. *Annual Review of Sociology,* 26: 611–39.

Berlet, C. and Nemiroff Lyons, M. (2000). *Right-Wing Populism in America: Too Close For Comfort.* New York: The Guilford Press.

Bershidsky, L. (2014). *Anti-War Russians, An Endangered Minority.* [online]

REFERENCES

Bloomberg. Available at: https://www.bloomberg.com/view/articles/2014-03-10/anti-war-russians-an-endangered-minority.

Birchall, C. (2006). *Knowledge Goes Pop. From Conspiracy Theories to Gossip.* Oxford: Berg.

Biriukova, L. and Zheleznova, M. (2013). *Blizkie k narodnomu frontu organizatsii raspredeliat prezidentskie granty.* [online] Available at: https://www.vedomosti.ru/politics/articles/2013/04/01/granty_doverennym.

Blake, H., Warren, T., Holmes, R., Leopold, J., Bradley, J., and Campbell, A. (2017). From Russia With Blood. [online] *Buzzfeed.* Available at: https://www.buzzfeed.com/heidiblake/from-russia-with-blood-14-suspected-hits-on-british-soil.

Blomfield, A. (2006). *Ambassador harassed by Putin youth wing.* [online] Telegraph. Available at: http://www.telegraph.co.uk/news/worldnews/1536439/Ambassador-harassed-by-Putin-youth-wing.html.

Bocharova, S. (2015). *Senator progovorilsia o soglasovanii 'patriotischeskogo stop-lista' s FSB.* [online] RBC. Available at: http://www.rbc.ru/politics/07/07/2015/559bbf869a794724f4be0361.

Bonnell, V. (1999). *Iconography of Power: Soviet Political Posters under Lenin and Stalin.* Berkeley: University of California Press.

Borenstein, E. (2017). *Plots against Russia: Conspiracy and Fantasy after Socialism.* [online] Available at: http://plotsagainstrussia.org/.

Borodina, A. (2008). *Kak smotreli 'Gibel' imperii. Uroki Vizantii'.* [online] Kommersant. Available at: http://kommersant.ru/doc/848071.

—— (2014). *Televizor Olimpiady i propagandy.* [online] Forbes. Available at: http://www.forbes.ru/mneniya-opinion/konkurentsiya/261539-televizor-olimpiady-i-ukrainy-rekordy-propagandy.

Boym, S. (1994). *Common places. Mythologies of Everyday Life in Russia.* Cambridge, MA: Harvard University Press.

Bratich, J. Z. (2008). *Conspiracy Panics: Political Rationality and Popular Culture.* Albany: State University of New York Press.

Brown, A. (1996). *The Gorbachev factor.* Oxford: Oxford University Press.

—— (2011). The Gorbachev Factor Revisited. *Problems of Post-Communism,* 58 (4–5): 56–65.

Brudny, Y. M. (1998). *Reinventing Russia. Russian Nationalism and the Soviet State, 1953–1991.* Cambridge: Harvard University Press.

Bryanski, G. and Grove, T. (2011). *Putin launches Kremlin bid with swipe at opponents.* [online] Reuters. Available at: http://www.reuters.com/article/us-russia-putin-presidency-idUSTRE7AQ05320111127.

Calabresi, M. (2017). Inside Russia's Social media War on America. [online] Time. Available at: http://time.com/4783932/inside-russia-social-media-war-america/.

Cassiday, J. A. and Johnson, E. D. (2010). Putin, Putiniana and the Question of a Post-Soviet Cult of Personality. *Slavonic and East European Review,* 88 (44): 681–707.

Chaulia, S. (2006). *Democratisation, NGOs and 'colour revolutions'.* [online] Open Democracy. Available at: https://www.opendemocracy.net/globalization-institutions_government/colour_revolutions_3196.jsp.

Clover, C. (2013). *Putin and the Monk.* [online] Financial Times. Available at: https://www.ft.com/content/f2fcba3e-65be-11e2-a3db-00144feab49a?mhq5j=e2.

REFERENCES

—— (2016). *Black Wind, White Snow. The Rise of Russia's New Nationalism.* New Haven: Yale University Press.

Cohen, Z. (2017). Russian politician: US spies slept while Russia elected Trump. [online] *CNN.* Available at: http://edition.cnn.com/2017/09/12/politics/russian-politician-us-election-intelligence/index.html.

Colton, T. (2008). *Yeltsin: A Life.* New York: Basic Books.

Colton, T. and Hale, H. (2014). Putin's Uneasy Return and Hybrid Regime Stability. *Problems of Post-Communism,* 61(2): 3–22.

Cowdock, B. (2017). Faulty Towers. Understanding the impact of overseas corruption on the London property market. [online] Transparency International. Available at: http://www.transparency.org.uk/publications/faulty-towers-understanding-the-impact-of-overseas-corruption-on-the-london-property-market/.

Crotty, J., Hall, S. M. and Ljubownikow, S. (2014). Post-Soviet Civil Society Development in the Russian Federation: The Impact of the NGO Law. *Europe-Asia Studies,* 66(8):1253–69.

Cullinane, S. (2015). *Putin's popularity at record high, government-funded poll says.* [online] CNN. Available at: http://edition.cnn.com/2015/10/22/europe/russia-putin-poll/.

Davis, D. B. (1971). *Fear of Conspiracy: Images of Un-American Subversion from the Revolution to the Present.* Ithaca: Cornell University Press.

Dawisha, K. (2015). *Putin's Kleptocracy.* New York: Simon & Schuster.

Dean, J. (2002). *Publicity's Secret: How Technoculture Capitalizes on Democracy.* Ithaca: Cornell University Press.

Deich, M. (2005). Zloveshchii 'Plan Dallesa'. [online]. *Moskovskii Komsomolets.* Available at: http://www.mk.ru/editions/daily/article/2005/01/20/200843-zloveschiy-plan-dallesa.html.

Dobson, M. (2009). *Khruschev's Cold Summer. GULAG Returnees, Crime, and the Fate of Reform After Stalin.* Ithaca: Cornell University Press.

Doktorov, B. Z., Oslon, A. A., Petrenko, E. S. (2002). *Ėpokha El'tsina: mneniia rossiian.* Moscow: Institut fonda 'Obshchestvenoe mnenie'.

Dolbilov, M. (2010). *Russkii krai, chuzhaia vera.* Moscow: Novoe literaturnoe obozrenie.

Dubin, B. (2011). Simvoly vozvrata vmesto simvolov peremen. *Pro et Contra,* 15 (5): 6–22.

Dudakov, S. (1993). *Istoriia odnogo mifa: ocherki russkoi literatury XIX-XX vv.* Moscow: Nauka.

Duncan, P. J. S. (2005). *Russian Messianism: Third Rome, Revolution, Communism and after.* London: Routledge.

—— (2013). Russia, the West and the 2007–8 Electoral Cycle: Did the Kremlin Really Fear a 'Coloured Revolution'? *Europe-Asia Studies,* 65(1): 1–25.

Dunlop, J. (2004). Aleksandr Dugin's Foundations of Geopolitics. *Democratizatsiia,* 12(1): 41–59.

Elder, M. (2011a). *Vladimir Putin accuses Hillary Clinton of encouraging Russian protests.* [online] Guardian. Available at: https://www.theguardian.com/world/2011/dec/08/vladimir-putin-hillary-clinton-russia.

—— (2011b). *Vladimir Putin mocks Moscow's 'condom-wearing' protesters.* [online] Guardian. Available at: https://www.theguardian.com/world/2011/dec/15/vladimir-putin-mocks-moscow-protesters.

Engelstein, L. (1993). Combined Underdevelopment: Discipline and the

REFERENCES

Law in Imperial and Soviet Russia. *American Historical Review*, 98(2): 338–53.

Etkind, A. and Yablokov, I. (2017, forthcoming). Global Crises as Western Conspiracies: Russian Theories of Oil Prices and the Ruble Exchange Rate. *Journal of Soviet and Post-Soviet Politics and Society*.

Evroaziatskii Evreiskii Kongress. (2016). *Antisemitizm v Rossii i stranakh SNG v 2015 godu*. [online] Available at: http://eajc.org/data//file/%D0%90%D0%BD%D1%82%D0%B8%D1%81%D0%B5%D0%BC%D0%B8%D1%82%D0%B8%D0%B7%D0%BC-15.doc.

Fedor, J. (2011). Chekists Look Back on the Cold War: The Polemical Literature. *Intelligence and National Security*, 26 (6): 842–63.

Fenster, M. (2008). *Conspiracy Theories: Secrecy and Power in American Culture*. Minneapolis: University of Minnesota Press.

Finkel, E. (2010). In Search of Lost Genocide: Historical Policy and International Politics in Post-1989 Eastern Europe. *Global Society*, 24(1): 51–70.

Finkel, E. and Brudny, Y. M. (2012). Russia and the Colour Revolutions. *Democratization*, 19(1): 15–36.

—— (2013). *Coloured Revolutions and Authoritarian Reactions*. London: Routledge.

Fishman, M. (2006). *A kamen' prosto otkryvalsia*. [online] Kommersant. Available at: http://kommersant.ru/doc/644690.

Fishman, M., Sedakov, P. and Alekseev, Iu. (2008). Demisezonnyi kandidat. *Russkii Newsweek* (6): 14–17.

Fitzpatrick, S. (2000). *Everyday Stalinism. Ordinary Life in Extraordinary Times: Soviet Russia in the 1930s*. New York: Oxford University Press.

Foreign Affairs. (2014). *Alexander Dugin*. [online] Available at: http://global thinkers.foreignpolicy.com/#agitators/detail/dugin.

Foucault, M. (1980). *Power/Knowledge: Selected Interviews and Other Writings 1972–1977*. Brighton: The Harvester Press.

Franchetti, M. (2008). *Jailed tycoon Mikhail Khodorkovsky Framed by key Putin Aide*. [online] Sunday Times. Available at: https://www.thetimes.co.uk/article/jailed-tycoon-mikhail-khodorkovsky-framed-by-key-putin-aide-935v8p982fg.

Fredheim, R. (2016). The Loyal Editor Effect: Russian Online Journalism After Independence. *Post-Soviet Affairs*, DOI: 10.1080/1060586X.2016.1200797.

Frye, T., Gehlbach, S., Marquardt, K. L. and Reuter, O. J. (2017). Is Putin's Popularity Real? *Post-Soviet Affairs*, 33(1): 1–15.

Fuller Jr, W. C. (2006). *The Foe Within: Fantasies of Treason and the End of Imperial Russia*. Ithaca and London: Cornell University Press.

Furman, B. (2007). *Problema 2008: Obshchee i osobennoe v protsessakh perekhoda postsovetskikh gosudarstv*. [online] Polit.ru. Available at: http://polit.ru/article/2007/10/19/furman/.

Gaidar, Y. (2007). *Collapse of an Empire. Lessons for Modern Russia*. Washington, DC: Brookings Institution Press.

Gaddis, J. L. (2005). *The Cold War*. London: Penguin.

Galbreath, D. J. (2009). Putting the Colour into Revolutions? The OSCE and Civil Society in the Post-Soviet Region. *Journal of Communist Studies and Transition Politics*, 25 (2–3): 161–80.

Galeotti, M. (1997). *Gorbachev and his Revolution*. London: Palgrave Macmillan.

REFERENCES

Gel'man, V. (2013). Cracks in the Wall. Challenges to Electoral Authoritarianism in Russia. *Problems of Post-Communism*, 60(2): 3–10.

—— (2015). *Authoritarian Russia: Analyzing Post-Soviet Regime Changes*. Pittsburgh: University of Pittsburgh Press.

—— (2016). The Politics of Fear. How Russia's Rulers Counter Their Rivals. *Russian Politics*, (1): 27–45.

Gill, G. (2013). Political Symbolism and the Fall of the USSR. *Europe-Asia Studies*, 65 (2): 244–63.

Goffman, E. (1974). *Frame Analysis: An Essay on the Organization of Experience*. Cambridge, MA: Harvard University Press.

Goldberg, R. A. (2001). *Enemies Within: The Culture of Conspiracy in Modern America*. New Haven: Yale University Press.

Golunov, S. (2012). *The 'Hidden Hand' of External Enemies*. [online] PONARS Eurasia. Available at: http://www.ponarseurasia.org/memo/hidden-hand-exter nal-enemies-use-conspiracy-theories-putins-regime.

—— (2015). *What Should Students Know about Russia's Enemies? Conspiracy Theories in Russian Geopolitical Textbooks*. [online] PONARS Eurasia. Available at: http://www.ponarseurasia.org/memo/conspiracy-theories-rus sian-geopolitical.

Gorlizki, Y. and Khlevniuk, O. (2004). *Cold Peace: Stalin and the Soviet Ruling Circle, 1945–1953*. New York: Oxford University Press.

Gorodetskaia, N. (2013). *Genprokuratura vynesla opredelenie politicheskoi deiatel'nosti*. [online] Kommersant. Available at: https://www.kommersant. ru/doc/2261048.

Goscillo, H., ed. (2011). *Putin as Celebrity and Cultural Icon*. London: Routledge.

Gray, M. (2010). *Conspiracy Theories in the Arab World: Sources and Politics*. London: Routledge.

Greene, S. A. (2014). *Moscow in Movement. Power and Opposition in Putin's Russia*. Stanford: Stanford University Press.

Greene, S. A. and Robertson, G. (2017). How Putin Wins Support. *Journal of Democracy*, 28(4): 86–100.

Greenfield, L. (1992). *Nationalism: Five Roads to Modernity*. Cambridge, MA: Harvard University Press.

Gudkov, L. D., Dubin, B. V. and Zorkaia, N. A. (2008). *Postsovetskii chelovek i grazhdanskoe obshchestvo* (Moscow: Moskovskaia shkola politicheskikh issledovanii).

Guriev, S. and Treisman, D. (2015). *How Modern Dictators Survive: An Information Theory of the New Authoritarianism*. [online] The National Bureau of Economic Research. Available at: http://www.nber.org/papers/ w21136.

Guseva, D. and Fishman, M. (2007). Soiuz sil'nykh pravykh. *Russkii Newsweek* (48): 26–8.

Gustaffson, T. (2012). *Wheel of Fortune. The Battle for Oil and Power in Russia*. Harvard: Harvard University Press.

Hagemeister, M. (2008). The Protocols of the Elders of Zion: Between History and Fiction. *New German Critique*, 35(1): 83–95.

Hale, H. (2015). *Patronal Politics: Eurasian Regime Dynamics in Comparative Perspective*. Cambridge: Cambridge University Press.

Halfin, I. (2001). The Demonization of the Opposition: Stalinist Memory and the 'Communist Archive' at Leningrad Communist University. *Kritika: Explorations in Russian and Eurasian History*, 2(1): 45–80.

Harambam, J. and Aupers, S. (2016). 'I am not a conspiracy theorist': Relational Identifications in the Dutch Conspiracy Milieu. *Cultural Sociology*, 11(1): 1–17.

Harris, J. R. (2015). *The Great Fear. Stalin's Terror of the 1930s*. Oxford: Oxford University Press.

Harrison, B. (2006). *The Resurgence of Anti-Semitism: Jews, Israel, and Liberal Opinion*. Lanham: Rowman & Littlefield Publishers.

Hemment, J. (2012). Nashi, Youth Voluntarism, and Potemkin NGOs: Making Sense of Civil Society in Post-Soviet Russia. *Slavic Review*, 71(2): 234–60.

Hofstadter, R. (1996). *The Paranoid Style in American Politics and Other Essays*. Cambridge: Harvard University Press.

Horvath, R. (2011). Putin's 'Preventive Counter-Revolution': Post-Soviet Authoritarianism and the Spectre of Velvet Revolution, *Europe-Asia Studies*, 63 (1): 1–25.

—— (2013). *Putin's 'Preventive Counter-Revolution': Post-Soviet Authoritarianism and the Spectre of Velvet Revolution*. London: Routledge.

Human Rights Watch. (2005). *Russia: Amended Law Threatens NGOs*. [online] Available at: https://www.hrw.org/news/2005/12/27/russia-amended-law-threatens-ngos.

Hutchings, S. and Rulyova, N. (2009). *Television and Culture in Putin's Russia: Remote Control*. London: Routledge.

Hutchings, S. and Szostek, J. (2015). Dominant Narratives in Russian Political and Media Discourse During the Ukraine Crisis. In Pikulicka-Wilczewska, A. and Sakwa, R., eds. *Ukraine and Russia: People, Politics, Propaganda and Perspectives*. Bristol: E-International Relations, pp. 183–96.

Hutchings, S. and Tolz, V. (2015). *Nation, Ethnicity and Race on Russian Television: Mediating Post-Soviet Difference*. London: Routledge.

Jablokov, I. (2015). Feinde, Verräter, Fünfte Kolonnen: Verschwörungstheorien in Russland. *Osteuropa*, (4): 99–114.

Johnston, T. (2011). *Being Soviet. Identity, Rumour, and Everyday life under Stalin, 1939–1953*. Oxford: Oxford University Press.

Jørgensen, M. and Phillips, L. (2002). *Discourse Analysis as Theory and Method*. London: Sage Publications.

Judah, B. (2013). *Fragile Empire. How Russia Fell In and Out of Love with Vladimir Putin*. New Haven and London: Yale University Press.

Kamyshev, D. (1999). *Otlichivshiesia i provinivshiesia*. [online] Kommersant. Available at: http://kommersant.ru/doc/218452.

—— (2002). 'Strategiia dolzhna byt' dostatochno tumannoi'. [online] Kommersant. Available at: https://www.kommersant.ru/doc/344734.

—— (2011). *Proekt 'Nu, pogodi!'* [online] Kommersant. Available at: http://www.kommersant.ru/Doc/1621193.

Kashin, O. (2005a). *Otriad vlastonogikh*. [online] Kommersant. Available at: http://kommersant.ru/doc/595759.

—— (2005b). *Znat' 'Nashikh'*. [online] *Kommersant*. Available at: http://kommersant.ru/doc/550696 [Accessed 26 June 2017].

—— (2012a). *Pravoslavnye, sovetskie liudi*. [online] Kommersant. Available at: http://www.kommersant.ru/doc-rss/1922059.

—— (2012b). 'Esli eto kamen', to eto kamen'. Esli shpion, to shpion'. *Arkadii*

REFERENCES

Mamontov o nravstvennosti i Pussy Riot. [online] Afisha. Available at: http://gorod.afisha.ru/archive/arkadij-mamontov-o-pussy-riot/.

Kates, G. (2011). *Russia Debates Whether Boos Were For Putin*. [online] The Lede. Available at: https://thelede.blogs.nytimes.com/2011/11/22/russia-debates-whether-boos-were-for-putin/.

Kay, J. (2011). *Among the Truthers: A Journey Through America's Growing Conspiracist Underground*. New York: HarperCollins.

Kessler, G. (2005). *Secretary Criticizes Russia's NGO Law*. [online] The Washington Post. Available at: http://www.washingtonpost.com/wp-dyn/content/article/2005/12/07/AR2005120701681.html.

Khlebnikov, M. (2012). *'Teoriia zagovora': opyt sotsiokul'turnogo issledovaniia*. Moscow: Kuchkovo pole.

Khlevniuk, O. (2009). *Master of the House: Stalin and his inner circle*. New Haven: Yale University Press.

Khodorkovskii, M., Gevorkian, N. (2012). *Tiur'ma i volia*. Moscow: Howard Roark.

Khrestin, I. (2006). *New NGO Law in Russia*. [online] American Enterprise Institute. Available at: https://www.aei.org/publication/new-ngo-law-in-russia/print/.

Klebnikov, P. (2001). *Godfather of the Kremlin: The Decline of Russia in the Age of Capitalism*. Orlando: Harvest Books.

Klier, J. D. (2014). *Russians, Jews, and the Pogroms of 1881–1882*. Cambridge: Cambridge University Press.

Knight, P. (2000). *Conspiracy Culture: American Paranoia from the Kennedy Assassination to The X-Files*. London: Routledge.

Koalitsiia pravozashchitnikov (2016). *Skhodstva i razlichiia zakonov SShA i Rossii ob 'inostrannykh agentakh'. Analiticheskaia zapiska*. [online]. Available at: https://hrdco.org/bez-rubriki/shodstva-i-otlichiya-zakonov-ssha-i-rossii-ob-inostrannyh-agentah-analiticheskaya-zapiska/.

Kolesnikov, A. (2015). *Russian Ideology After Crimea*. [online] Carnegie.ru. Available at: http://carnegie.ru/2015/09/22/russian-ideology-after-crimea/ihzq.

Kolonitskii, B. (2010). *'Tragicheskaia erotika': obrazy imperatorskoi sem'i v gody pervoi mirovoi voiny*. Moscow: Novoe Literaturnoe Obozrenie.

Korchenkova, N. and Goriashko, S. (2015a). *S nechistogo lista*. [online] Kommersant. Available at: http://www.kommersant.ru/Doc/2763526.

—— (2015b). *Senatory zapolniaiut ist preduprezhdenii*. [online] Available at: https://www.kommersant.ru/doc/2761543.

Korey, W. (2004). *Russian Antisemitism, Pamyat, and the Demonology of Zionism*. London: Routledge.

Korobov, P. (2005). Raznostoronnee dvizhenie. *Kommersant*. [online] Available at: http://kommersant.ru/doc/595759.

—— (2008). *'Vlast' zdes' ne pri chem'*. [online] Kommersant. Available at: http://kommersant.ru/doc/847876.

Koshar, R. (1993). Foucault and Social History: Comments on 'Combined Underdevelopment'. *American Historical Review*, 98(2): 354–63.

Koshkin, P. (2015). *The Kremlin might create a list of 'undesired' foreign organizations*. [online] Russia Direct. Available at: http://www.russia-direct.org/analysis/kremlin-might-create-list-undesired-foreign-organizations.

Kostyrchenko, G. (2010). *Stalin protiv 'kosmopolitov'. Vlast' i evreiskaia intelligentsia v SSSR*. Moscow: ROSSPEN.

REFERENCES

Kotkin, S. (1995). *Magnetic Mountain: Stalinism as a Civilization*. Berkeley: University of California Press.

Kozlov, V., Galimova, N., Rozhdestvenskii, I., Sardzhveladze, S., Feinberg, A. and Alekhina, M. (2017). *S uchastnikami priamoi linii s Putinym proveli instruktazh*. [online] RBC. Available at: http://www.rbc.ru/politics/14/06/2017/594012e89a79472052f8b7fa.

Krastev, I. (2011). Paradoxes of the New Authoritarianism. *Journal of Democracy*, 22(2): 5–16.

Krastev, I. and Leonard, M. (2014). *The New European Disorder*. [online] European Council on Foreign Relations. Available at: http://www.ecfr.eu/page/-/ECFR117_TheNewEuropeanDisorder_ESSAY.pdf.

Krechetnikov, A. (2015). 'Rusofob' Olbrait i 'kremlevskii Merlin'. [online] *BBC*. Available at: http://www.bbc.com/russian/international/2015/06/150622_pat rushev_interview_albright.

Kukolevskii, A. (2011). *'Éffekt Monsona'*. [online] Kommersant. Available at: http://www.kommersant.ru/doc/1816701.

Kurnosov, A. A. (2006). Ob odnom iz èpizodov razgroma istoricheskoi nauki 1960-1970-kh gg. (Po materialam Tsentra khraneniia sovremennoi dokumen tatsii). *Voprosy obrazovaniia* (4): 363–89.

Kuvakin, I. (2015). *Dvorkovich dopustil zagovor protiv Rossii kak prichinu padeniia tsen na neft'*. [online] RBC. Available at: http://www.rbc.ru/econom ics/17/02/2015/54e2760b9a7947ea2a641f0a.

Labott, E. (2011). *Clinton cites 'serious concerns' about Russian election*. [online] Available at: http://edition.cnn.com/2011/12/06/world/europe/russia-elections-clinton/index.html.

Laclau, E. (2005a). *On Populist Reason*. London: Verso.

—— (2005b). Populism: What's in the Name? In Panizza, F., ed., *Populism and the Mirror of Democracy*. London: Verso, pp. 32–49.

Laquer, W. (1993). *Black Hundreds: The Rise of the Extreme Right in Russia*. New York: Harper Collins.

Laruelle, M. (2007). The Orient in Russian Thought at the Turn of the Century. In Shlyapentokh, D., ed., *Russia between East and West: scholarly debates on Eurasianism*. Leiden: Brill, pp. 9–39.

—— (2008). *Russian Eurasianism: An Ideology of Empire*. Washington: Woodrow Wilson Center Press.

—— (2012). Conspiracy and Alternate History in Russia: A Nationalist Equation for Success? *Russian Review*, 71(4): 565–80.

—— (2016a). The Izborsky Club, or the New Conservative Avant-Garde in Russia. *Russian Review*, 75: 626–44.

—— (2016b). The Three Colours of Novorossiya, or the Russian nationalist mythmaking of the Ukraine crisis. *Post-Soviet Affairs*, 32(1): 55–74.

Lasslia, J. (2014). *The Quest for an Ideal Youth in Putin's Russia II*. Stuttgart: Ibidem Press.

Lenta. (2014). *Putin zaiavil o krakhe mirovoi ekonomiki pri tsene nefti 80 dollarov*. [online] Available at: https://lenta.ru/news/2014/10/17/krahmira/.

Levada-tsentr. (2007). *Rossiiane o Putine*. [online] Available at: http://www.levada.ru/2007/08/06/rossiyane-o-putine/.

—— (2009). *Otnoshenie rossiian k NATO*. [online] Available at: http://www.levada.ru/2009/03/31/otnoshenie-rossiyan-k-nato/.

—— (2012). *O protestuiushchikh, otkaze v registratsii G.Iavlinskomu, kontrole*

za vyborami-chast'-2. [online] Available at: http://www.levada.ru/2012/02/07/o-protestuyushhih-otkaze-v-registratsii-g-yavlinskomu-kontrole-za-vyborami-chast-2/.
—— (2013a). *GKChP v pamiati rossiian.* [online] Available at: http://www.levada.ru/19-08-2013/gkchp-v-pamyati-rossiyan.
—— (2013b). *Obshchestvennoe mnenie ob NKO s inostrannym finansirovaniem.* [online] Available at: http://www.levada.ru/2013/05/17/obshhestvennoe-mnenie-ob-nko-s-inostrannym-finansirovaniem/.
—— (2013c). *Otkuda rossiiane uznaiut novosti.* [online] Available at: http://www.levada.ru/08-07-2013/otkuda-rossiyane-uznayut-novosti.
—— (2015). *Otnoshenie rossiian k drugim stranam.* [online] Available at: http://www.levada.ru/2015/04/02/otnoshenie-k-drugim-stranam/.
—— (2016a). *Avgustovskii putch i GKChP.* [online] Available at: http://www.levada.ru/2016/08/15/avgustovskij-putch-i-gkchp/.
—— (2016b). *Elektoral'nye reitingi partii.* [online] Available at: http://www.levada.ru/2016/07/01/elektoralnye-rejtingi-partij-2/.
—— (2017). 'Druz'ia' i 'vragi' Rossii. [online] Available at: https://www.levada.ru/2017/06/05/druzya-i-vragi-rossii-2/.
Livers, K. (2010). The Tower or the Labyrinth: Conspiracy, Occult, and Empire-Nostalgia in the Work of Viktor Pelevin and Aleksandr Prokhanov. *Russian Review,* 69(3): 477–503.
Ljubownikow, S., Crotty, J. and Rodgers, P. (2013). The state and civil society in Post-Soviet Russia: The development of a Russian-style civil society. *Progress in Development Studies,* 13(2): 153–66.
Lo, B. (2003). *Vladimir Putin and the Evolution of Russian Foreign Policy.* Oxford: Blackwell Publishing Ltd.
Lohr, E. (2003). *Nationalizing the Russian Empire. The Campaign against Enemy Aliens during World War I.* Cambridge: Harvard University Press.
Lowe, H.-D. (1993). *The Tsars and the Jews. Reform, Reaction and Anti-Semitism in Imperial Russia, 1772–1917.* London: Routledge.
Lukyanov, F. (2016). Putin's Foreign Policy: The Quest to Restore Russia's Rightful Place. *Foreign Affairs,* 95(3): 30–7.
MacAskill, E. (2014). Putin calls internet a 'CIA project' renewing fears of web breakup. [online] *Guardian.* Available at: https://www.theguardian.com/world/2014/apr/24/vladimir-putin-web-breakup-internet-cia.
McFaul, M., Petrov, N. and Ryabov, A. (2004). *Between Dictatorship and Democracy: Russian Post-Communist Political Reform.* Washington DC: Carnegie Endowment for International Peace.
Mackinder, H. J. (1904). The Geographical Pivot of History. *The Geographical Journal* 23(4): 421–37.
Makfol, M. and Pozner, V. (2012). *Pozner.* [online] Channel One. Available at: https://www.1tv.ru/shows/pozner/vypuski/gost-maykl-makfol-pozner-vypusk-ot-31-01-2012.
Mäkinen, S. (2011). Surkovian Narrative on the Future of Russia: Making Russia a World Leader. *Journal of Communist Studies and Transition Politics,* 27 (2): 143–65.
Makutina, M., Tagaeva, L. and Khimshishvili, P. (2015). *Genprokuraturu poprosili zakryt' pervye piat' nezhelatel'nykh organizatsii.* [online] RBC. Available at: http://www.rbc.ru/politics/25/05/2015/5563152d9a79470ee203a065.

Malinova, O. (2012). Simvolicheskoe edinstvo natsii? Reprezentatsiia makropoliticheskogo soobscshestva v predvybornoi ritorike Vladimira Putina. *Pro et Contra*, 16(3): 76–93.

Malkina, T. (2012). Andrei Loshak: 'To, chto telenachal'stvo dalo dobro na "Polnoe zatmenie", absurdno samo po sebe'. [online] *Bol'shoi gorod*. Available at: http://bg.ru/society/andrey_loshak_to_chto_telenachalstvo_dalo_dobro_na-11711/.

March, L. (2002). *The Communist Party in Post-Soviet Russia*. Manchester: Manchester University Press.

Markedonov, S. (2013). *The North Caucasus: The Value and Costs for Russia*. [online] Russia in Global Affairs. Available at: http://eng.globalaffairs.ru/number/The-North-Caucasus-The-Value-and-Costs-for-Russia-16287.

Masci, D. (2017). *In Russia, nostalgia for Soviet Union and positive feelings about Stalin*. [online] Pew Research Center. Available at: http://www.pewresearch.org/fact-tank/2017/06/29/in-russia-nostalgia-for-soviet-union-and-positive-feelings-about-stalin/.

Masis, J. (2016). *Russia Quietly Strips Emigres of Dual Citizenship*. [online] Forward. Available at: http://forward.com/news/world/342136/russia-quietly-strips-emigres-of-dual-citizenship/.

Maxwell, N. (2015). *From Russia With Cash*. [online] Transparency Inernational. Available at: http://www.transparency.org.uk/from-russia-with-cash/#.Wf9QG9ucYU0.

Meduza. (2016a). *Besedy 'Sergeia Glaz'eva' o Kryme i besporiadkakh na vostoke Ukrainy*. [online] Available at: https://meduza.io/feature/2016/08/22/besedy-sergeya-glazieva-o-kryme-i-besporyadkah-na-vostoke-ukrainy-rasshifrovka.

—— (2016b). *Chetvert' rossiian nazvali 'Vesti Nedeli' s Kiselevym luchshei analiticheskoi peredachei*. [online] Available at: https://meduza.io/news/2016/08/27/chetvert-rossiyan-nazvali-vesti-nedeli-s-Kiselevym-luchshey-analiticheskoy-peredachey.

—— (2016c). *Kak v Rossii presleduiut za prizyvy vernut' Krym Ukraine*. [online] Available at: https://meduza.io/cards/kak-v-rossii-presleduyut-za-prizyvy-vernut-krym-ukraine.

Melley, T. (2000). *Empire of Conspiracy: The Culture of Paranoia in Postwar America*. New York: Cornell University Press.

—— (2008). Brainwashed! Conspiracy Theory and Ideology in the Postwar United States. *New German Critique*, 35(1): 145–64.

Merzlikin, P. (2017). *Viacheslav Mal'tsev s 2013 goda obeshchaet revoliutsiiu v Rossii. Ego soratnikov zaderzhivaiut i arestovyvaiut po vsei strane*. [online] Meduza. Available at: https://meduza.io/feature/2017/11/02/vyacheslav-maltsev-s-2013-goda-obeschaet-revolyutsiyu-v-rossii-ego-soratnikov-zaderzhivayut-i-arestovyvayut-po-vsey-strane.

Meteleva, S. and Raskin, A. (2006). Spetskor upolnomochen zaiavit'. *Russkii Newsweek*, (4): 14–20.

Meyer, H. and Ant, O. (2017). *The One Russian Linking Putin, Erdogan and Trump*. [online] Bloomberg. Available at: https://www.bloomberg.com/news/articles/2017-02-03/who-is-alexander-dugin-the-man-linking-putin-erdogan-and-trump.

Miller, A. (2009). *Istoricheskaia politika: update*. [online] Polit.ru. Available at: http://polit.ru/article/2009/11/05/istpolit/.

—— (2012a). Istoricheskaia politika v Rossii: novyi povorot? In Miller, A. and

REFERENCES

Lipman, M., eds., *Istoricheskaia politika v XXI veke*. Moscow: Novoe literaturnoe obozrenie, pp. 328–67.

—— (2012b). *Istoriia poniatiia 'natsiia' v Rossii*. [online] Otechestvennye zapiski. Available at: http://www.strana-oz.ru/2012/1/istoriya-ponyatiya-naciya-v-rossii.

—— (2012c). Izobretenie traditsii. *Pro et Contra*, 16(3): 94–100.

Mills, S. (2003). *Michel Foucault*. London: Routledge.

Mitrokhin, N. (2003). *Russkaia Partiia. Dvizhenie russkikh natsionalistov v SSSR 1953–1985 gody*. Moscow: Novoe literaturnoe obozrenie.

Moldes, C. (2017). *In Offhand Remark, Putin Says Someone is Harvesting Russians' Biological Material*. [online] Global Voices. Available at: https://globalvoices.org/2017/11/01/in-offhand-remark-putin-says-someone-is-harvesting-russians-biological-material/.

Morar', N. (2007). *VTSIOM: korruptsiia v obmen na loial'nost'*. [online] The New Times. Available at: https://newtimes.ru/stati/others/archive-7767-vcuom-korrypcuya-v-obmen-na-loyalnost.html.

Mudde, C. (2007). *Populist Radical Right Parties in Europe*. Cambridge: Cambridge University Press.

Mukhametshina, E. (2015). *Vse bol'she rossiian khotiat pereizbraniia Vladimira Putina na chetvertyi srok*. [online] Vedomosti. Available at: https://www.vedomosti.ru/newspaper/articles/2015/03/04/putin-stanovitsya-bezalternativnee.

Ó Beacháin, D. and Polese A., eds. (2010). *The Colour Revolutions in the Former Soviet Republics: successes and failures*. London: Routledge.

Olmsted, K. S. (2009). *Real Enemies: Conspiracy Theories and American Democracy, World War I to 9/11*. New York: Oxford University Press.

O'Loughlin, J., Toal, G. and Kolosov, V. (2017). The Rise and Fall of 'Novorossiya': examining support for a separatist geopolitical imaginary in southeast Ukraine. *Post-Soviet Affairs*, 33(2): 124–44.

Ortmann, S. and Heathershaw, J. (2012). Conspiracy Theories in the Post-Soviet Space. *The Russian Review*, 71(4): 551–64.

Oushakine, S. A. (2000). In the State of Post-Soviet Aphasia: Symbolic Development in Contemporary Russia. *Europe-Asia Studies*, 52(6): 991–1016.

—— (2009a). 'Stop the Invasion!': Money, Patriotism, and Conspiracy in Russia. *Social Research*, 76(1): 71–116.

—— (2009b). *The Patriotism of Despair: Nation, War and Loss in Russia*. Ithaca and London: Cornell University Press.

Panchenko, A. (2015). Komp'iuter po imeni Zver': eskhatologiia i konspirologiia v sovremennykh religioznykh kul'takh. *Antropologicheskii forum* (25): 122–41.

Panizza, F. (2005). Introduction: Populism and the Mirror of Democracy. In Panizza, F., ed., *Populism and the Mirror of Democracy*. London: Verso, pp. 1–31.

Papkova, I. (2011). *The Orthodox Church in Russian Politics*. New York: Oxford University Press.

Parland, T. (2005). *The Extreme Nationalist Threat in Russia: The Growing Influence of Western Rightist Ideas*. London and New York: Routledge Curzon.

Parfitt, T. (2017). *Culture Minister should lose faulty PhD*. [online] The Times. Available at: https://www.thetimes.co.uk/article/russian-culture-minister-vladimir-medinsky-should-lose-faulty-phd-nx0vqv2ml.

REFERENCES

Paterson, T. (2014). *Ukraine crisis: Angry Angela Merkel questions whether Putin is in 'touch with reality'*. [online] Telegraph. Available at: http://www.telegraph.co.uk/news/worldnews/europe/ukraine/10673235/Ukraine-crisis-Angry-Angela-Merkel-questions-whether-Putin-is-in-touch-with-reality.html.

Petrov, N., Lipman, M. and Hale, H. (2014). Three Dilemmas of Hybrid Regime Governance: Russia from Putin to Putin. *Post-Soviet Affairs*, 30 (1): 1–30.

Phillips, N. and Hardy, C. (2002). *Discourse Analysis: Investigating Processes of Social Construction*. Thousand Oaks: Sage Publications.

Pipes, D. (1997). *Conspiracy: How the Paranoid Style Flourishes and Where it Comes From*. New York: Free Press.

—— (1998). *The Hidden Hand: Middle East Fears of Conspiracy*. New York: Griffin.

Plamper, J. (2002). Foucault's Gulag. *Kritika: Explorations in Russian and Eurasian History*, 3(2): 255–80.

Plokhy, S. (2014). *The Last Empire. The Final Days of the Soviet Union*. New York: Basic Books.

Poe, M. (2000). Izobretenie kontseptsii 'Moskva – Tretii Rim'. *Ab Imperio*, (2): 61–86.

Pomerantsev, P. (2013). *Cracks in the kremlin Matrix*. [online] Eurozine. Available at: http://www.eurozine.com/cracks-in-the-kremlin-matrix/.

Popper, K. R. (1973). *The Open Society and Its Enemies*. Volume 2. London: Routledge and Kegan Paul.

Przeworski, A., ed. (2015). *Democracy in a Russian Mirror*. Cambridge: Cambridge University Press.

Radio Free Europe/Radio Liberty. (2017). *Russian Police Arrest Blogger, Others Over Alleged Violence At Rally*. [online] Available at: https://www.rferl.org/a/russian-police-arrest-blogger-other-protesters-over-alleged-violence-march-26-anti-corruption-rally-navalny-maltsev/28429019.html.

Radnitz, S. (2016). Paranoia with a purpose: conspiracy theory and political coalitions in Kyrgyzstan. *Post-Soviet Affairs*, 32 (5): 474–89.

Razuvalova, A. (2015). Konspirologicheskii siuzhet v fil'me 'Lermontov' i 'Dnevnike rezhissera' N. Burliaeva: k voprosu ob 'etnografii emotsii' natsional'no-konservativnogo obshchestva. *Antropologicheskii forum*, (25): 95–121.

Remnick, D. (1998). *Resurrection: The Struggle for a New Russia*. New York: Vintage Books.

Rhodes, E. (1997). Origins of a Tragedy: Joseph Stalin's Cycle of Abuse. *The Journal of Psychohistory*, 24 (4): 377–89.

Riabov, P. (2010). Mikhail Katkov ili Ideologiia Okhranki: po povodu odnogo sbornika statei. *Forum noveishei vostochnoevropeiskoi istorii i kul'tury*, (2): 35–68.

Rights in Russia. (2012). *Ludmila Alekseeva answers Arkady Mamontov*. [online] Available at: http://hro.rightsinrussia.info/archive/ngos/mamontov/alekseeva.

Risen, J. (2015). *Joe Biden, His Son and the Case against a Ukrainian Oligarch*. [online] New York Times. Available at: https://www.nytimes.com/2015/12/09/world/europe/corruption-ukraine-joe-biden-son-hunter-biden-ties.html.

Rittersporn, G. T. (2014). *Anguish, Anger, and Folkways in Soviet Russia*. Pittsburgh: University of Pittsburgh Press.

Robins, R. S. and Post, J. M. (1987). The Paranoid Political Actor. *Biography*, 10 (1): 1–19.

REFERENCES

—— (1997). *Political Paranoia: The Psychopolitics of Hatred.* New Haven and London: Yale University Press.
Rogin, M. P. (1987). *Ronald Reagan, The Movie and Other Episodes in Political Demonology.* Berkeley: University of California Press.
Rogov, K. (2013). Sverkhbol'shinstvo dlia sverkhprezidentstva. *Pro et Contra,* 17, (3–4): 102–25.
—— (2015). 'Krymskii sindrom': mekhanizmy avtoritarnoi mobilizatsii. *Kontrapunkt,* (1): 1–15.
Ross, C. (2009). *Local Politics and Democratization in Russia.* London: Routledge.
—— ed. (2016). *Systemic and Non-Systemic Opposition in the Russian Federation. Civil Society Awakens?* London: Routledge.
Rossman, V. (2002). *Russian Intellectual Antisemitism in the Post-Communist Era.* Lincoln: The University of Nebraska Press.
Rozhdestvenskii, I., Mikhailova, A., Rustamova, F., Glikin, M. and Makarenko, G. (2016). Armiia Zolotova: zachem i kakim obrazom sozdaetsia natsional'naia gvardiia. [online] RBC. Available at: http://www.rbc.ru/politics/05/04/2016/5703ed1d9a794798356bbca1.
Sakva, N. (no date). Chto takoe 'plan Dallesa?' [online]. Available at: http://sakva.ru/Nick/DullPlan.html.
Sakwa, R. (2005). The 2003–2004 Russian Elections and Prospects for Democracy. *Europe-Asia Studies,* 57 (3): 369–98.
—— (2009). *The Quality of Freedom: Khodorkovsky, Putin, and the Yukos Affair.* Oxford: Oxford University Press.
—— (2011). Surkov: Dark Prince of the Kremlin [online] *Open Democracy Russia.* Available at: https://www.opendemocracy.net/od-russia/richard-sakwa/surkov-dark-prince-of-kremlin.
—— (2012). Conspiracy Narratives as a Mode of Engagement in International Politics: The Case of the 2008 Russo-Georgian War. *Russian Review,* 71(4): 581–609.
—— (2014). *Putin and the Oligarch: The Khodorkovsky-Yukos Affair.* London: I. B. Tauris.
Samarina, A. (2004). Moskovskie degustatory ukrainskogo sala. [online] *Nezavisimaia gazeta.* Available at: http://www.ng.ru/ideas/2004-12-07/1_pavlovskiy.html.
Samoilenko, S. A. and Erzikova, E. (2017). Media, political advertising and election campaigning in Russia. In C. Holtz-Bacha and M. Just, eds., *Handbook of Political Advertising.* Routledge, London, pp. 253–68.
Saradzhyan, S. and Schreck C. (2005). *NGOs a Cover for Spying in Russia.* [online] Global Research. Available at: http://www.globalresearch.ca/ngos-a-cover-for-spying-in-russia/139.
Schimmelpenninck Van Der Oye, D. (2001). *Toward the rising sun: Russian ideologies of empire and the path to war with Japan.* DeKalb, IL: Northern Illinois University Press.
Schimpfossl, E. and Yablokov, I. (2014). Coercion or Conformism? Censorship and Self-Censorship among Russian Media Personalities and Reporters in the 2010s. *Demokratizatsiya: The Journal of Post-Soviet Democratization,* 22(2): 295–312.
Schmidt, D. (2006). *Russia's NGO Legislation: New (and Old) Developments.* [online] Russian Analytical Digest. Available at: https://www.files.ethz.ch/isn/

REFERENCES

19048/Russian_Analytical_Digest_3.pdf.

Schmidt, M. L., Mazzetti, M. and Apuzzo, M. (2017). Trump Campaign Aides Had Repeated Contacts With Russian Intelligence. [online] *New York Times*. Available at: https://www.nytimes.com/2017/02/14/us/politics/russia-intelligence-communications-trump.html.

Sedakov, P., Vernidub, A. and Guseva, D. (2007). Kul'tiverovanie. *Russkii Newsweek*, (41): 32–5.

Shcherbal', M. (2010). *Ekonomicheskaia situatsiia v strane i lichnoe material'noe polozhenie glazami rossiian: dinamika otsenok naseleniia (2005–2010)*. Monitoring obshchestvennogo mneniia (5): 252–64.

Sheiko, K. and Brown, S. (2014). *History as Therapy: Alternative History and Nationalist Imaginings in Russia*. Stuttgart: Ibidem Press.

Shekhovtsov, A. (2015). Western Sources of Neo-Eurasianism: Recent Findings on Alexander Dugin and the European New Right, 1989–1994. In M. Laruelle, ed. *Eurasianism and the European Far Right: Reshaping the Europe–Russia Relationship*. Lanham: Lexington Books, pp. 35–53.

—— (2018). *Russia and the Western Far Right*. London: Routledge.

Shenfield, S. D. (2001). *Russian Fascism: Traditions, Tendencies, Movements*. Armonk: M. E. Sharpe.

Sherlock, T. (2011). Confronting the Stalinist Past: The Politics of Memory in Russia. *The Washington Quarterly*, 34(2): 93–109.

Shevel, O. (2011). Russian Nation-building from Yel'tsin to Medvedev: Ethnic, Civic or Purposefully Ambiguous? *Europe-Asia Studies*, 63(2): 179–202.

Shevtsova, L. (1999). *El'tsin's Russia: Myths and Reality*. Washington, DC: Carnegie Endowment for International Peace.

—— (2005). *Putin's Russia*. Washington, DC: Carnegie Endowment for International Peace.

—— (2015). Forward to the Past in Russia. *Jouranl of Democracy*, 26(2): 22–37.

Shnirel'man, V. (2002). *The Myth of the Khazars and Intellectual Antisemitism in Russia, 1970s–1990s*. Jerusalem: The Hebrew University of Jerusalem.

—— (2006). *Byt' alanami. Intellektualy i politika na Severnom Kavkaze v XX veke*. Moscow: Novoe literaturnoe obozrenie.

—— (2012). *Khazarskii mif: ideologiia politicheskogo radikalizma v Rossii i eë istoki*. Moscow: Mosty kultury.

—— (2017). *Koleno Danovo. Eskhatologiia i antisemitizm v sovremennoi Rossii*. Moscow: Izdatel'stvo BBI.

Sidorenko, A. (2011). *Russia: Creators of Election Violation Map Come Under Attack*. [online] Global Voices. Available at: https://globalvoices.org/2011/11/30/russia-creators-of-election-violation-map-come-under-attack/.

Sigelman, L. and Shiraev, E. (2002). The Rational Attacker in Russia? Negative Campaigning in Russian Presidential Elections. *The Journal of Politics*, 64(1): 45–62.

Smirnov, S. (2012). *Medvedev: 'V slove "agent" net nichego plokhogo'*. [online] Vedomosti. Available at: http://www.vedomosti.ru/politics/news/6930971/medvedev_v_slove_agent_net_nichego_plohogo#ixzz2EMGZkLnk.

Smith, D. (1999). *Working the Rough Stone: Freemasonry and Society in Eighteenth Century Russia*. De Kalb: Northern Illinois University Press.

Smith, K. (2002). *Mythmaking in the New Russia: politics and memory during the Yeltsin era*. Ithaca: Cornell University Press.

Smolchenko, A. (2007). *Putting Words in Albright's Mouth*. [online] The

REFERENCES

Moscow Times. Available at: http://www.themoscowtimes.com/news/article/putting-words-in-albrights-mouth/193094.html.

Snyder, T. (2015). Integration amd Disintegration: Europe, Ukraine and the World. *Slavic Review*, 74(4): 695–707.

Soldatov, A. and Borogan, I. (2015) *The Red Web: The Struggle between Russia's Digital Dictators and the New Online Revolutionaries*. New York: Public Affairs.

Sperling, V. (2015). *Sex, Politics, and Putin: political legitimacy in Russia.* Oxford: Oxford University Press.

Spillius, A. (2011). *Vladimir Putin calls John McCain 'nuts' in outspoken attack.* [online] Telegraph. Available at: http://www.telegraph.co.uk/news/worldnews/europe/russia/8958294/Vladimir-Putin-calls-John-McCain-nuts-in-outspoken-attack.html.

Stal, M. (2013). Psychopathology of Joseph Stalin. *Psychology*, 4, 1–4.

Staryi televizor (2012). *Interv'iu Andreia Loshaka, pridumavshego proekt 'Rossiia: Polnoe zatmenie'. Avtor podrobno rasskazal zachem i kak vse snimalos'.* [online] Available at: http://staroetv.su/news/2012-09-01-1866.

Stott, M. (2007). *Putin appeals for Russian voters, opponents criticise.* [online] Available at: http://www.reuters.com/article/us-russia-vote-idUSL2946083720071129.

Suny, R. G. (1993). *The Revenge of the Past. Nationalism, Revolution and the Collapse of the Soviet Union.* Stanford: Stanford University Press.

Tolz, V. (1998). Forging the Nation: National Identity and Nation Building in Post-Communist Russia. *Europe-Asia Studies*, 50(6): 993–1022.

—— (2001). *Russia*. London: Arnold.

—— (2014). Modern Russian Memory of the Great War, 1914–1920. In E. Lohr, A. Semyonov and V. Tolz, eds. *Nation and Empire at War.* Bloomington: Slavica Press, pp. 257–86.

Topping, A. and Elder, M. (2012). Britain admits 'fake rock' plot to spy on Russians. [online] *Guardian*. Available at: https://www.theguardian.com/world/2012/jan/19/fake-rock-plot-spy-russians.

Toynbee, A. J. (1947). Russia's Byzantine Heritage. In Connoly, C., ed. *Horizon* XVI (91): 82–95.

Treisman, D. (2007). Putin's Silovarchs. *Orbis*, 51 (1): 141–53.

—— (2011). *The Return: Russia's Journey from Gorbachev to Medvedev.* New York: Free Press.

—— (2013). Can Putin Keep His Grip on Power? *Current History*, (10): 251–8.

Trenin, D. (2011). Overview of the History of Russian Foreign Policy, (1992–2010). In Bubnova, N., ed., *20 Years Without the Berlin Wall: A Breakthrough to Freedom.* Moscow: ROSSPEN.

Tsygankov, A. (2009). *Russophobia. Anti-Russian Lobby and American Foreign Policy.* New York: Palgrave Macmillan.

Turkova, K. (2013). *'Levada tsentru' zakazyvaiut issledovaniia s tsel'iu vneshnego upravleniii nashei stranoi'.* [online] Kommersant FM. Available at: http://kommersant.ru/doc/2185439/print.

Utekhin, I. (2004). *Ocherki kommunal'nogo byta.* Moscow: Novoe literaturnoe obozrenie.

Umland, A. (2007). *Post-Soviet 'Uncivil Society' and the Rise of Aleksandr Dugin: A Case Study of the Extraparliamentary Radical Right in Contemporary*

REFERENCES

Russia. PhD. Cambridge University.

—— (2009). Patologicheskie tendentsii v russkom 'neoevraziistve'. O znachenii vzleta Aleksandra Dugina dlia interpretatsii obshchestvennoi zhizni sovremennoi Rossii. *Forum noveishei vostochnoevropeiskoi istorii i kul'tury* (2): 127–41.

—— (2010). Aleksandr Dugin's transformation from a lunatic fringe figure into a mainstream political publicist, 1980–1998: A case study in the rise of late and post-Soviet Russian fascism. *Journal of Eurasian Studies*, 1: 144–152.

—— (2011). Fascist Tendencies in Russian Higher Education: The Rise of Aleksandr Dugin and the Faculty of Sociology of Moscow State University. *Democratizatsiya*, [online] Available at: http://www.academia.edu/854121/Fascist_Tendencies_in_Russian_Higher_Education_The_Rise_of_Aleksandr_Dugin_and_the_Faculty_of_Sociology_of_Moscow_State_University.

Vanhala-Aniszewski, M. and Siilin, L. (2013). The Representation of Mikhail Gorbachev in the Twenty-First Century Russian Media. *Europe-Asia Studies*, 65 (2): 221–43.

Vasil'ev, I. (2007). *Vot stoit ona pered nami*. [online] Ogonek. Available at: https://www.kommersant.ru/doc/2299668.

Vedomosti. (2016). *'Levada-tsentr': 56% rossiian sozhaleiut o raspade SSSR*. [online] Available at: https://www.vedomosti.ru/politics/news/2016/12/05/668109-levada-tsentr-sssr.

Verkhovsky, A. (2016). Radical nationalists from the start of Medvedev's presidency to the war in Donbas: True till Death? in Kolsto P. and Blakkisrud, H., ed., *The New Russian Nationalism: Imperialism, Ethnicity and Authoritarianism, 2000–2015*, Edinburgh: Edinburgh University Press, pp. 75–103.

Viderker, S. (2010). 'Kontinent Evraziia': klassicheskoe evraziistvo i geopolitika v izlozhenii Aleksandra Dugina. *Forum noveishei vostochnoevropeiskoi istorii i kul'tury*, (1): 5–14.

Volkov, V. (2008). Standard Oil and Yukos in the Context of Early Capitalism in the United States and Russia. *Demokratizasiya*, 16 (3): 240–64.

—— (2012). Protestnye mitingi v Rossii kontsa 2011-nachala 2012 gg.: zapros na demokratizatsiiu politicheskikh institutov. *Vestnik obshchestvennogo mneniia* (2): 73–86.

—— (2015). 86% Putina: verit' ili net? [online] Vedomosti. Available at: http://www.vedomosti.ru/opinion/articles/2015/12/09/620191-86-putina.

—— (2016). *Russian Elite Opinion After the Crimea*. [online] Carnegie endowment for international piece. Available at: http://carnegieendowment.org/files/CP_Volkov_WEB_Eng.pdf.

Volkov, D. and Goncharov, S. (2014). *Rossiiskii media-landshaft: televidenie, pressa, internet*. [online] Levada-tsentr. Available at http://www.levada.ru/2014/06/17/rossijskij-media-landshaft-televidenie-pressa-internet/.

von Bieberstein, J. R. (2008). *Der Mythos von der Verschwörung: Philosophen, Freimaurer, Juden, Liberale und Sozialisten als Verschwörer gegen die Sozialordnung*. Marix Verlag.

Voronin, N. (2013). *Surkov rasskazal v Londone, chto mechtaet o zastoe*. [online] BBC Russian. Available at: http://www.bbc.com/russian/russia/2013/05/130501_surkov_lse_russia_lecture.shtml.

Weaver, C. (2012). *Unorthodox behaviour rattles Russian church*. [online] Financial Times. Available at: http://www.ft.com/intl/cms/s/0/8da92478-8573-11e1-a75a-00144feab49a.html#axzz1sErQuxqp.

Weir, F. (2005). *Russian government sets sights on 'subversion'*. [online] The

REFERENCES

Christian Science Monitor. Available at: http://www.csmonitor.com/2005/0601/p06s02-woeu.html/(page)/2.
White, S. (2011). *Understanding Russian Politics*. Cambridge: Cambridge University Press.
Wikileaks. (2010). *Cable 10Moscow184: The Evolving Role and Influence of Vladislav Surkov*. [online] Available at: http://wikileaks.org/cable/2010/01/10MOSCOW184.html.
Wilson, A. (2005). *Virtual Politics: Faking Democracy in the Post-Soviet World*. New Haven: Yale University Press.
—— (2014). *Ukraine Crisis: What it Means for the West?* New Haven: Yale University Press.
Yablokov, I. (2014). Pussy Riot as Agent Provocateur: Conspiracy Theories and the Media Construction of Nation in Putin's Russia. *Nationalities Papers*, 42 (4): 622–36.
—— (2015). Conspiracy Theories as Russia's Public Diplomacy Tool: The Case of 'Russia Today' (RT). *Politics*, 35 (3–4): 301–15.
Yanov, A. (2010). Istoriia odnogo otrecheniia: pochemu v Rossii ne budet fashizma. *Forum noveishei vostochnoevropeiskoi istorii i kul'tury* (2): 187–214.
Yeltsin, Boris (1994). *Zapiski prezidenta*. Moscow: Ogonek.
Young, K. (2007). US 'Atomic Capability' and the British Forward Bases in the Early Cold War. *Journal of Contemporary History*, 42 (1): 117–36.
Zakharov, D. (2011). *Proekt 'Vtoraia svezhest'*. [online] Kommersant. Available at: http://kommersant.ru/doc/1586150.
Zheleznova, M. (2013). *Proverki NKO okazalis' masshtabnee ozhidanii*. [online] Vedomosti. Available at: http://www.vedomosti.ru/politics/news/11182771/proverki_ne_vremya_dlya_dialoga.
Zhukov, M. and Samoilova, N. (1999). *Iliukhin nashel scheta El'tsina*. [online] Kommersant. Available at: http://kommersant.ru/doc/215417.
Zorin, A. (2001). *Kormia dvuglavogo orla. Literatura i gosudarstvennaia ideologiia v Rossii v poslednei treti XVIII – pervoi treti XIX veka*. Moscow: Novoe literaturnoe obozrenie.
Zubok, V. (2009). *A Failed Empire. The Soviet Union in the Cold War from Stalin to Gorbachev*. Chapel Hill: The University of North Carolina Press.
Zygar', M. (2006). *Sviazannye odnoi lentoi*. [online] Kommersant. Available at: http://kommersant.ru/doc/673083.
—— (2016). *All the Kremlin's Men*. New York: Public Affairs.
—— (2017). *Putin Likes to Pretend 1917 Never Happened*. [online] The Atlantic. Available at: https://www.theatlantic.com/international/archive/2017/04/russia-putin-revolution-lenin-nicholas-1917/521571/.

Index

'agents of influence' 51, 53, 60–1
Albright, Madeleine 92–3, 167
Alekseeva, Liudmila 123–4, 126
American Council for International Relations 67
Anatomy of Protest 152
Andropov, Iurii 60–1
Antimaidan 175, 182
August 1991 coup 1, 50–1, 63, 68, 76–7, 94

Belovezha accords 28–9, 44, 66–8
Berezovskii, Boris 30, 105, 140, 149
Biden, Joe 166–8
Bilderberg club 67
'Black Hundreds' 19
Bolotnaia Square 149, 151–2, 156, 158
Book of the Kahal 18
Burbulis, Gennadii 64
Byzantine Empire 96–9

Cathedral of Christ the Saviour 100–2
Clinton, Bill 63, 69
Clinton, Hillary 154
colour revolution 80, 82, 86, 110, 113, 117, 129–30, 136–7, 144–5, 148, 154–5, 175, 180–1, 183, 186, 190, 192
Council for National Strategy 114
Crimea 32, 75, 124, 162–4, 169–71, 174, 176, 178, 186–7, 189, 193
Crimean War 5, 15

Danilevskii, Nikolai 16
Dostoevsky, Fedor 16
Dugin, Aleksandr 32–6
  The Iuzhinskii circle 32
  The Foundations of Geopolitics 33, 36–7
  Conspirology 33
  Alain de Benoist 35
  Moscow State University 177
  The Great Game 36
  electoral campaigns 135–6
  the war in Georgia 37
Dulles Plan 61–3

'enemy of the people' 19

fake structures 139–41
Fedorov, Evgenii 128
Femen 104
Freemasons 14
Froianov, Igor' 24, 53

Gefter, Mikhail 27–8, 31
Glaz'ev, Sergei 91, 115, 178, 184
Golos 147–8
Gorbachev, Mikhail 24, 28, 51, 53, 56–60, 64–5, 67, 81, 87, 133, 152, 155,
  and forgeries 60, 62
gosdep 154
Grigor'ev, Maksim 139–41

Iakovlev, Aleksandr 53
Iliukhin, Viktor 59, 67–9

INDEX

impeachment to Yeltsin 66–72
Information warfare 106

Kara-Murza, Sergei 55–6
Kas'ianov, Mikhail 140, 173
Kasparov, Garry 173
Katkov, Mikhail 17
Kholmanskikh, Igor' 150–151
Kiselev, Dmitrii 99, 165–6, 168, 171–3, 176, 182
Krasheninnikova, Veronika 91, 125–7, 181
Kratkii kurs VKPb 21
Kriuchkov, Vladimir 53, 65
Kurginian, Sergei 53–4, 56, 152

Leont'ev, Mikhail 36, 151, 154–5, 157
Levada-tsentr 128
Limonov, Eduard 170, 172

Mamontov, Arkadii 101–103, 105–6, 120–2, 124, 128
Mal'tsev, Viacheslav 193
Markov, Sergei 101, 119
McFaul, Michael 133, 154–6
Medvedev, Dmitrii 37, 42, 117, 145–6, 151, 159, 167, 186
Moscow Helsinki Group 121, 123

Narochnitskaia, Natalia 37–41
Nashi 93–96
National-traitors 170
natural resources 57, 77, 83, 109, 115, 117, 119, 153, 158, 167–8, 190
Navalny, Aleksei 62, 149, 155, 171, 177,
Nevzorov, Aleksandr 94
New World Order 34–5, 39, 53, 67, 90, 109, 116, 176, 185, 187, 190
Novorossiia 176–7
Nuland, Victoria 166

'occupational government' 70
oligarchs 30, 54, 87, 95, 97, 114–16, 139, 141, 145, 177, 186
Open Russia 114, 140
Operation Golgotha 60

Orthodox Christianity 39, 67, 90, 97–8, 103
OSCE 141–2, 148

Panarin, Igor' 52–3, 155
paranoid style 6, 25
Patriarch Kirill 100–1, 104, 107
Patrushev, Nikolai 118, 121, 167, 179
Pavlov, Valentin 65–6
Pavlovskii, Gleb 26–32, 48–9, 88, 94, 117, 135, 139–40, 189
  Foundation of Effective Politics 27
  Orange Revolution 80
  Dugin, Aleksandr 36
perestroika 28, 32–3, 51–4, 60, 64–5, 87, 146, 155, 181
perestroika-2 152
Petrov, Vasilii 14
Peskov, Dmitrii 59, 146, 163
Poklonnaia Hill 156, 159
Popov, Gavriil 65
Popper, Karl 6
Powell, Jonathan 122–4
Protocols of the Elders of Zion 18
Provocateurs (film) 102
Pushkov, Aleksei 91
Pussy Riot 100–8, 110–11
Putin, Vladimir
  In Putin's support movement 13
  NGOs 118–20, 122, 179
  Pavlovskii 27–30
  rallies 113, 142
  sanctions 171, 175–6
  successor 27, 80, 82, 167
  the Soviet collapse 50, 72–6, 135
  popularity 29–30, 88, 135, 137, 159–60, 186
  press-conference 92, 149
  Putin's plan 136
Putin's enemies 119, 139–41, 143
political rallies 95, 110–12, 123, 138, 142–4, 149, 150, 152, 155–8, 175, 181
Prokhanov, Aleksandr 33, 66, 189

Ratnikov, Boris 92, 167
Rice, Condoleezza 116, 121,
Roberts, Paul Craig 106
Rogozin, Dmitrii 90–1, 115

Rockefellers 52, 114
ruling circles of the USA 90
Russia: The Full Eclipse 62

sanctions against Russia 165, 169, 171–4, 178
Second World War 21, 40, 69–70, 94–5, 127, 182–3
Sechin, Igor' 114
Shevchenko, Maksim 42–7
  the Caucasus 42–4
  Israel 45–6
Shevkunov, Tikhon 97–8
Shironin, Viacheslav 52–3
Sidiakin, Aleksandr 125–7
siloviki 114, 117
Slavophiles 5, 15–16, 40, 87
Special correspondent 103
spy rock 120–3
St George ribbon 126–7
Starikov, Nikolai 56–8, 148–9, 175, 179
State and the Oligarchy 116
State Committee of the State of Emergency (*GKChP*) 64–6, 76, 94
Strelkov, Igor' 176–8
Surkov, Vladislav 80–90, 98, 108, 109, 116, 159, 168, 177, 190

Trilateral Commission 35, 52–3, 67
tumultuous '90s 138

Ukraine
  2014 crisis 32, 36, 75, 111, 133, 159, 162–5, 172, 174–82, 186
  2004 elections 27, 30–1, 80, 86, 93, 112, 117–18, 121, 127, 134, 148, 155
  Soviet collapse 58
  'the puppet state' 165–9
Union of Right Forces 144
United Russia 59, 83, 96, 134, 136–7, 139, 142–6, 148
Utkin, Anatolii 24, 58

Vesti Nedeli 126, 165–6, 170, 172–5, 180, 182

Washington Regional Party Committee 90
white ribbon 127, 148–50
'wrecking' 20

Yanukovich, Viktor 27, 30, 80, 162, 165–6, 171, 179, 183
Yukos 112–17, 130, 140

Zor'kin, Valerii 90
Zyuganov, Gennadii 67